Presented
to
Tulsa City-County Library
by the

Col. David K. E. Bruce, 1898–1977. Courtesy of Mrs. David K. E. Bruce.

OSS
against the
Reich

*The World War II Diaries
of Colonel David K. E. Bruce*

edited by

Nelson Douglas Lankford

The Kent State University Press
Kent, Ohio, and London, England

© 1991 by The Kent State University Press, Kent, Ohio 44242
All rights reserved
Library of Congress Catalog Card Number 90-47719
ISBN 0-87338-427-X
Manufactured in the United States of America

Library of Congress Cataloging-in-Publication Data

Bruce, David Kirkpatrick Este.
  OSS against the Reich : the World War II diaries of Colonel David
K. E. Bruce / edited by Nelson Douglas Lankford.
    p.   cm.
  Includes bibliographical references and index.
  ISBN 0-87338-427-X (alk. paper) ∞
  1. Bruce, David Kirkpatrick Este—Diaries.   2. World War,
1939–1945—Personal narratives, American.   3. United States. Office
of Strategic Services—Biography.   4. Intelligence officers—United
States—Diaries.   I. Lankford, Nelson D.   II. Title.
D811.B82   1991
940.54'8173'092—dc20   90-47719

British Library Cataloging-in-Publication data are available.

For my mother and father

Contents

Preface

In the spring of 1986 a collection of decorations in a museum case—an American Presidential Medal of Freedom, medals of a Commander of the British Empire, and assorted Continental orders—caught my eye. These items formed a small part of an exhibition that my colleagues at the Virginia Historical Society had assembled to display the diversity of recent acquisitions. With the medals was a faded typewritten letter recounting in bemused good humor the author's ordeal of being dragged by William J. "Wild Bill" Donovan into the French hedgerows, well in advance of Allied lines and under fire from a German machine gun, only a day after the invasion of Normandy in 1944. This was my introduction to David K. E. Bruce, raconteur. I soon discovered the wealth of material he had given to the society. Although work on another book occupied my time that spring, I did not forget this glimpse into the varied life of this attractive, urbane, and gifted diplomat who, despite birth in Maryland and service abroad for many years, always counted himself a Virginian. That introduction, sparked by medals in an exhibit case, led to this book.

Because of that exhibition and because of their many kindnesses, I would first like to thank my colleagues at the Virginia Historical Society, especially Sara B. Bearss, who compiled the index for this book; Howson W. Cole; John H. Hanson; Frances Pollard; Sarah Sartain; and Paulette Thomas. The society's director at the beginning of my research, the late Donald Haynes, gave me permission to publish the diaries. His successor, Charles F. Bryan, Jr., endorsed my work with characteristic enthusiasm and, as a student of World War II himself, gave consistent, wholehearted support for my work. Throughout the course of the project, I have benefited from the sensible advice of the society's director emeritus, John Melville Jennings, whose own skillful diplomacy in the early 1970s convinced Ambassador Bruce that his papers would find a good home at the society.

The staffs of several libraries assisted my research, including those at Alderman Library, University of Virginia; Boatwright Library, University of Richmond; James Branch Cabell Library, Virginia Commonwealth University; the National Archives, Washington, D.C.; the Richmond Public Library; and the U.S. Military History Institute, Carlisle Barracks, Pennsylvania. Many people at these repositories aided my work, especially at the National Archives, where John Taylor shared his deep knowledge of the OSS official records, and Sim Smiley shared her knowledge of OSS, gleaned from her work on William Casey's posthumously published memoirs.

Members of the Bruce family showed me many kindnesses during my research. The ambassador's widow, Evangeline, gave my work her warm and enthusiastic endorsement and helped to identify some of the people mentioned in the diaries. The ambassador's son, David S. Bruce, introduced my wife and me to the legendary Bruce hospitality at Staunton Hill and gave me the benefit of his wide reading in the history of American intelligence activities.

My wife, Judy, gave the manuscript repeated, sharp readings and encouraged me throughout the writing. Many others have given me advice, information, and support, for which I am grateful. Any errors that remain are my own.

The diaries presented here chronicle the war through the eyes of only one man. With the accounts of others, however, Bruce's journal can help readers who did not live through that period begin to understand what it was like for those who did. I hope, too, that these pages will help evoke the memory of a particular time for readers of the World War II generation, for whom that great conflict was the formative event of their youth. Among them are two people, my parents, to whom I owe much; I dedicate this book to them.

For David Bruce, the war and his response to it marked him for leadership in his nation's foreign affairs after the conflict was over. That is another story, however, one that I plan to tell in another book. For the present, I hope readers of David Bruce's exploits in OSS will be as much rewarded by these diaries as I have been.

Editorial Note

The World War II diaries of David Bruce presented in this book are transcribed from documents in the David K. E. Bruce Papers, owned by the Virginia Historical Society in Richmond, Virginia. These documents are typescripts (both a ribbon copy and a carbon copy); no handwritten versions of the diaries are known to exist. Chapters 1 and 2 are taken from loose sheets of typescript in the Bruce Papers. Chapters 3 through 12 are taken from a bound folder of typescript that bears a title page reading "*PERSONAL DIARY DAVID K. E. BRUCE Colonel, GSC July 7, 1943, to December 6, 1944.*" The typeface in the folder is the same throughout. Internal evidence suggests that Bruce had all of the entries in the folder re-typed some time after December 6, 1944, probably a number of years later. At the U.S. Military History Institute at Carlisle Barracks, Pennsylvania, the William J. Donovan Papers contain another version of Chapter 4. Internal evidence suggests that this version is a fragment of the original text of Bruce's diaries. The principal differences between these two versions of Chapter 4 are explained in the notes. Quite possibly other portions of the original are extant, but research in OSS papers at the National Archives, the Bruce Papers at the Virginia Historical Society, and the Donovan Papers at the U.S. Military History Institute has failed to turn up any such documents.

Although transcription may appear to pose few problems when the original is typewritten, some problems are inevitable, and a statement of editorial method is necessary. The transcription policy followed in this book retains the exact wording of the typed original—almost. Some inconsistencies have been standardized, though not those of spelling or incorrect grammar. For example, a.m. and A.M. are rendered a.m. throughout; U.S. and U. S. appear as U.S. Bruce's original page numbers and running heads do not appear. The dates separating diary entries have been put in a standard form. The typescript contains a number of handwritten corrections, perhaps one per page, all in Bruce's hand. These changes are nearly all minor stylistic ones—for example, deleting excessive use of the word "very"—and have been ignored in favor of the original typescript. Exceptions are explained in the notes, unless it was obvious that Bruce was correcting a spelling error made by the typist, in which case the handwritten correction is silently incorporated into the text of this book.

The chapter divisions are arbitrary because no such breaks appear in Bruce's typescript. The decision where to make a chapter division was guided by logical breaks in the narrative of the diaries rather than desirable length of chapter. As a result chapters vary greatly in length. When there is a gap of a day or more between entries in the diaries, an editorial note appears in brackets to indicate the omission. In the case of long gaps, a summary of Bruce's activities appears in these editorial notes.

OSS against the Reich

he returned to Maryland to pass the bar, even winning a seat in the state legislature at age twenty-six—thanks to charm, ready wit, and family connection—the allure of life abroad had captured his imagination.

Europe claimed him again two years later when, newly engaged to Ailsa Mellon, the daughter of Pittsburgh financier and treasury secretary Andrew W. Mellon, Bruce sat for the examination to enter the United States consular service. In 1926 the newlyweds spent their honeymoon on the way to his posting as vice-consul in Rome. Only a year later, however, his wife's poor health and her unhappiness with life abroad led him to resign. He returned to private life in America and, it would seem, abandoned his vision of a career in foreign service.

There were compensations. Entree into the privileged world of the Mellons opened doors to Bruce that would otherwise have remained closed and brought him to the attention of men in high places who would not forget in later years the favorable impression he had made. By the 1930s Bruce sat on the boards of some of America's largest corporations. Andrew Mellon turned increasingly to him for advice. Bruce played an important supporting role in the creation of Mellon's gift to the nation, the National Gallery of Art, where the collections today include many paintings acquired through Bruce's initiative. After Mellon died in 1937, with the National Gallery still under construction, his son Paul and his son-in-law helped bring the dream to life, each serving in turn as president of the museum's board of trustees.

By the late 1930s, as he passed his fortieth year, David Bruce could take satisfaction in these accomplishments and others. Historical biography intrigued him, as it had his father, and he wrote a book of essays on each president from Washington to Lincoln. He bought back Staunton Hill, renewing his ancestral ties with Virginia, leading to election in 1939 to that state's legislature. As the decade ended, he could add this rising political role to his standing in the museum and philanthropic circles of Washington and New York. And yet, the charmed life that great wealth made possible did not provide the fulfillment it might have for a man of another temperament. If external events had not intruded, he might have continued this life of honeyed privilege, chafing at its subtle limitations but never doing what he really wanted to do. But the old hankering for service abroad simmered at the back of his consciousness, ready, when circumstances changed, to reclaim its former primacy among his youthful ambitions.

In the same month that Bruce won his primary election in Virginia, the seeds he had seen the diplomats plant at Versailles in 1919, and that isolationists, pacifists, and appeasers had nurtured in the meantime, produced a terrible crop that ripened in the August sun. In that month Stalin gave his blessing to Hitler's war in return for a share of the spoils, and the Western democracies at last began to learn the folly of their ways.

The familiar story of the events that followed is quickly told. After Hitler crushed Poland in September 1939, however, the remaining antagonists settled back to a twilight war, confining themselves to small-scale air raids and isolated clashes at sea. Chamberlain was still at Number 10 Downing Street, the French still snug behind their Maginot line. The spring of 1940 changed all that. After smashing Denmark and Norway, Hitler turned westward on the tenth of May. In five days his panzers shattered the opposing defenses. In five more they reached the English Channel, dividing the Allied armies and forcing them to face total ruin and defeat. Churchill, prime minister at last, gasped when he learned that after less than a fortnight's campaigning the French were ready to surrender their country and their honor. By the end of June, England faced a hostile Continent. Stalin befriended Hitler; America embraced neutrality.

No one on either side of the Atlantic knew that summer whether British stubbornness and Churchill's splendid rhetoric could repel the expected German assault. Many Americans believed the swastika would displace the Union Jack in Whitehall before the year was out. The rush of events was hard to comprehend. Congress had given voice to popular sentiment with the Neutrality Law of 1937. In the country, the powerful midwestern wing of the Republican party cherished its ideal of an isolationist America, impervious to the quarrels of the Old World. As in Britain, many on the left scorned military preparedness as something dangerous and even immoral.

Isolationists redoubled their campaign to avoid entangling alliances, and the Nazi-Soviet pact revealed to all but hardened fellow travelers the true face of Lenin's heir. There was another group of Americans worth noting for their response to the war. They were disposed by kinship, commerce, or affinity for the Allies, and their vision of world affairs came to be called internationalist. Because their view triumphed, a sense of inevitability often colors accounts of their role, and a self-serving mythology has grown up overstating both their prescience and their contribution. Their role was nevertheless crucial, and what can be said about this group, which included both Republicans and Democrats, conservatives and liberals, is that its members shared the conviction that in its defiance of Hitler Britain was fighting America's fight. To this group David Bruce gave his allegiance, like them unwilling to turn inward and abandon England in the dark days of 1940–41.

Another American who shared some of the internationalists' sentiments, though he did not subscribe to their desire for an immediate, unilateral declaration of war against Germany, was Franklin D. Roosevelt. The president had always taken a global view. After Germany defeated France and threatened England, Roosevelt saw the folly of thinking America could stand aloof. He could go only so far and so fast in his effort to aid Britain, however, or he would outpace the willingness of the public to follow and risk losing the presidential election in November 1940.

Although FDR instinctively sympathized with the British and wanted to help them as much as possible, he needed to know if they were likely to hold out. One thing he did know: he could no longer trust his ambassador in London to give him sound advice. A shrewd, self-made man, and a power in the Massachusetts Democratic party, Joseph P. Kennedy thought the British were finished. He broadcast his opinions openly in London, sent home defeatist cables, and suggested that America think about living with a Europe dominated by Hitler. Roosevelt, therefore, needed other sources of information about conditions in Britain, and the most famous observer whose advice he heeded in the summer of 1940 was William Joseph Donovan.

America's most decorated hero of World War I, a successful Wall Street lawyer, and a former official in the Coolidge administration, "Wild Bill" Donovan seemed an unlikely confidant for the architect of the New Deal. Despite their differences, FDR sensed that the Republican Donovan could bring the White House a candid assessment of affairs in Britain. Donovan spent three weeks in London that summer, as the opposing air forces struggled for mastery of the skies over southern England. He returned to Washington and told FDR that Kennedy was wrong. Britain would hold out. It could not win, however, without American aid.

Donovan was only the most celebrated envoy to provide Washington with intelligence on the war. Others included American military men sent on official business and private individuals who had reason to be in England. One of them was David Bruce.

The events of May and June 1940 jolted Bruce but did not stun him into inactivity or convince him that salvation lay in neutrality. He joined the American Red Cross as a member of its war relief committee and prepared immediately for an inspection tour across

As a Red Cross official, Bruce (in the civilian hat), watches planes of the RAF and the Luftwaffe duel over the cliffs of Dover in August 1940, a month before the bombing of London began. The group in the photograph consisted of American journalists who went to the south coast of England for a view of the fighting. The two women were Bruce's friends Virginia Cowles of the *New York Herald Tribune* (to the left of Bruce) and Helen Kirkpatrick of the *Chicago Daily News.* Courtesy of the Virginia Historical Society.

the Atlantic. Bruce embarked from New York on June 28, the only American passenger on an ocean liner that was delayed in sailing because U-boats had unnerved the crew on the previous crossing and made them reluctant to reenter the war zone.

He found London remarkably calm. As the conflict between the Luftwaffe and the RAF intensified, he wrote that "the people at home are laboring under a complete misapprehension about conditions here. The spirit of the people is very high indeed. . . . Personally, I believe that England is impregnable against a German invasion."[2] Red Cross duties did not prevent a personal assessment of military conditions, as a British magazine of the day revealed in a photograph that showed him standing on the cliffs at Dover watching the aerial combat that raged overhead. In years to come Bruce could share, as could few other Americans, the British national memory of that summer—after an overcast July, a break in the weather, and a progression of days of cloudless, china-blue skies streaked with the contrails of hundreds of airplanes. And then the Blitz.

When the focus of German attack shifted, providentially, from airfields and radar stations to the great sprawl of London, Bruce observed the mettle of Britons under fire. His Red Cross office at the north end of Waterloo Bridge, a favorite Luftwaffe target halfway between Westminster and the dome of St. Paul's, gave him a daily vantage point for viewing the destruction. He shared the danger with Londoners and during nights in the air raid shelters witnessed their stoicism first hand. Like many others, he began to look on the cramped discomfort of evenings underground as an unnecessary burden. He therefore decided to take his chances sleeping in his own rooms in Queen Anne's Gate, near the official residence of the head of British secret intelligence and midway between two other nearby favorite German targets—Buckingham Palace and the Houses of Parliament.

When he returned home in the autumn, as the fury of Goering's bombers reached a climax, Bruce spoke on the radio about Red Cross efforts and praised the resolution of London's citizens during the Blitz. Early in the New Year he visited London again, flying by special State Department dispensation, as his dog-eared passport testifies, to Lisbon and then, on board a blacked-out flying boat, from that spy-ridden neutral port to western England. On his return he exhorted the national Red Cross convention to continue aiding "that extraordinarily brave and gallant race" of Britons.[3]

While Bruce, Donovan, and others did their part to support the British and keep Washington informed on the war, American opinion began to shift, though not as much as internationalists wished. After France fell and England stood alone, most Americans acknowledged the need for more defense spending but still recoiled from the thought of war with Germany. The 1941 bill to extend conscription, originally approved during the Battle of Britain the previous year, passed in the House of Representatives by a single vote. The president himself, far from plotting deviously for war as conspiracy folklore would have it, still had doubts about entering the conflict.

While America hesitated, a greater, if less visible peril than the Blitz threatened Britain in 1941: it was losing the war at sea. By May, U-boats were sinking merchantmen at several times the capacity

In a letter written to his mother from London on August 22, 1940, Bruce expressed his conviction that it was not likely London would ever be bombed. Sixteen days later a photographer captured this scene near Tower Bridge, not far downstream on the Thames from Bruce's office, during the first mass air raid on the city. Courtesy of the National Archives.

of British and American shipyards to replace them. If the battle of the Atlantic was lost, all the aid given would be in vain. Despite the efforts of David Bruce's Red Cross, Churchill's island nation would starve.

As Britain's requirements for the matériel of war grew desperate, so did the parallel need for intelligence. In the aftermath of Dunkirk, Canadian industrialist William Stephenson, better known by his code name "Intrepid," went to New York to head British intelligence activities in the Americas. One of the first men he spoke to was Donovan, whose trips to Britain later that year may have resulted in part from the prompting of "Intrepid." The murky origins of British-American cooperation in intelligence matters are made no clearer by the heroic mythology surrounding the founding fathers of modern espionage. It appears that through Stephenson's reports and Donovan's visits, the British came to believe that "Wild Bill" had Roosevelt's ear. They also believed he was the best man to create an American covert intelligence organization that could work in tandem with their own hard-pressed service. They revealed to him the operations of their secret agencies with remarkable openness, at least in the early days before he became serious competition.

The same ideas percolated in Donovan's mind. After he returned from another foreign tour in early 1941, he lobbied in Washington for creation of a central agency entrusted with gathering intelligence. Powerful opponents, especially in the military, lobbied just as vigorously against him. After months of intrigue, on July 11, 1941, Roosevelt created the agency Donovan desired, with Donovan at its head, and called it the office of the Coordinator of Information. It was not the only intelligence service—the army, navy, and FBI had theirs—and it was not the centralized operation of Donovan's dreams, but it gave him the base he needed.

At its inception the COI consisted of two parts, a foreign information service and, more important, a research and analysis division. The former dealt in propaganda, while the latter collated information on subjects that might be of use in the event war came to America. Fortunately, espionage and related skullduggery were not the first priorities, for the COI found coordination of even nonsecret data into usable form difficult. Donovan's personality provided the source of both the agency's creative energy and many of its difficulties. Like other men of action, he neglected good habits of administration and fostered much of the organizational chaos that beset the COI in its early days.

If "Wild Bill" earned his nickname anew and offended powerful men in Washington, he also cultivated friendships in the right places, especially the White House. And the Donovan force of will that brought the agency into being in the first place also attracted a gifted staff and infused them with his own enthusiasm for the work. Without regard to political philosophy or the conventions of the civil service, he assembled in months a glittering pool of talent—academics, entrepreneurs, Ivy League Republican bankers, left-wing labor attorneys, anyone with a particular skill to contribute. That, at least, is the myth of creation COI veterans like to tell, and there is some truth in it.

One of those Donovan tapped for leadership in the COI was David Bruce. The steps leading to his recruitment went back several years.

Well before the war, Donovan knew of Bruce's talents and British sympathies and saw both confirmed by his Red Cross work in London. When Donovan reached England on his celebrated fact-finding trip in the summer of 1940, Bruce was already there. He was staying, in fact, with a member of Parliament who was an old friend of both Americans and who generously opened his house in Queen Anne's Gate to both men that summer. Bruce and Donovan probably kept in close touch from that point forward. Later, in the same month that Bruce addressed the Red Cross national convention, he joined a new pressure group, called the Fight for Freedom committee, composed of leading internationalists, including Donovan, who tried to combat isolationist opinion. One of the largest financial contributions to the committee came from Bruce's wife. To his Red Cross speeches praising the bravery of Londoners, Bruce added lectures calling for American rearmament and the defeat of Hitler.

As a committed internationalist who had seen the Battle of Britain and the Blitz for himself, who enjoyed widespread contacts in establishment circles in both England and America, and who had the personal charm and character needed for a leadership role, Bruce was an appealing choice for Donovan. He may have lacked the full-time administrative experience of the Wall Street executives Donovan also hired, but "Wild Bill" suspected that the tall, articulate Southerner would rise to the occasion. And so, on October 10, 1941, David Bruce officially began work for the COI. As head of the newly created Secret Intelligence branch in Washington, he supervised the information-gathering component of the organization, known in the early days as "Special Activities—Bruce," or SA-B for short.

Little time remained to prepare for the conflict that many of Bruce's COI colleagues believed could not be avoided. The draft, the defense buildup, and Lend-Lease all moved the nation closer to hostilities, though by themselves they did not make war inevitable. And for all their efforts to convince the American public to support the struggle against Germany, the internationalists could not do what their isolationist foes accused them of doing—drag the nation unwillingly into war. Where the internationalists failed, carrier-based Japanese planes succeeded.

Pearl Harbor disrupted many plans, including David Bruce's. For him and others of his views, however, at least the future after that December Sunday became less complicated. The events of that day— with assistance from Hitler four days later when he declared war on America—relieved them of the need to continue cajoling their fellow citizens. No longer did they need to press such arguments as those found in a draft resolution that Bruce intended to present to the Virginia legislature when it convened in January 1942. Embracing a thoroughly internationalist, pro-British view of affairs, Bruce ended the resolution with an argument he hoped would persuade his colleagues to call for a declaration of war against Germany. Like other opponents of isolationism, Bruce had come to believe that in order to preserve Western civilization, America must abandon the futile pursuit of neutrality and, with open eyes, choose war.

The COI's few months of peacetime building had ended, but the organization's growing pains had not. If anything, once the nation was at war, bureaucratic infighting at the COI's expense intensified. Such concern arose among Donovan's British supporters for the survival of his organization that early in 1942 they sent several missions to Washington to assess its chances. One delegation, consisting of journalist Ritchie Calder and David Bowes-Lyon, brother-in-law of George VI, described the COI with some accuracy as "an amorphous group of activities which has developed out of the personality of Colonel Donovan."[4] They concluded, however, that the agency would survive.

Again Donovan avoided the daggers of his Washington opponents when Roosevelt gave American secret intelligence a second birth, on June 13, 1942, reincarnating the COI as the Office of Strategic Services, directly under the Joint Chiefs of Staff. Although in the reorganization it lost the "white," or overt, propaganda function to another agency, the OSS grew to embrace five major branches— Secret Intelligence (SI), Research and Analysis (R&A), Counterespionage (X-2), Special Operations (SO), and Morale Operations (MO)—and at its peak employed more than 13,000 men and women around the world.

That growth, however, was in the future. In early 1942, while the COI fought to survive bureaucratic wars, America, Britain, and Russia—betrayed by its German ally in June 1941—staggered from catastrophes on the real battlefield. In quick succession after Pearl Harbor came the fall of Hong Kong, Manila, and Singapore. The Wehrmacht, recovered from its first taste of Russian winter, raced toward the Caucasus. Rommel approached his zenith in North Africa. The battle of the Atlantic increased in ferocity, threatening to undo all the schemes and plans—for they were as yet no more than that—for Allied victory. The reality of war soon came home to Americans. Before Pearl Harbor, Hitler had withheld his submarines from hunting in the western Atlantic. During the spring of 1942, Americans living along the East Coast could look out and see just off shore the grim smudges of smoke marking each tally in the season of the war known as the U-boat paradise.

In early 1942, Donovan's agency had little to offer—merely the promise of future applications of secret intelligence and clandestine operations. Thanks to cooperation between Donovan and the heads of British intelligence, the latter, with years of experience and no lack of lessons learned the hard way, opened their doors to the untested American agency. Donovan and his associates had much to learn, even if they never subscribed to the remark, attributed to Secretary of War Henry Stimson but probably apocryphal, that "gentlemen do not read each other's mail." Malcolm Muggeridge's faintly condescending recollection captures a sense of the times: "Ah, those first O.S.S. arrivals in London! How well I remember them—arriving like *jeunes filles en fleur* straight from a finishing school, all fresh and innocent, to start work in our frowsty old intelligence brothel! All too soon they were ravished and corrupted, becoming indistinguishable from seasoned pros who had been in the game for a quarter of a century and more."[5] That they learned quickly and contributed to the war effort, even Muggeridge had to admit.

As one of Donovan's two key deputies in the spring of 1942, forty-four-year-old David Bruce faced the most important challenge of his life, one that would soon take him abroad and propel him back to the career in foreign service that had beckoned at the end of the last war. More than he could have imagined in 1942, the travails and achievements of the next three years would determine the course of his own life as dramatically as they did that of his country.

In that spring the disorderly growth of Bruce's command continued, as his team ordered the file cabinets, typewriters, and stationery on which all bureaucracies subsist and interviewed the prospective new employees needed to fill a vastly expanded complement of personnel. These people were the woolly-headed academics, would-be spies, and "staff of Jewish scribblers" denounced by Goebbels in the early months of the COI.[6] By the following spring, SI, no longer the embryonic "Special Activities—Bruce," did not just consume paper and office space but began to make its existence known in Washington with a stream of intelligence reports. By that time too, Bruce's operation had begun to spin out the first of many webs of agent networks, especially, in the early days, in sub-Saharan Africa, along the supply routes from the New World to Britain's forces in Egypt.

In the midst of this activity, Bruce began to record his daily experiences, at first only when he was away from the office on inspection trips. His first wartime diaries recount three such trips in 1942—to London, Cairo, and London again—made while he was still based in Washington. Later, in the summer of 1943 after Donovan had sent him to expand OSS's base in the United Kingdom, Bruce described an excursion away from his London office to newly liberated North Africa and the front in Sicily. Thereafter his accounts described his work in London and on the Continent, as head of OSS in the European theater of operations, almost continually from D-day to the Battle of the Bulge. Such extensive diaries by a high-ranking officer in intelligence work are exceedingly rare.

As the first diary opens, Bruce has just begun the perilous journey by air across the North Atlantic, via Newfoundland and neutral Eire, to England. In London he, Donovan, and other COI officials would meet to negotiate an operational protocol for cooperation with their British counterparts. None of the Americans even knew whether their organization would survive their trip. The outcome of the political struggle in Washington over intelligence matters was still in doubt. Not until shortly after Bruce's arrival in London does word come that FDR has signed an executive order creating OSS and giving new life to America's first independent secret intelligence agency.

1

Some Most Interesting Sights

London, May 18 to June 25, 1942

May 18

We left LaGuardia Airport, New York City, at 8:05 a.m. by Pan American Clipper, and arrived at Shediac, New Brunswick, at 1:25 p.m., a distance of about 600 land miles. I was travelling under orders from the Coordinator of Information and the Army Air Corps. The Clipper was stripped of most of her furnishings, but was withal comfortable. Most of the passengers were American Air Officers, as well as General Sicey and two other Frenchmen.

Shediac is a small, unpretentious town of about two thousand inhabitants. Its chief industry appears to be lobster canning. The chopping up of these poor boiled crustaceans is done by women, whose deftness in extracting the meat from the shells is almost miraculous. Thousands of live lobsters are confined at the wharfside in water tanks, and the sorters handle them with insouciant dexterity, although, to be sure, they wear gloves.

We spent the night at Shediac in a large ramshackle frame hotel—the Shediac Inn.

May 19

We left this morning at 9:05 a.m., arriving at Botwood, Newfoundland, four hundred miles away, at 12:30 p.m. Here we lunched, and walked about in the beautiful spring weather. Botwood is a scene of considerable activity. Blasting is going on at rock quarries, concrete highways are being laid out, the waitresses are collecting autographs, and the streets of the dilapidated village are streaming with trucks. The appearance of the inhabitants is poverty-stricken in the extreme, the houses being in a bad state of repair and wearing a general air of dilapidation. There are no signs of agricultural enterprise—the soil is rocky and barren, and the pasturage not nearly as lush as at Shediac. There is said to be excellent trout and salmon fishing in the vicinity. The local people, especially the children, look undernourished, but are amiable and polite.

May 20

We left Botwood at 6:35 p.m. on the 19th, and arrived in the greenery of Foynes, Ireland, at 7:35 a.m. on the morning of the 20th. All of these hours are calculated on New York time. To my great surprise, Nancy Adare, Helen Kirkpatrick, and our charming American Minister, David Gray, were at the dock, expecting another friend who was not on the plane. Actually, most of our passengers were U.S. Army Air Corp officers, none of whom, with the exception of Larry Callahan and King Douglas,[1] I had known before. Because of unexpected Irish regulations, we had been obliged to travel in civilian clothes, and an odd assortment they were, bought hurriedly from Jewish second-hand clothes dealers in New York. I received a message from Dick Ellis,[2] whom I had particularly intended to see, stating he was enroute to Egypt, and was spending the day at the Dunraven Arms at Adare. Thither, Gray motored me with the two girls, and I lunched with Dick and had a long talk with him before boarding the 4:15 p.m. land plane for Bristol. At Bristol, the prospect of a long train journey was removed by the kindness of the British SIS in having sent Air Commodore Payne to meet me. We flew up the Thames River Valley and an hour later, were at Hendon where Fisher Howe[3] had a car for me. We passed low over Bath and, although the destruction was bad enough, it was not as general as newspaper accounts of the German raids there had led me to anticipate. What a lovely old city it is, with its pump room and its leisurely Eighteenth Century atmosphere.

It seemed very natural to be back at the Ritz, with its usual hall porters, indestructible old servants, and moths flying out of every stuffed chair.

May 21

London, although still marred by the effects of bombing, had undergone no air raids since I was last here. It had improved in appearance, for much debris had been removed, shattered windows had been boarded up, and the naturally tidy instinct of the British had reasserted itself. I found that the Coordinator of Information Offices were in the Embassy Building at Grosvenor Square, and was delighted to find my friend, from old Roman days, Percy Winner[4] amongst the other occupants. I spent the afternoon with Brigadier M.[5] at Broadway discussing matters of mutual interest, and dined with Lady Colefax at the Dorchester, in a glaringly decorated private room, in company with Oliver Lyttleton, Oliver Stanley, the Mountbattens,[6] the Casa Mauris,[7] Mrs. Hamilton, the RAB Butlers and Victor Cazalet.[8] Oliver Lyttleton, until recently, represented the Cabinet in the Middle East, Oliver Stanley—once Secretary of War— is now a Colonel in Army Intelligence, Mountbatten is Chief of Combined Operations—the most interesting war position in England—, Butler is Minister of Education, Victor Cazalet is a liaison officer with the Poles, and Frieda Casa Mauri was the toast of my generation fifteen years ago, although I had never known her. Mrs. Hamilton was very agreeable and is, I should judge, a female politician.

May 22

I went to Baker St. to see the SOE people, and had a satisfactory conversation with Sir Charles Hambro, Tony Keswick and Major Glynn. After emerging from a veritable rabbit-warren of offices, I went off to lunch at the Savoy with the ever charming David Bowes-Lyon, Percy Winner and Ritchie Calder[9] who had recently been with David in the United States representing the Political Warfare Executive. I called on Ambassador Winant, whose sincerity is always refreshing, and my old friend, Averell Harriman, whom I found recovering from a severe illness. Rabagliati, a friend of Dick Ellis, stopped in to see me. I had a long talk with Bill Whitney,[10] and dined with Audrey Bouverie.[11]

May 23

After lunching with Virginia Cowles,[12] Frieda Casa Mauri, and Tommy Hitchcock,[13] at an attractive little Parisian-inspired restaurant off Curzon Street, named Le Bon Viveur, Tommy, Virginia, Lady Long[14] and myself motored down to spend the night at Barbie Wallace's[15] place in Sussex. Since Euan's death, she has had to vacate the big house and is now ensconced in a lovely cottage looking onto Lavington Park. We spent the night there with Esmond Rothermere, Lady O'Neale and others, and Tommy and I drove up to London on Sunday afternoon. The dynamic Raymond Guest was in town, so we stopped to see him and Harold Fowler and had dinner with Bunny Carter[16] at White's, where the food and wine, although considerably more expensive, seemed as good as ever. In fact, for those who can afford to eat in the best hotels, clubs, and restaurants, the provender of England appears excellent, until one begins to remark on its lack of variety. Cheese is, as it has been for a long time, almost unprocurable in the cities, as are oranges and lemons, and a

Among the many friends Bruce encountered in London in 1942 was Lt. Comdr. Raymond R. Guest, who later became chief of the Maritime Unit of OSS in the European theater of operations. Courtesy of the National Archives.

variety of foods which are commonplace at home. In private houses of every degree, except in the country, the ration card enables one to buy enough to sustain life in not too straitened a manner, but does not afford one any relief from gastronomic monotony. A few concessions have been made to established national tastes, such as maintaining the fiction that pork sausages can still be bought. And indeed they can, but they contain almost every stuffing except pork.

May 24

Tommy and I motored back to London after lunch today—a 2½ hour run—and stopped in to see Raymond Guest, who is with the minesweepers, and Harold Fowler, now a Colonel in the Air Corps, whose exploit in flying through the opening in the Arc de' Triomphe after the 1918 Armistice aroused such excitement. Raymond was his usual ebullient self, as if he contained in his own person enough vitamins to supply a nation of people with vitality. Tommy,

Bunny Carter and I dined at White's, on smoked salmon, lamb, brussels sprouts, potatoes, prune tart, cocktails, a 1924 Chateau Margaux, and vintage port.

May 25

This is Whitsun holiday, so all the shops and most of the Government departments are closed. I had a quiet day at the office. I went to see Colonel Robert L. Bacon this morning, the Intelligence Officer for General Spaatz's[17] new air force unit, and then lunched with Nonie Griggs at Bucks Club, where we enjoyed gulls eggs, potted shrimp, liver, asparagus as well as an enlivening bottle of claret. There is, of course, a real shortage of wines and spirits. Scotch whiskey costs almost 23 shillings a bottle, and wine is almost unpurchasable except in a comparatively small number of places. Virginia cigarettes are not numerous, and the tobacconists impose a rather capricious limitation on purchases, which does not seriously affect favored customers. A black market in food is said to exist, but the practice of private individuals purchasing its products is frowned upon. The rationing of gasoline has made automobile traffic a shadow of what it once was, but during daylight hours there is no difficulty in finding taxicabs. The rationing of clothing prevents one from buying more than a minimum of clothing, but abundant supplies of cloth and haberdashery seem to exist in the shops. There is, of course, no new construction of importance being done in London, nor any attempt made to replace shattered glass or refurbish the dingy exteriors of existing buildings. Went to see Admiral Godfrey, the British Director of Naval Intelligence, this afternoon, and he took me through the new underground portion of the Admiralty Building where there were some most instructive sights. I went to see Eva and Robert Lutyens at the Dorchester this afternoon, to discuss with them their plans to bring their boy back from the United States, and dined with Wallace Phillips[18] at Claridges, where we had a marvellous bottle of Chateau Margaux 1920.

May 26

I called on Tony Biddle, the only Ambassador in the history of diplomacy to five nations at one time. He was as always charming with his delightful manners and cordiality. I then went to see Admiral Alan Kirk who has returned here as Chief of Staff to Admiral Stark, as well as principal Naval Attache. I lunched at Boodles Club with Tony Keswick and Major Glynn of SOE, and then went to see Major Desmond Morton, the Prime Minister's Special Assistant.

Had tea with Betty Cranborne,[19] and dined at White's with Brigadier Menzies—an instructive and fruitful evening.

May 27

Lunched with General "Pug" Ismay[20] at the Ritz, the PM's military assistant who told fascinating stories about his Chief. Garland Williams, Hanbury Williams[21] and myself motored down this afternoon to Southampton, and saw some unusual secret[22] installations in the country. We spent the night, arriving back at London in time to lunch with Fisher Howe at the Connaught. I went to call on Lord Selborne this afternoon. He is the Minister of Economic Warfare, having replaced Dr. Dalton. Had a drink with Adele Cavendish,[23] and dined tonight, after a Katharine Hepburn movie, with Colonel Head[24] and his wife, and Betty and Bobbity Cranborne[25] who, since I was last here, has become Minister of the Dominions. Their boy Robert is recovering from a frightful wound incurred on Salisbury Plain when during a demonstration, a British aeroplane, piloted by a Canadian, mistook the spectators for his target and killed twenty-five or more of them and wounded three times as many.

May 29

Saw Bill Stevenson of the American Red Cross, Nonie Griggs of the Navy and Major Wilkinson, MacArthur's friend from the Philippines, whom I had met in Washington. Lunched with Captain Taylor at Bucks. Had a talk this afternoon with Ambassador Winant and dined at Claridges with Helen Fitzgerald.[26]

May 30

Lunched with Lord and Lady Louis Mountbatten on Chester Street. A very abundant meal served by a Navy Yeoman. There was a Canadian Colonel, the jolly Crown Prince of Norway[27] and an aged but charming Princess—nationality unknown—with a guttural accent and all her own teeth. Went down this afternoon to stay at Dytchley with Nancy.[28] The others were the Cranbornes, Jeremy Tree, Major Wilkinson, Juby Lancaster, Adele Cavendish, Hamish Hamilton[29] (a Publisher) and his Italian wife.

May 31

Motored up Sunday afternoon in the Embassy Car—a great convenience in this country where gasoline rationing is so strict—and dined tonight at the Berkeley with Tommy Hitchcock, King Douglas,

Larry Callahan and Adele Cavendish. Later we went around to Raymond Guest's flat, and saw Harold Fowler and some other people.

June 1

Saw Captain Taylor and Colonel Stebeni. Lunched at the Savoy at the Monday Lunch Club—an American organization—where I met several old friends. Had a call from Boergner[30] of the Free French Delegation, and dined with Admiral Godfrey at the Royal Thames Yacht Club.

June 2

Called on Tony Biddle to introduce Whitney Shepardson,[31] who arrived last week-end. Then went to see Lady Reading.[32] Sybil Colefax came to see me. Lunched with Bettine Abingdon at the Connaught, met the de Traffords late this afternoon, and had an excellent dinner tonight at the Bagatelle with Air Vice Marshal Medhurst[33] and Air Commodore Payne, winding up at White's Club.

June 3

An air raid alarm about three in the morning, but nothing happened. Called on Colonel Gambia-Parry, and lunched at the Connaught with Whitney Shepardson, Colonel Munn and Brigadier Gubbins. Went to see Commander Fleming at DNI, had tea with Nancy Astor[34] and went early to bed.

June 4

Called on Admiral Kirk. Lunched at the Carlton Grill—all that is left of the hotel, thanks to bombing—with Cyril Radcliffe of MOI and Bruce Lockhart, Director of PWE. Saw Nancy Tree, and dined at the Dorchester with Nonie Griggs, Dorothy Beatty, Bill Stevenson, Barbie Wallace and the Duchess of Westminster.[35]

June 5

Went to St. Albans to see Major Cowgill[36] and others. Lunched at Bucks with Air Commodore Payne. Had a call from my old friend Hope of the British Red Cross, and dined at Pastoria with Helen Kirkpatrick, where we found a good bottle of Moselle for what is now not the immoderate cost of two pounds.

June 6

At the office all day. Lunched at Bucks with my old schoolmate, Doc Matthews,[37] who is now Counsellor at the Embassy. Had a talk with Major Henderson and Major Wallenstein and went early to bed.

June 7

Motored to Ascot to have lunch with Kay and Rudolph de Trafford. Dorothy Beatty, Michael Colefax, David Margesson, Major Brooker, Helen and Evelyn Fitzgerald, and Nonie Griggs were there. Afterwards Sheila Milbanke came in. I went over on my way home to see Aunt Rita Fitzgerald and Margaretta Winchilsea,[38] and dined at the Cafe Royale with Ed Johnston, where since one is now rationed to two dishes the atmosphere of gastronomic splendor has suffered a decline.

June 8

Lunched with Air Commodore Payne at Whites, talked to the Ambassador, and dined after that with Lady Reading, whose WVS now numbers over a million members. She is one of the really extraordinary women of the world, with great ability and charming in conversation.

June 9

Lunched at the Connaught with Lloyd Steere,[39] the Agriculture Attaché at the Embassy who has the best knowledge of anyone I know regarding food conditions in Europe. The last time I saw him was going to Newfoundland on a bomber London bound. At Gander, Newfoundland he took off on a British bomber an hour before we were due to leave on a more comfortable American bomber. After his departure the weather changed and we were detained for a week in Gander while he arrived safely the next morning in Scotland. Went down to Cranborne this evening and spent night there—lovely drive over the Downs.

June 10

Lunched at Claridges with Field-Marshal Sir Philip Chetwode, Sir John Kennedy[40] and Mr. Hope of the British Red Cross. Spent afternoon with Brigadier Gubbins and dined tonight at the Carlton Grill with Sir Charles Hambro. Had kummel at 10 shillings a glass.[41]

June 11

Flew from Northolt in a Hornet with Air Commodore Payne to an Aerodrome further North where we spent the day and saw many interesting secret[42] things. We spent the night at Babe Barnato's[43] house and returned to London in the morning.

June 12

Lunch at Lansdowne Restaurant with Colonel Dancey[44] deputy to "C" in SIS and Major Henderson. Met Bill Donovan on his arrival at

Hendon Airport, and dined at Claridge's with him, Bill Stephenson (head of British secret activities in the Western Hemisphere),[45] Preston Goodfellow, Fisher Howe and Irving Pflaum.[46]

June 13[47]

Lunched at Claridges with Colonel Donovan and a large group, and dined with Sir Charles Hambro and some of the key men in his organization.

June 14

Lunched with Bill Stephenson, Bill Donovan, Goodfellow, etc., and went to the country to meet David Bowes-Lyon and see some installations there. Dined at the Ritz with the two Bills, Stuart Menzies and Colonel Dancey.

June 15

Lunched with General Chaney, General Bolte,[48] Colonel Donovan, Preston Goodfellow, Whitney Shepardson, Garland Williams. Afternoon at interesting place in the country. Dined with Colonel Donovan, Bill Stephenson, Preston Goodfellow and Air Vice-Marshal Medhurst.

June 16[49]

A medley of engagements of various kinds. Expedition to country.

June 17

Lunch Lansdowne Restaurant Commander Cohen[50] and Major Henderson. Dinner at Claridges with large group.

June 18

Am. Foreign Office—Cavendish-Bentick.[51]
Various engagements.

June 19

Lunch Le Bon Viveur, Howe and Murphy. Dinner with Menzies, Goodfellow, et al.

June 20

Interesting day and lunch in the Whaddon Chase country. Stopped at Major Cowgill's place, and saw Ferguson, Philby and Captain Mills. Taken around installations by Colonel Gambia-Parry. Bill Stephenson took us out to dinner at Sound Studios with Norman Loudon, Miss Preston, Dick Ellis and Jimmy Murphy. In the afternoon, Col. D. and I went to 20 Grosvenor Square to see Admiral Stark, Commander Paul Hammond, Captain Creasy and Air Chief Marshal Joubert.[52]

June 21

Julian Allen,[53] who is here with A-2, came to see me this morning. Spent most of the day at office. Lunched with Colonel Donovan, Ellis, Howe, Murphy, Goodfellow, etc. Afternoon at office. Dined with Ed Johnston, Harold Fowler, King Douglas and Pete Hamilton, all in Army Air Corps.

June 22

Lunch at Coach and Horses, London. Left immediately afterwards with Major Clarke-Coke, and Major Alistair Campbell, both British, and Preston Goodfellow. Stayed the night at the Antelope Inn in Dorchester, Dorset.

June 23

Got up at 2:30 a.m. and attended some highly interesting exercises (rehearsal for Dieppe raids).[54] Lunched at Cranborne. Returned to London in later afternoon. Cocktails with Payne and Barnato, and dinner at the Ritz with Howe and Dick Heppner.[55]

June 24[56]

Left Hendon in a Fokker at 3:30
Arrived Prestwick at 7:45
Drank a lot of beer, had dinner & left at 10:45 on a B-24.

June 25

Arrived Gander Newfoundland at 12 noon.
Left Gander at 1:10 p.m.
Temperature 8° above zero at 11000 feet.
40 mile head wind—ground speed 180 miles per hour.
Arrived Montreal 6 p.m.
Left 6:50 p.m. on a privately chartered American Airlines plane and arrived in New York at 8:30 p.m.

2

Thunder of the Guns in the Distance

Africa, the Western Desert, and London,
August 11 to September 26, 1942

[Editor's note: No diary survives for the period between June 25 and August 11, 1942.]

August 11
Left Washington at 6:20 p.m. on the Seaboard Air Line for Miami.

August 12
Arrived Miami at 4:30 p.m. This city is almost given over to soldiers and sailors. The last time I was here the harbor and canals contained numbers of cargo vessels, yachts and pleasure craft. Now there is little shipping in evidence, and the only yachts are derelict looking objects of small size.[1]

August 13
After a night at the Columbus Hotel—if so short a stay could be called night—we were called at 3:00 a.m. We waited at the airport until 5:35 a.m. when we took off with 20 passengers on a DC3. Lieutenant Colonel Clabagh,[2] Lieutenant Colonel Kirchhoff, and Major Holliday were aboard. We arrived at Porto Rico at 11:45 a.m., left there at 12:50 p.m. and reached Trinidad at 5:00 p.m. where we spent the night in an officers' barracks. I have had a chance to do more reading than I have enjoyed for months, and finished today the *ABC Murders* by Agatha Christie and the *Strategy of Terror* by Edmund Taylor.

August 14
Called at 5:00 a.m. Left Trinidad at 6:30 a.m.; arrived Georgetown at 8:45; left at 9:30 and, after an intermediate stop, reached Belem, Brazil at 5:35, to spend the night in another barracks.
Read *While Rome Burns* by Alexander Woolcott and *Nana* by Emile Zola.

August 15
Up at 3:30 a.m. but did not leave Belem until 5:30 a.m. Arrived Natal[3] at 11:30 a.m. after reading the *Adventures of Ellery Queen*. The airport here is large and busy with a personnel of American soldiers, sailors and marines. An Egyptian-like sand storm covers everything with dust. The barracks are as usual. We are not allowed in the city because of certain unfortunate recent episodes between Americans and natives, in which drunkenness, assault, and battery were involved.

August 16
A lazy day at the airport which is itself, however, a scene of incessant activity, with planes of every type coming and going. We are staying in an officers' barracks. The mess is moderately good—all the food except beef is imported from the states. This afternoon we motored into Natal—a moderate sized, but most unattractive city. There are two old American gunboats in the harbor, but little else except three American Clippers. A fine modern road is being constructed, between Natal and the airport, which is a boon to native labor.
Read Van Loon's *Story of Mankind*.

August 17
The weather has been cool and delicious since our arrival, with the exception of dust storms in the afternoons. Under one blanket at night it is still chilly, despite the comparative nearness to the Equator.
We left at 4:45 p.m., and I spent a not uncomfortable night on the floor of the Clipper. There were forty passengers.
Read the *Army Officers' Manual*.

August 18
After a quiet crossing we arrived at Fisherman's Lake, Liberia, at 6:00 a.m., Natal time. Pan American has built an encampment here, in what was formerly dense jungle. The food, sanitary arrangements and equipment of every sort are excellent. This is the rainy season, but the weather is not immoderate. I have met several Pan American employees whom I had known elsewhere, and am staying in their quarters, which are clean and as adequately fitted up as would be rooms in any small hotel at home. The type of personnel throughout the Pan American system is a fine one, and they make better representatives of our country than do many of our diplomatic, consular, army and navy officers.[4]

August 19
We left Fisherman's Lake at 11:30 a.m., African time, and after a half hour stop at the fine Roberts Field Airport (near Monrovia) adjoining the Firestone Rubber Plantation, went on to Accra which we reached at 5:35 p.m. I was sorry not to see more of Liberia, and to learn to what extent the descendants of the American slaves who were manumitted and sent there, a century ago, have or have not prospered. The natives whom we saw at the Lake were gay, jolly, and appeared to be sturdy, although considerably smaller in stature and bulk than colored people in Virginia.

Finished *Van Loon* and read the *Tempest* and *Two Gentleman of Verona; The Forgiveness of Proteas* by Valentine imposes quite a strain on the reader's credulity.

August 20
Up at 4:00 a.m. Had a long talk with Tom Early at the airport. On account of engine trouble we did not leave until 8:45 a.m. One of the motors soon began to splutter and we returned to Accra at 9:30 a.m. Mr. Anderson[5] the Vice Consul, brought me a message from Hutcheson. We started again at 10:45 and arrived at Lagos at 12:15, where I saw Watts. Left Lagos at 12:45 and reached Kano at 4:45, a distance of 524 miles. We ran into a bad thunderstorm which delayed us and threw us around a bit.

Read H. G. Wells' *History of the World.*

Tonight we drove in to see Kano—a most interesting place architecturally—said to be one of the world's oldest walled cities.

August 21
Up at 4:00 a.m. A heavy rain. We did not leave until 5:50. Nigeria is a beautiful country to fly over. There are large areas in cultivation and I have seen some exceptionally fine crops of Indian corn and sorghum. Arrived Maiduguri 7:45 a.m., and had coffee there while we refuelled. We left at 8:30 and made slow time (150 m.p.h.) against strong head winds, reaching El Geneina at 1:05 p.m. We spent the night there. The place was infested with flies, like a Biblical plague. We are now in the Sudan. Went out in a truck this afternoon to hunt gazelles—the truck stuck in the mud and with the assistance of natives we pulled it out with ropes. I walked home. The hunters saw some game but killed nothing. Read Allan Michie's *Retreat to Victory.*[6]

August 22

Up at 4:45 a.m., Egyptian time, and took off at 6:05, shortly after daylight. We were all glad to leave this place, which is simply a desert station, and this morning was totally without water. We are now down to nine passengers and a good deal of freight. Arrived at Khartoum at 10:20, left at 11:40 and reached Luxor, which abounds with American beer and cigarettes; at 3:55 p.m., we went to see the magnificent ruins of Karnak. Read the *Black Camel*—a Charlie Chan mystery.

August 23

Called at 5:00 a.m. Left Luxor 6:45. Finished Wells, and read *The Merry Wives of Windsor*. Arrived Cairo at 9:15, and was met by Turner McBaine and Joe Leete. They took me to the Mena House[7] for lunch. I dined with Minister Kirk on his houseboat on the Nile.

Air raid alarm announced by what sounded like cracked cow-bells. Many lights were not even extinguished. The Heliopolis airport has been bombed, but never the city proper.

August 24

Saw Generals Brereton and Maxwell, Sonny Whitney and Lord Glenconner. Lunched with Kirk at a fine town house that he uses only for luncheon. Dined with McBaine, Leete, Bowlby, Commander Bremner, and Lieutenant Colonel Teague[8] (the last three are all Britishers).

Cairo is something of a shock in that life seems completely normal. One can buy anything in the shops—in fact in some respects goods seem more plentiful than at home. The front is only 120 miles away but the city swarms with apparently carefree British officers and men.

Air raid alarm.

August 25

Lunched with John de Salis and Hussanein[9] (the head of the Royal Cabinet) who was a classmate of John at Oxford. Excellent food and drink at the Mohammed Ali Club.

Dined with Kirk in his third house, at Mena. We were served on the immense roof which gives a gorgeous view of the Pyramids under a full moon. He had a lot of high British officers there, and we heard the thunder of the guns in the distance.[10]

August 26

Lunched at Michael Wright's (British Embassy). Henry Hopkinson[11] and their wives and two French officers were there.

I am staying at Shepheards, in rooms that must have been magnificent in Victorian days.

Dined with Turner and Joe at an attractive restaurant—the Auberge.

August 27

Saw Paul West[12] and Morde.[13] Lunched with Alex Kirk and dined with Bowlby and some of his friends. Got to bed at 2:00 a.m. The working hours in Cairo are usually from 9:00 to 1:00 and from 5:00 to 8:00 so dinner is usually at a later hour. Have finished my business with Kirk. He is a queer fellow, uncooperative and seemingly uninterested in intelligence matters. His mind is quick, his wit mordant, but he is ill attuned to the times, particularly to matters pertaining to war.[14]

August 28

Up at 4:45. Left Heliopolis airport at 7:15 and reached Khartoum at 1:25 p.m. Left at 2:55 and arrived at El Fasher at 6:00 p.m. Read *The Sapphire* by A. E. W. Mason, *Why Didn't They Ask Evans* by Agatha Christie, and *Queen's Folly* by Stanley Weyman. 12 passengers on the plane, which I thought was going to crash in the Khartoum takeoff.

Am very sleepy after less than 3 hours last night.

August 29

Up at 4:15 a.m., found it raining and blowing hard. Left El Fasher at 7:15 a.m. Arrived El Geneina 8:30. Left at 9:10, arrived Maiduguri at 12:40, left there at 1:15, reached Lagos at 5:15, left Lagos at 5:45 and arrived Accra at 7:30. Aubrey Hutcheson joined me at Lagos and we spent the night at Accra's Sea Breeze Hotel. I have had a raging fever all day with chills, etc.

Read *Salute to Adventurers*—excellent—by John Buchan, and *Step by Step, 1936–1939* by Winston Churchill.

August 30

High fever again today. Breakfasted on tea and beer, lunched at American Consulate with Hutch and Anderson, spent afternoon with British Pero officers (Political Economic Research Organization) and went out to the camp. I was due to leave tonight but the plane that was to take us has not arrived. I went to bed supperless, having no appetite, but full of aches, pains and fever.

August 31

Loafed around with frequent visits to the airport to see if there is any chance of getting off. Still have fever. Took a blood test for malaria—result negative.

These Nigerians are sturdy looking people. Their posture is superb, probably due to their habit of carrying burdens on their heads.

Went in to see Hutch this morning, and met the Police Commissioner, a fine looking British officer named Nottingham. Had a long talk after lunch with Captain Turkel,[15] Air Transport Command Intelligence Officer.

September 1

Still waiting at Accra. At last received word I was going on a bomber tonight. In my hurry to get through the camp in the dusk (no lights owing to the blackout) I fell into an air raid cement trench and skinned both legs. Learning nothing by experience, a few minutes later I fell into another, and arrived at the airport with my trousers bloody and torn. We left on a B-24 (Captain Reed, a former T.W.A. pilot) at 9:00 p.m. in the rain. There was only one other passenger and a large cargo of mica. I slept somehow with my head on a machine gun and my feet on a box ominously labelled "explosives."

September 2

Arrived Natal 8:45 a.m. (5:45 Natal time). Left at 7:50 a.m., after breakfasting with Lieutenant Skeffington. Arrived at Belem at 12:30. The crew went to bed, and Mr. Stolee—the only other passenger—and myself visited the city which I had seen about a year ago, and which had not improved in the interval. The crew consists of 5—Captains Reed and Byrne, Lieutenant Williams, a radio sergeant and a mechanic. We had the usual gorgeous tropical sunset and went to bed at seven.

September 3

Up at 4:30, left at 6:30 and flew all morning above the clouds, which were ranged beneath us like jagged white mountain ridges. Favored by a tail wind we averaged over 230 miles an hour at 12,000 feet, and reached Borinquen Field, Porto Rico, 1990 miles non-stop from Belem at 3:10 p.m. To bed at 8:00.

September 4

Up at 5:00 a.m. This installation with swimming pools, golf course, tennis courts, barracks and houses is the best we have seen anywhere enroute.

We left at 7:10 and 7:25 sighted a German submarine about 1½ miles away on our port side. We reported its position. Have read recently *Measure For Measure, The Comedy of Errors, Much Ado About Nothing, Midsummer Night's Dream, Love's Labour's Lost, Merchant of Venice, As you Like It, Taming of the Shrew, All's Well that Ends Well, Twelfth Night* and *The Winter's Tale.* The pilot told me, his only passenger, he could return to Washington by any route I wished. I suggested we fly over Staunton Hill which we did. It looked tiny and odd, nestling in the trees.[16]

[Editor's note: No diary entries exist for the days between Bruce's return from Africa on September 4 and his departure for London six days later.]

September 10

Up at 4:30. Went out into the water from La Guardia Field on an American Export Airline ship, and sat there in the fog until 12:00 o'clock, when the pilot, despairing of any satisfactory visibility, sent us home.

September 11 and 12

Up at 5:00. Left at 7:55 a.m. This is a very comfortable plane with peacetime fittings. Colonel Lory (from the Johns Hopkins), George Burnham and Warwick Potter[17] are all aboard. We have fifteen passengers and a crew of eleven. We arrived at Botwood at 2:45 p.m., left there at 4:15, and after three hours sleep arrived at Foynes at 2:50 a.m., New York time. We had a brisk walk, an excellent breakfast, and went by bus to the Limerick Airport, which we left at 7:30, reaching Bristol at 9:30 a.m. We left Bristol at 11:30 by special train and arrived at London at 1:30 (6:30 London time). Bill Phillips, Whitney Shepardson, Bill Stephenson, Colonel Franck, Fisher Howe and David Williamson[18] all very kindly met me at the station and took me to Claridges, where Colonel Donovan had an enormous dinner for the O.S.S. people, and some additional guests. I sat up until 2:00 a.m. and got a good many things accomplished, including the drinking of a pitcher of beer.

On the route back from Africa in September 1942, Bruce asked the pilot to fly over the Bruce family's country estate, Staunton Hill, an antebellum Gothic Revival house in Charlotte County, Virginia, southwest of Richmond. Courtesy of the Virginia Division of Historic Landmarks.

September 16

Went to see Averell Harriman. Lunched at Bill Phillips' apartment. Called on Captain Taylor, Tony Biddle and at the Embassy. Dined with Bill Stephenson, Erritt Cord,[19] Brigadier Gubbins, Colonel Franck, and Major Glyn.

September 17

Called on Air Vice Marshal Medhurst. Lunched at Bucks with Brigadier Menzies. Went to see Mr. Herbert,[20] Chief of Censorship. Stopped by American Red Cross on Grosvenor Square. Dined with Cranbornes.

September 21

Saw a variety of people. Went to the train and put everything aboard. As it was due to leave the station, we were told that the plane, with which we were to connect, was cancelled. Returned to Claridges and dined with Gunther, Huntington[21] and Shepardson.

September 25

Left Bristol at 9:05 a.m. in a de Havilland and reached Irish airport at 11:15 a.m. It is a one and one-half hour drive by bus from the airport to the Dunraven Arms at Adare, where we lunched. Saw Nancy Adare there.[22]

Left Foynes at 6:15 p.m. on the Pan-American—20 passengers—Captain Vaughan commanding.

September 26

Arrived at Botwood 11:20 a.m. Left Botwood 1:05 p.m. Arrived Shediac 4:35 p.m. Left 5:30 p.m. arriving at La Guardia Airport, New York, at 9:50 p.m. After a long customs examination, I went to Syosset.[23]

3

That Challenge

North Africa and Sicily, July 7 to 24, 1943

[Editor's note: Since the last diary entry, Bruce had been appointed head of OSS/Europe, and moved from Washington to London. By the summer of 1943 the Axis powers had reached their high-water mark and began to recede in the face of quickening, though not yet overwhelming, Allied power on all the major fronts. In the Mediterranean, the Allies had ejected Rommel's Afrika Korps from Egypt, Libya, and Tunisia, and in July were about to expel the Germans from Sicily as well. On the eve of the invasion of that island, Donovan summoned Bruce to inspect the Mediterranean theater of operations first hand. Donovan himself was aboard an American command ship where he could observe the assault, which occurred on July 10. Bruce's jurisdiction within the OSS domain did not encompass North Africa or Italy, and so he could record the disarray he observed in OSS organization in that theater with more bemused detachment than would otherwise have been the case. Internal evidence suggests that he edited the diary for the trip recorded in this chapter before it was typed but not long after it was written.]

July 7

I left London tonight for Scotland. This was in response to a series of cables from General Donovan at Algiers stating that if I came there immediately, I would have an opportunity to participate in the Sicilian campaign. In true OSS fashion I responded to what, whenever a trip is mentioned, we are accustomed to call "that challenge." My orders are completely indefinite and only authorize me to report to our own headquarters in North Africa—from then on one must improvise.

July 8

I arrived at Kilmarnock at five in the morning, and motored to Prestwick, whence I walked to Ayr and came back on foot, occasionally quenching my thirst with a beaker of beer. At 9:45 p.m. we took off in a C-54, with bucket seats. Bucket seats inspire terror in the soul—as well as the bottom—of the most hardened air traveler. No matter how one tries, it is impossible to extract any comfort from them. During the day, pressed tightly in a serried row of human sardines, one cannot lean back without impaling the spine on an obtruding strut or jut. At nights, the ridges between the seats make reclining a torture such as only the mediaeval rack can parallel. However, I excavated a cave beneath the piles of cargo that covered the floor of the plane, crept into the cavern and lay, almost blissfully, there throughout the night, my sleep somewhat disturbed by the rhythmic response of the aluminum beneath me to the throb of the engines.

The 2100 statute miles to Marrakesh were covered by 7:45 a.m. on the morning of July 9th, and at 10:05 a.m. I left for Algiers, where I arrived at 2:30 p.m. I soon quailed at the seemingly hopeless prospect of locating our organization or any of its members. Either it was so obscure, or else had gone so completely underground, that I could find no trace of it.

Sitting patiently on my kitbag in the entrance way of Army Air headquarters, I awaited the sight of a friendly face, and was finally rewarded by Don Coster's appearance. He gave me the telephone number of Bill Eddy,[1] Chief of OSS, Algiers. I telephoned Eddy, but was told by his secretary that he had not only left the city but had left no address behind him; moreover, she said General Donovan had done the same. Further, there was no message for me. The challenge had presented itself even sooner than I had expected.

I finally discovered that, except for Eddy's apartment and office in town, OSS was located in two villas on the outskirts of the city, and in a training area on the seacoast. In one of these, I found John Williams and various friends; in another Arthur Roseborough, Ted Ryan and a numerous company, including Charlie Vanderblue.[2] Since Charlie and I intended to go to Sicily together, I felt quite relieved at the sight of him, but discovered that neither he nor any of our personnel knew how to communicate with the General or Eddy, and that no arrangements whatever had been made for our trip.

Charlie had discovered a colony of fleas in his bed at the villa and had taken up his quarters elsewhere. He whisked me off to stay at the Hotel Valetti, a gaudy hostelry supposedly reserved for Generals. It was the first instance of the magic so often to be worked in the next few days by my companion's agreeable, friendly personality superimposed on his West Point ring. Whenever Charlie told me: "I have an idea," I knew that little time would elapse before the idea would be translated into something tangible, such as travel orders, seats on planes, food in the desert, wine from the air. We had been in Algiers only a few hours when, like a conjuror, he had equipped us cap à pied from steel helmets to leggings and boots, to say nothing of hanging ever-scarce pistols around our waists.

July 10
  Charlie and I spent the day at OSS installations. In the afternoon we called on David King, at the training station, and spent a large part of the afternoon swimming—Paul Van der Stricht[3] sharing the warm waves with us. That night our combined British-American parachute school put on a small show. Planes came overhead, and out of them leaped quantities of bodies, only barely discernible against the sunset afterglow, until their chutes opened into billowy clusters looking like floating, inverted mushrooms, or the sort of gigantic white umbrellas that one used to see in photographs, sheltering naked, black African potentates from the sun.

July 11
  We left Algiers by plane at 8:30 p.m. and arrived at Tunis at 12:30 p.m. Had it not been for Charlie's whipping up a close acquaintanceship during the trip with a young officer in the Signal Corps, we would have been stranded in Tunis, for we found no hotel accommodations or transportation available. C. telephoned his new friend, who sent a jeep for us, and we were taken to La Marsa, where Signal Headquarters was installed in the same villa as General Eisenhower.[4] Here our lack of proper orders began to embarrass us, and if we were ever to get to Sicily, it looked as if we would have to hitchhike there. Moreover, we had meanwhile no unit to which we could attach ourselves for billeting and messing. C. found a former West Point classmate in this villa who gave us a meal and took us swimming, but beyond that could not do much to help us. Prospects looked dark indeed, until we found that General Spaatz was somewhere in the vicinity. We borrowed a jeep and called on him. Fortunately, I had with me a letter to him from his daughter, Tatty,[5] who had worked for a while as my secretary in Washington. He very kindly told us that we could be attached for some days to his headquarters. A very supercilious young billeting officer then

said there was no remaining place to sleep except in a villa at Sidi Bou Said which was reserved for high-ranking British and American officers, and that if we pleased, we could try to induce the owner, who still resided there, to give us one of the rooms reserved for her. When I found that the owner was Baroness d'Erlanger,[6] my friend Leo's mother, the rest was easy. The Baroness, a most charming, beautiful lady in her seventies, was delighted to see a friend of her son's. The villa was extremely fine, with a superb view over the Bay of Tunis. Inside, it was very large, and had a little canal of running water traversing the lower floor. The Germans had occupied it, leaving a small apartment for the Baroness' own use, and there she had remained throughout the battles in Tunisia. The Germans had stripped the house of some of its furnishings and silver, but Charlie and I spent the night in a glorious Moorish room, which possessed every convenience except bedclothing.

Before going to bed we found Jack Kellogg, from Chicago, living in the adjoining guest house. I had not seen him for years, and certainly not since he had joined the Navy. He very generously took us under his wing and supplied us with transport and food, since there were no messing arrangements for us at the Villa. He could not have been more considerate and helpful.

We spent our time buttonholing high officers in an attempt to have them issue orders sending us to Sicily, but to no avail. Whenever we went to an American officer and explained that we were engaged in irregular activities, we would find ourselves referred to a British officer who took a dim view of our participating in them in Sicily. Quite rightly, they said we could not go unless we previously secured General Patton's[7] approval. As we had no sponsor who could cable for us to General Patton, we seemed to be in a hopeless impasse.

July 12

Having failed in our attempts through normal channels to achieve our ends, we decided to have recourse to more unorthodox methods. Lt. Colonel Pantaleoni[8] unexpectedly made his appearance, and happy as we were to see him, we were still more pleased to find him in possession of a jeep. Accordingly, the three of us set forth for Bizerta and rocked through countryside over wretched and dusty roads. Carcasses of tanks and burned-out vehicles showed how bitterly contested parts of this terrain had lately been. Arrived at Bizerta, we found Bill Eddy, who we had thought had already reached Sicily, still there, and with him John Whittaker, Corvo[9] and several Italian agents, all hidden away in a barracks. We wrestled manfully with Bill's reluctance to take us with him, on account of our lack of

During his trip to North Africa and Sicily in July 1943, under irregular orders and without proper papers, Bruce knew it would be wise to avoid Maj. Gen. George S. Patton, who was well known for his strict discipline and short fuse. Patton (the one with his mouth open) is shown here going ashore during the landing in North Africa. Courtesy of the National Archives.

proper orders. He drew a grim picture of how, if this were discovered after our arrival there, General Patton, who had been known to discipline a man for wearing a cotton instead of a woolen shirt, might make short shrift of the OSS detachment and throw it out of his theatre. At last Charlie, impatient of this obduracy, discovered as usual an old friend, this time a General in charge of transportation. He readily agreed to load us on one of his boats early the next morning, on condition that Eddy would give us a brief note saying we were attached to his command. This Eddy agreed to do, and we thought we had come to the end of our trail.

July 13

At three o'clock in the morning I was awakened by Bill, who had tracked me down with his torchlight. He said he had been unable to sleep through worrying lest our presence would so embarrass his position that his whole work would be ruined. There was no use arguing further with him, and Charlie and I resigned ourselves with as good grace as possible to our keen disappointment. Pants, who was to go to Sicily later (where he was wounded, captured by the Germans, and has since not been heard from) drove us back to La Marsa, where we inflicted ourselves once again on the Signal Corps. Once more we took a swim, cadged a meal at General Spaatz' table, and crept unaccredited back into our still unsheeted beds at the d'Erlanger villa.

July 14

Charlie spent the morning trying to waylay General Eisenhower in a last attempt to secure orders to go to Sicily. The General was not to be trapped, but Charlie did see the Chief of Staff, and his request was flatly rejected. We abandoned our battle gear and thumbed a ride in a jeep to the Tunis airport. There Charlie and I separated, he to take a plane to Cairo and I bound for Algiers and thence, so I expected, to London.

Upon entering my plane, just before its departure, I found it loaded with so many passengers, and so laden with freight and baggage that it seemed incredible to me that anything overburdened to this extent could ever leave the ground. My worst fears were confirmed when the pilot came back and addressed us from the door of his cabin, saying: "I have come from Cairo today and I am starting for Algiers at once. This plane is overloaded and may crash. Do any of you want to get off?" There was no answer, so he continued, "O.K., boys, hold everything. In five minutes you will be safely in the air or you will all be dead." With difficulty we became airborne, and in two and a half hours reached Algiers where I went to stay in Don Coster's commodious apartment.

July 15

After a good night's rest, my hopes again revived. I called up Ted Curtis, General Spaatz' Chief of Staff, found he was stationed in Constantine, and, after calling on General Bedell Smith, went by air to Constantine, a trip of an hour and a half. There I found George MacDonald,[10] John Mitchell, Cookie, and a most agreeable company.

July 16

At breakfast, having happened to mention to Ted my fruitless journey from England, and bewailing my lack of orders, he at once volunteered to arrange the whole thing for me. Since I was an officer in the Air Corps, he said he would have me sent over as an Air observer to Sicily. We went in his own plane (a French one) to Tunis, where he took me to General Spaatz' headquarters, wrote out my orders, arranged with Colonel Bagby of the Airborne Troops to furnish me transportation, and deposited me in a small guest house on the La Marsa beach.

July 17

I left El Alawein (the Tunis airport) on a C-47 at 9:30 a.m. this morning. We arrived at Cap Bon at 10:15 and left there at 11:30, arriving in Sicily near Gela at 1:00 p.m. No babe deposited in a desert could have been more lost than I was. I did not know where any American Army units were located, I had no transportation, and my orders attached me to nobody for messing and billeting. In the distance on a hill was Gela; in the foreground, sitting on a heavy kit bag, in the blazing sun, was myself. Finally, as there seemed to be no jeeps in sight, I shouldered my gas mask and musette bag, donned my steel helmet and pistol belt, picked up my bag, and started across a wheat field. A couple of little boys popped unexpectedly from a ditch and asked me, in Italian, for chewing gum. Having satisfied them, they then insisted on carrying most of my equipment to the nearest road. There I hailed a passing Duck and clambered up alongside the driver. I asked where he was going. He replied, "Out the road to my camp." He volunteered to drop me near Gela. I waited on the roadside until I secured a ride on a jeep which left me at the City Hall. The city bore few marks of shelling and bombing, and, to my relief, was full of American soldiers. I went to the nearest headquarters and asked what Divisions or other formations were located near there. Learning that General Patton's headquarters was only a couple of miles away, I caught a ride on a truck and was dropped at the gate, where I left my baggage under a tree while I made a reconnaissance. Carefully avoiding anyone who looked like what I thought General Patton would look like, I was rounding a tent when I ran smack into Bunny Carter, who is in G-2. From him I learned that General Donovan had left Sicily that afternoon for Algiers. Next, I saw Charlie Codman,[11] who turned out to be Patton's aide. A few minutes later, John Whittaker appeared, and then I knew all was well. John piled me into a jeep and we drove what seemed to be a vast distance to a little Italian town where he had the local printing presses working overtime on propaganda leaflets. Except (in true Sicilian fashion) for continually asking for cigarettes, money, chewing gum, chocolate, one's clothes, equipment and revolver, the local population seemed apathetic, and very evidently had no sense of shame about the sorry performance of their soldiers, or apprehension that their conquerors would be harsh to them.

Later that evening, we drove to a communal school building beyond Gela where Bill Eddy and some of his cohorts were installed. Now that I had arrived with appropriate orders he was most cordial and cooperative. Bill is a very fine man. He was born in the Near East, and is an excellent Arabic and French scholar. He had a brilliant record in the last war in the U.S. Marine Corps, and still limps badly as a result of a serious wound received at that time. His services for OSS in Tangiers and North Africa were very effective. His present position as Strategic Services Officer in the North African theatre, and the consequent administrative responsibilities attaching to that duty, are distasteful to him. In civil life, he was President of a college—I think it was Hobart. It is impossible to know Bill and not to respect him.

July 19

Eddy and I started off early in a jeep, and drove toward the sector where the American First Division is fighting. The traffic on the road was not excessive and we made good time. There was no evidence of current battle along the way, except for occasional shell-fire. We found First Division headquarters situated in an olive grove. Having, as usual, no place to stay or to mess, Bill and I sat on our bedding-rolls alongside the road, hoping for a friend to turn up. While we were smoking and chatting, a small car with no top came whizzing along, and behind the wheel was a man with an unmistakable, flaming, red head. It was Knickerbocker,[12] the newspaper correspondent. I hailed him, and told him I wanted to get up to the front, had no transportation and would he help me. He readily assented. So, leaving Bill and our luggage behind, I went off, not with him since his car was crowded, but with Don Whitehead,[13] the A.P. correspondent, who was in possession of a small captured Italian automobile. As it happened, I did not see Knick again, but Don, having been imposed upon in this summary fashion, was good enough not only to take charge of me but to treat me thenceforth with the greatest amiability and kindness. He had heard that Enna, a tenaciously-held German strongpoint, had just fallen, and proposed we go there at once. So we did, trying as best we could when we neared Enna to avoid the sides of the road which, it was to be presumed, had been mined. The explosion of a land mine under a jeep or a small car is comparatively violent, and it is likely to relieve the occupants of their feet and often of their legs as well. At any rate, we arrived safely and found ourselves in time to receive unearned plaudits and flowers from the local population who had, no doubt, similarly greeted the Germans when they first made their entry. The town was not badly damaged. We made for the leading hotel, and found that the proprietor spoke English. He asserted he was anti-Fascist and had locked up about thirty Italian officers in one of his large rooms. Sure enough he had, and an American Corporal who had wandered in was standing, or rather sitting, guard over them. The Corporal did not speak Italian, but somehow he must have terrified them, because, when we entered, they looked as if they expected a speedy and brutal judgment to be delivered against them. They surrendered all over again, and were an abject, unshaven, ill-disciplined, cowardly-looking lot of men from whom braggadocio had entirely departed. They seemed more concerned about having missed their lunch than anything else. Don and I had not eaten for many hours and went on a foraging expedition, but found the cupboards and cellars cleaned out. Our hotel proprietor beckoned to us with a great air of mystery, and told us that in another room he had locked up the leading Italian secret service man in that district. We went to see him. The prisoner, who was in an officer's uniform, evidently expected his end was approaching. He was excessively nervous, burst out crying, and his story about himself was thin and feeble. We did nothing to relieve his apprehensions, and placed him under guard.

From the hotel we went to the Governor's palace, a large and fine example of Mussolini architecture, which was completely undamaged. In its garage, where we were ferreting about for spare parts for our car, we found, in a tool chest, an up-to-date and detailed plan of all Italian and German defenses in Sicily.

The courtyard was crowded with GI's, who were sitting about waiting for orders. Some Civil Affairs officers entered into conversation with a group of gaily caparisoned Sicilians who looked like bandits. I was squatting quietly on the steps trying to read a local broadsheet when I was forced to look up by a loud clicking of spurs, immediately followed by a gush of Italian language. I found that the local dignitary confronting me was head of the Enna police force, and he was surrendering to me as the ranking American officer present. I arose and greeted him with what dignity I could muster. To my dismay, he suddenly drew out a comic-opera sword, more tassels than steel, and presented the hilt to me. I grasped it, not quite sure whether I was expected to run it through him, or keep it as a souvenir. Another spate of language flowed from him so I reversed the role and presented it back to him, whereupon his entourage of police officers all clicked their heels, gave in unison what sounded like a grunt, and saluted. At this point the Civil Affairs officers who had gone off for a few minutes to investigate the contents of a huge wine butt reappeared on the scene and assumed possession of him.

Don and I decided to chug off, and had great difficulty in getting under way, since an Italian soldier whose importunities to surrender to us we had previously resisted again waylaid us. We left him disconsolate and dejected in the square, a picture of shattered military pride, a prize nobody wanted.

To date I had seen no member of the First Division except at a distance. We were searching for its command post, and had drawn off for a moment into an olive grove to read our map. Alone under a tree, lying on a blanket, at four o'clock on this hot afternoon was a man clad in parts of an American uniform, but hatless, tieless, with his sleeves rolled up and sound asleep. Don walked over to look at him, and informed me it was Terry Allen,[14] General of the First. We tactfully woke him up. He rubbed his eyes and asked if we would like to breakfast with him, which we gladly accepted. An orderly and bacon and eggs materialized from the nearby bushes.

General Allen is a very attractive man, with immense drive and vitality. He made some suggestions as to where we might go in search of excitement, and told me to attach myself to his personal mess at headquarters. Again Don and I set off and got mixed up with some desultory patrols, who were firing in a desultory way at some desultory German patrols. We decided to try to buy some wine, and went to several farm houses with this purpose in mind, but to no avail. The local farmers were all barricaded in their houses or their barns, since they never felt sure in this territory whether they were being approached by Americans or by Germans.

We returned to Division Headquarters just in time for me to join Eddy, who was taking off a couple of agents for infiltration that night through the German lines. One was a young fellow, and the other an elderly man. We went to a village near the lines, made arrangements to clear them with the local American regimental commander, bought them a couple of small mules (which even at the time I personally believed to be a mistake) and left them in the custody of one of Eddy's junior officers. Bill and I returned late to camp, and spent a heavenly night under the trees.

July 20

This morning we were told that the two agents had been captured last night, but had later made their escape, and would be infiltrated shortly, through the lines, in another locality. What had happened was that while being interrogated by a German sentry, a strolling Italian had, in the moonlight, recognized one of the mules as belonging to his brother-in-law and had denounced its strange rider as a thief!

Headquarters was shifted forward this morning, and we spent the day scouring around the countryside. As General Allen believed in attacking only at night,[15] the days were rather quiet, except for sniping, patrol clashes, and mild artillery fire. Allen was most cordial to me, took me about and described vividly the course of the campaign, his ideas about intelligence, his views as to the proper use of OSS personnel, etc. His staff seemed absolutely tip-top and the morale of his officers and men was wonderful. I was particularly impressed by the ability of his G-2, Lt. Colonel Porter, who had gathered in his Section a wonderful assortment of people, including a Russian and a Chinaman. Paper work was reduced to a minimum in the First Division and it was a streamlined fighting machine, in which all officers and men were encouraged to take combat risks, and, under all circumstances, to keep pushing ahead. We slept that night happily in another grove of olives.

July 21

I heard that Teddy Roosevelt[16] had returned last night from a patrol and went to hunt for him. I found him just getting up, and injudiciously lent him my steel helmet for his shaving water. An hour later I tried to recover it, but it had vanished, leaving me feeling very naked, indeed. Bill and I breakfasted with Ted, General Allen and others. After breakfast, I had a long talk with General Allen, who asked me if I would take some despatches and letters for him to London. He said the next few days would be very quiet in his sector, and if I had to go, I might as well go soon. This was stated in the most cordial terms, and I welcomed his offer to lend us his command car. Our only jeep was busy with the agents, and Bill and I were at a definite loss for transportation. Accordingly, we rode in the General's car from Villa Rosa to Gela where again I had to improvise in order to secure transportation to North Africa. The method I adopted was to have myself dumped with my kit in the middle of an empty air field. I reached there about 3:00 p.m. and sat on my bedding-roll reading. Shortly a plane came in. I accosted the pilot and asked if he would take me back with him when he returned to Tunis. He said he would be glad to do so, and that he was leaving in three days. I moved into the plane, sat on my bedding-roll and resumed my reading. Another plane came in and I repeated the performance, moving into it, since it was leaving in the morning. A third plane arrived and out of it stepped George MacDonald and Eric Warburg. They were returning almost immediately with some German prisoners. I joined them.

An hour and a half later we reached El Alawein. Tunis was as usual overcrowded, but Eric took me to the house where he lived with a French family, and I had a luxurious bath and sleep.

July 22

I left El Alawein at 7:30 a.m., arrived at Telegma at 9:15, left there at 10:00, and reached Algiers at 11:30 a.m. It was a rough ride.

I dined that night with Captain Cuthbert Bowlby, in his lovely villa, with his SIS men, and spent the night with Don Coster.

July 23

Charlie Vanderblue had returned from Cairo, so we left Algiers together at 11:10 a.m. on a C-54. Arrived at Oran at 12:45, lunched there, and left at 1:45 p.m. We stopped at Casablanca at 4:45 p.m., left there at 5:10, and arrived safely at Marrakesh. There we decided to visit Mrs. Nicholson's famous villa. We revelled in its sunken marble bathtubs, and washed the dust from our throats with Charlie's excellent Bourbon. We were sorry to have to leave on the 8:45 plane, and exchange the villa's comfortable padded chairs for the ATC bucket seats.

July 24

We arrived at Prestwick at 9:10 in the morning, and left on the courier plane at 4:45 p.m. Frances Day[17] kept all the passengers amused by her gayety and witticisms, and we landed outside London just before seven o'clock.

4

The Prospect of Giving and Receiving Punishment Is Formidable

The Invasion of Normandy, May 30 to June 9, 1944

[Editor's note: In the ten months since his last diary, Bruce had been immersed in the task of building OSS in London to its peak strength in preparation for the Normandy invasion.]

May 30

General Donovan and I left Paddington on the 11:30 p.m. train, our cover story being that we were going to make visits to various friends of his in British Army field units.

Reaching Plymouth at 7:30 a.m. May 31, we were met by a launch and breakfasted with Admiral Kirk, Commanding Task Force 122, on the heavy cruiser Augusta. His Chief of Staff, Admiral Strubel,[1] was also there. After a tour of the harbor, which was crowded with shipping of every variety, we boarded the destroyer "Davis,"[2] and got under way at 12:30 p.m. Her skipper, Commander Dunn, had chaperoned a convoy across from N.Y. and reached Plymouth only four days previously. He had not been briefed on the plans, was without bombardment practice, and had no crystals for communications. Five other destroyers which had arrived from the Mediterranean a week ago were in the same plight. However, the Commander was in no way disheartened, nor were his excellent young officers, although they were naturally somewhat bewildered.

June 1[3]

Dropped anchor at Belfast at 10:30 a.m. We took a launch to the "Tuscaloosa," where we were very comfortably installed, General Donovan in Admiral Deyo's[4] cabin, and myself in Capt. Waller's emergency cabin. The Admiral was most hospitable and very interesting on many subjects of mutual concern. General D. and he had made a trip with Secretary Knox to Pearl Harbor in September 1940, and they had much to say about conditions there at that

Bruce and Donovan started their voyage to the Normandy invasion by breakfasting on May 30, 1944, with Rear Admiral Alan G. Kirk on board the USS *Augusta*. Kirk (left) is shown here on his ship's bridge with General Bradley (second from left) nine days after Bruce and Donovan's visit. Courtesy of the U.S. Navy Department.

period and afterwards. They felt that Admiral Kimmel[5] was an unimaginative man of narrow views, but an indefatigable worker and a conscientious officer. (His relationship, and coordination of naval activities, with the army functions of General Short had been far closer than is customary. Secretary Knox had never wanted to put Kimmel in command and the appointment had been dictated by the President. Undoubtedly there was negligence on the part of both Kimmel and Gen. Short,[6] but the Court Martial had to find "goats" and they were the obvious choice.) Immediately after the Japanese attack, Kimmel went to pieces and was not competent to carry on with his duties, being completely crushed by the affair. (There seems little doubt that considerable blame should attach not only to those two officers, but to their superiors in the War and Navy Departments.) We all agreed that the Jap attack was a blessing—even though well disguised at the time—to the United States, and forced us out of our lethargy in a manner that a less disastrous incident would not have accomplished.

After lunch, General D. and myself went to Belfast, where, under the skilful guidance of the Port officer, Commander Keane, who is more Blarneyish than the Irish themselves, we were taken to Belfast Castle to see Admiral Bevan, the senior British Naval Officer in Northern Ireland, and afterwards to see Lt. Gen. Cunningham,[7] who is the chief British military officer in the Northern Ireland command. General Cunningham had been in charge of the British forces in Abyssinia, where he had conducted a brilliant campaign, but had incurred disfavor during his later operations in the Middle East under Auchinlech,[8] and is believed unlikely to see further active service. His views regarding the late Major General Wingate[9] were illuminating. Both General D. and himself felt that Wingate resembled, in some of his eccentricities and sentiments of revolt against constituted authority, T. E. Lawrence, whose relative he is said to have been. (Gen C had known him well in Abyssinia, and had found him difficult to deal with, although a man of great energy, ability, and courage. He strongly espoused the cause of the natives of the countries in which he was working and over-exaggerated their contributions to military operations. [It sounds to me as if he had been, in his views of British Imperialism, much like Wilfrid Scawen Blunt.][10]) General C. felt that in one respect his death occurred opportunely for his reputation—that he could not have gone along much longer without becoming engaged in serious quarrels with his superiors. General D. had known Wingate in Burma and thought his outfit there somewhat undisciplined and sloppy. We returned to the ship at 6:30 and after dinner saw a movie of the life of Gentleman Jim Corbett.

Although participation by the U.S. Navy in the forthcoming operation has been outlined in a series of directives, its situation leaves much to be desired. It was apparently settled at the Teheran Conference[11] that the British Navy, together with the Tactical Air Force, would furnish the great majority of the necessary protection and support to the assault forces. As time went on, it became evident that, in spite of British representations, the available resources of the British Navy were grossly inadequate to the task. Our own naval authorities in Washington were reluctant to increase the size of their endeavour, being obsessed by their commitment in the Pacific and perhaps not unwilling if things go wrong to have the British Navy bear the lion's share of the blame. Admiral Kirk pleaded in the most urgent and strongest terms for reinforcements, which have been supplied in considerable quantity, although grudgingly and late. Even tonight, officers of some vessels are being briefed for the first time on their intricate tasks in the great operation; and certain of the ships recently arrived from America are lacking necessary equipment, including such items as crystals, smoke floats and their igniters, and sufficient supplies of ammunition to continue their duties, unless the landing is quickly successful.

The "Tuscaloosa" is surrounded by fighting craft and merchant vessels of every description—battle ships, heavy and light cruisers, destroyers, trawlers, transports, gay, even beneath a leaden sky, with vari-colored signal flags and the Stars & Stripes or Union Jack. The "Tuscaloosa" carries a complement of about 1,200 officers and men and is a well run and "happy" ship.

June 2

Awakened early to the tune of vigorous deck-scrubbing and sea chanteys. The day is beautifully crisp and clear. We have our meals and sit in the Admiral's cabin, where he very kindly permits us to listen to his conversations with captains from his various ships, who at this late hour are struggling to keep abreast of the torrent of literature on invasion plans that daily pours across their desks. Went ashore at 9:30 a.m. in the "Bird of Dawning," whose flight is very slow. We met Commander Keane and his driver, Miss Diana Kirkpatrick, and motored out to see the Governor of Northern Ireland, the Duke of Abercorn,[12] a charming man of 75 with a purple nose and a fondness for port, who has occupied his position for the past 23 years. His official residence, the former home of Lord Downshire, is a stately and attractive Georgian house. We then went to lunch at Newcastle with Major General Irwin of the 5th Division, Brigadier General Warnick[13] (Deputy Division Commander), and Colonel Franson, Chief of Staff, to whom we gave a sketch of OSS activities. From there we returned to Belfast and called on the Prime Minister, Sir Basil Brooke,[14] a cousin of General Alan Brooke. We also paid a call on Miss Kirkpatrick's mother, whose husband, a naval reserve officer, is Master of the local stag hounds. In the late afternoon we went to Clandeboye, a huge house belonging to the Marquis of Dufferin and Ava.[15] Lady D. gave us the usual tea, whiskey, jam, cakes and conversation.

We arrived back in time for dinner on the Tuscaloosa, and later resumed study of the Overlord and Neptune plans.

June 3[16]

Bright and clear. We had a long talk after breakfast with Commander South, Admiral Deyo's Chief of Staff. (Once again the old story was repeated. The British Navy had originally undertaken to support Overlord, and, late in the day, was unable to meet its commitments. The US Navy Dept. interested in the Pacific, almost to the exclusion of other theatres, had at last consented to send help that may prove to be too little and too late.) The Allied Air Forces, once confident that they could deal almost alone with German coastal defenses, were now apprehensive of the result, and had requested more and more assistance from their naval colleagues. General Collins,[17] commanding the American assault forces, which the "Tuscaloosa" was to support, was reported to be fully satisfied that his mission would be successfully completed. Last minute changes were being constantly made in the plans. The American airborne troops, conveyed in C-47's, are now to be routed directly over U.S. naval vessels, and will pass and repass for a period of many hours on D-day. The U.S. Navy has been instructed to fire at no planes, unless clearly identified as belonging to the enemy, at a range greater than 1,000 feet. This should either afford German bombers an excellent opportunity to slip in, or the Sicilian misfortune of our ships firing on our own transport aircraft may be repeated. Perhaps, however, these plans will again be altered at the last moment, and a more satisfactory procedure devised.

(General Donovan feels that too easy an optimism over the success of the assault prevails, and that the architects of Overlord were lacking in a realization of the actual combat conditions that may confront the Allies. He himself has always favored a thrust from the Mediterranean and through the Balkans, a view shared by many high-ranking British strategists. He told me last night that PM Churchill had not long ago cabled to the British Embassy in Wash a message for transmission to Pres. Roosevelt, denying the allegations that once a cross-channel attack had been decided upon, the PM had expressed discontent over the decision, or pessimism over the result. He did however, at the same time, again place himself on record as having preferred ever since 1941, when Gen D discussed the matter with him, an attack via the Mediterranean, instead of across the English Channel.)

Captain Waller has now moved to his emergency quarters, as he will hereafter pass most of his time on the bridge, and I have fallen heir to his spacious cabin. Adjoining it is a large saloon which is to be used by Commander Williamson (A Public Relations Officer) and by Willard Shadel of the CBS. At lunch today Shadel, who was at the Italian Front this spring, said that General Mark Clark is very given to personal publicity, and is not highly regarded by those who serve under him. He added that General Eaker[18] of the AAF is similarly addicted to self-advertisement. When the Army AF announced the complete destruction of Cassino[19]—a statement later belied after the doughboys found it still infested by Germans—the comment was that "as usual Eaker reached for the microphone too quickly." Shadel reported that Patton enjoyed a fine reputation as a driving, forceful leader, and that General Truscott[20] was held in warm esteem. He thought the American troops in Italy were boastful, and many of them homesick and querulous, in contrast to their British comrades, about the hardships to which they were exposed. He found that they fought well offensively, especially where an attack required dash, but were not so effective where qualities of routine persistence were required. He told the story of a bridge built by a company of American engineers. When finished, a placard was affixed to it reading: "This bridge was commenced by the ——— Co. of U.S. Engineers at 10 a.m. on May 2, 1944. All materials are on hand at 4 p.m. on the same date. Bridge completed at 6 p.m. on May 3 and in service at 6:30 p.m. May 3." A little further down the river the British Royal Engineers erected a bridge a few days later. When it was finished they nailed on it a placard reading: "Built by the Royal Engineers. There is nothing remarkable about this Bridge."

The Western Naval Task Force, of which the Tuscaloosa forms part, is commanded by Rear Admiral Alan Kirk and includes Assault Force O (under Rear Admiral J. L. Hall, whose duty is to assist the landing in the "Omaha" area) and Assault Force U (under Rear Admiral D. P. Moon,[21] who is to care for the "Utah" area which extends northward from the mouth of the River Vire). We are in the U group of vessels.

An airborne division, (the 82nd) will be dropped behind the Utah beaches prior to H hour on D-day to assist the seaborne landing, and another airborne division (the 101st) will follow later in the day. The Army Commander of Assault Force U (7th Corps) is Major General Collins (on board the Bayfield) and the Deputy Commander of the 7th Corps is Major General Landrum (on board an LCI).

The landing force of the U.S. Army for the Utah beaches is the 4th Infantry Division (reenforced) under Major General Barton, with Brigadier General Barber[22] as his second in command.

Admiral Deyo has the supporting force to Admiral Moon, with responsibility for the counter-battery work, and the destruction or neutralization of other enemy defenses that oppose landing, such as searchlights, etc. He is also to protect the minesweeping group, assist in preventing the egress of enemy light naval forces from the Carentan estuary, and support the movements of the VII Corps along the coast. The Utah beach extends for 5,300 yards along the lower Eastern shore of the Cotentin Peninsula on the Western side of the Baie de la Seine. The midpoint between the assault beaches is 24.5 air miles from Cherbourg, and 129 miles from Plymouth.

It is interesting to hear the concern expressed by these naval officers on the post-war future of the U.S. Navy. They feel that the Army AF has, through publicity channels, exaggerated its real achievements in this war, and popularized its position at the expense of the Navy, the exploits of which, in Admiral Deyo's opinion, have been throttled by censorship, or not sufficiently recorded due to the Navy's own unimaginative conduct of public relations. (The Admiral fears that a single Government Department for National Defense might discriminate against the Navy. General Donovan believes, on the other hand, that over-all control by a judicious and fair-minded civilian is the only method by which the contending demands of the Services might be satisfactorily adjusted within a peacetime economy. The resentment of all officers that one meets here against the bureaucratic methods, and lack of vision in the State Dept. is striking. The admiral fears that unless it undergoes a radical internal reorganization, involving a drastic housecleaning of present personnel, and the attraction to it of new blood, it will prove incapable of coping with its vastly increased responsibilities, and make our country seem unfit to meet its obligations as the greatest world power.)

June 4

We arrived off Falmouth early this morning, and at 6:30 a.m. received orders that, owning to bad weather conditions in the channel, the invasion had been postponed for 24 hours and, if it could not be carried out then it might be further postponed for two weeks. This incident again highlights what General D. has so often said about the nature of the tremendous gamble the Allies are making. Only for a few days in each month are the moon, the tides, the light, the weather and sea conditions propitious for a long cross-channel invasion. On today's choppy seas the landing boats would be tossed about like cockleshells, and would probably arrive at the French coast off schedule, partially filled with water, if indeed they were not swamped, and their human freight suffering from the aftermath of seasickness. In the previous landings in which American troops have participated, good luck has played a determining part, nor have any of them been directed against a strong opposition and defenses such as are now to be expected. Underwater obstacles with mines attached, beach mines, light and heavy coastal batteries, machine gun nests, and strong points of every description, supposedly have long been prepared against such an assault, and behind them is a mobile striking force of panzer and infantry divisions, composed of excellent soldiers. The fickle British climate is the true mistress of these seas.

We cruised about all day and went somewhat beyond Bristol before making a turn. This afternoon I counted over 75 warships and transports within a radius of a few miles, and it is probable that German reconnaissance planes have done the same. Tonight it has cleared, and although the sea is still disturbed we are hopeful the invasion date need not once more be set back. This short trip has afforded an opportunity to read with some degree of care the Navy, Army, and Air Force plans for Neptune (the assault landing phase of Overlord). They impress one with the complexity of an amphibious operation and the numerous contingencies that must be provided for. The success of this assault would appear to hinge largely on a series of optimistic assumptions. For example, the efficacy of the fire from the larger naval guns against the principal enemy batteries will depend primarily on the Air Force spotters detailed to this work. They will be flying far from their bases, and can remain for only a limited period of time over their targets. Therefore, they will be constantly shifting, and replacing one another. Some will be adept in directing fire and observing results, others may misjudge the situation entirely. For an amphibious operation, proper cloud conditions are essential for accurate support of every kind by airplanes—at one time they will be heavily bombing objectives removed only 500 yards from our own landing forces. Enfilading fire by the enemy on the beaches, unless eliminated, might well destroy our entire attempt. And so one could go on almost ad infinitum. Perhaps too much hope has been founded on the element of surprise. We have selected for the attack the most obviously favorable points of attack. In spite of the projected diversions, it might be assumed that the enemy, seldom notorious for deficiency in staff work, has reached a generally correct estimate as to its direction. Nor does it seem possible for a huge armada, some slow elements of which must commence this journey 24 hours or more ahead of H-hour, to escape unfriendly observation long before its arrival at its destination. Security control, so far as mastering the German espionage system in the U.K. is involved, has, I believe, done a thorough job. Another most important assumption which it will be interesting to examine after the event is that the German build-up will proceed at a pace approximately no faster than our own. Father Neptune himself may have a voice in this matter, and other vagaries of Fortune may be more unfavorable to our expectations than to those of our land-based opponents.

June 5

The weather has improved this morning and, being about opposite Bristol, we are now retracing our way to Plymouth. The sight of these cruisers and battleships in line, flanked by destroyers, is majestic. About noon we passed through two large convoys of transports laden with troops; one of them was flying 67 barrage balloons. In this operation there will be about 3,200 ships and thousands of small craft employed against a 90-mile front. Amongst them are numbered six battleships (3 of them American: the Nevada, Texas and Arkansas; and the other three British: the Ramillies, Warspite and Rodney); 2 Gunboats (Dutch); 2 Monitors (British); 27 Cruisers (21 of them British, 2 French, 1 Polish, and 3 American: the Tuscaloosa, Augusta and Quincy); 124 Destroyers (mostly British, about 30 being American with some Dutch, Polish and French); 143 Minesweepers; 8 Headquarters ships (4 British and 4 American: the Bayfield, Maloy, Achenar and another); 9 Assault Group Headquarters ships (British); 13 PT boats (American); 150 MTB boats (British); and a host of other escort and auxiliary craft.

The fire power of this fleet will be immense. The Tuscaloosa has nine 8" guns, eight 5"25' guns, six 40 mm quads and 18 20 mms.

At one point we pass 5-½ miles of LCT's, four rows wide in the Channel. Included in our firepower will be 5,000 rockets, to be fired from five rocket ships in clusters of one thousand each.

Altogether, the prospect of giving and receiving punishment is formidable. General D. and myself are most fortunate to be on this ship with her charming Admiral and his very fine officers, all of whom, without exception, appear to be intelligent, able and agreeable. Captain Waller is from Norfolk, Virginia, Commander South, the Chief of Staff, from Arkansas, and Lieutenant Brooks, the Flag Lieutenant, from Massachusetts (he is a graduate of Williams College and a former pupil of Jim Baxter;[23] the other officers mentioned are Annapolis men). These make up, with us, the quintet which take their meals in the Admiral's cabin, Captain Waller not being counted, as he now stays continuously on or near the Bridge.

9 p.m. The wind has freshened, and the seas, instead of quieting down, are rising higher. There are heavy cloud banks above us and toward France. However, the authorities who control this expedition must be satisfied over the weather prospects for tonight and tomorrow morning, since we have now definitely set our course for the Utah beaches. Admiral Moon has flashed a signal exhorting all hands to be brave and cheerful and make a touchdown on the French coast. No doubt General Eisenhower's and General Montgomery's declarations calling on God to help man are now being circulated on the transports.[24] Breakfast has been ordered on the Tuscaloosa for 9:30 tonight, so it is to be inferred that meals will be very irregular from now on. General D.'s colored cabin boy, who has never before been in action, is tripping about the decks in a blue woolen cap and a field jacket, patting the guns, and interviewing the Marines. This afternoon a submarine was reported on the Radar as being about 20 miles away. We have had Spitfire escort thus far on our journey, but have seen no hostile planes, although it would be easy for them to hide in the lowering clouds. The radio reported from London a rumor circulating there this morning that the Americans and British had already landed in France. The German radio denied this rumor. The BBC stated that the Allies had victoriously entered Rome. The German radio said the Germans had evacuated the Holy City, and the Allies had fallen into the trap and made the great strategical error of entering the Capital. Except for the radio war, all is quiet and peaceful on this ship, except that this instant we are hearing on the radio a transcription of the Allied tanks rumbling into Rome, and the cheers of the populace. The men of the Tuscaloosa are on the alert, many of them smoking their pipes and cigarettes, telling stories, and looking quite happy at the prospect of excitement. The Admiral has exercised by pounding the punching bag in his cabin, has taken a bath, had dinner with us, which consisted of mock turtle soup, excellent steak and vegetables, vanilla ice cream with chocolate sauce, and is now up above surveying his domain. I feel that something will soon happen, for General D., freshly shaven and bathed, has buttoned his trousers about his ankles, put on his rubber-soled shoes, taken out his olive wool cap, and is calmly eating an apple. Those who have been with him before on similar occasions tell me that when General D. puts on that costume one should be prepared for trouble. Everyone is now wearing or carrying life belts and steel helmets. The cabins have been stripped of glass, and movables have been lashed down. For security reasons, our ships have been sealed for some days—in the case of the Tuscaloosa, before we

left Belfast. Almost no messages from the outside world have been received by us although, to deceive the Germans, there has been no marked diminution of wire traffic, the gaps being filled with meaningless cypher groups. 10:30 p.m.—General D. and I had bacon and eggs. 11:45 p.m.—Ack Ack fire, probably over land, at airplanes on starboard side. Lasted about 15 minutes. Strange ships making 25 knots about 11 miles away appear on Radar screen. Are finally designated as friendly. On starboard side, four star shells shot into air at great distance, reason unknown.

June 6

1 a.m. Returning C-47's, probably those which dropped the Pathfinder Paratroopers, are passing over us. Feel sorry for the paratroopers tonight; there is a high wind and they will probably be badly scattered in landing. 20 miles off the port side there are flashes as if from heavy guns. 1:05 a.m. Cloudy but enough moon to see fairly well. We have been passing up a lane lined with buoys dropped by the minesweepers. On our port side is a seemingly endless row of landing craft. Some of them are tiny, and the troops, doubtless miserably cold and uncomfortable, have been on them for more than 24 hours. Our navigation has been excellent.

1:30 a.m. Large number of C-47's passing over us, returning from dropping personnel in France. Have been almost all over ship poking about. CIC (Combat Information Centre) is a most interesting place. It is a system only recently installed on American ships for calculating and centralizing combat intelligence, and its Radar control and mechanical detection devices are miracles of inventiveness. 1:55 a.m. Wind is 32 knots off port bow. Sea looks rough. It is quite cold, and everyone is muffled up in sweaters and heavy jackets. 2:35 a.m. Tuscaloosa has dropped anchor and will rest awhile. We slept from 3:00 to 4:10 a.m. and were on deck again at 4:15 a.m. It is astonishing that, with this vast force surrounding us, such quiet and blackout on the craft can prevail. Signals are given from ship to ship by carefully screened spotlights. Our deployment is all made. Each vessel has taken up its appointed position. Close to the shore, at 2,500 to 3,000 yards are the destroyers, whose job it is to breach the sea wall where our troops must land, and stop as far as possible any German fire directed against and along the beaches. The Tuscaloosa was in position at 5 a.m. but our instructions are not to open up until 5:18 a.m. and not to fire until 5:50 unless we are meanwhile attacked. Actually, about 5:30 some of our vessels became engaged with shore batteries, and by the time the Tuscaloosa opened at 5:45

While on board ship in the early hours of D day, Bruce observed the hundreds of C-47s returning from France and worried that high winds would scatter the paratroops they had just dropped behind German lines. Here troop-carrying gliders can be seen in the French fields while transport planes circle overhead. Courtesy of the National Archives.

Seeing "a seemingly endless row of landing craft" early on D day, Bruce realized the soldiers had been huddled on these small, open vessels for over twenty-four hours. Courtesy of the National Archives.

there had been fierce interchanges between the naval forces and the shore batteries. During the night there had been heavy bombing by the RAF, which was scheduled to drop 4,000 tons of high explosives. Early this morning they were followed by about 1,000 medium and heavy American bombers who were to attempt to saturate enemy defenses. It is still cold and windy, and the overcast is heavy so that our men are bombing through cloud. Minesweepers, one of which was torpedoed and sunk on the way over, reported no mines encountered in the American area. When daylight came, the activity was intense. As bomb loads were discharged, great flashes of fire shot toward the sky, followed by columns of dust and smoke, whilst, overhead, tracers from Ack Ack made golden sparkling showers amid the dark or silver planes. Once a Marauder, in the midst of a tight formation, received a hit, and flamed like a huge Bunsen

Burner for a minute before being reduced to a small globule of black soot that hung for a time high in the sky. Throughout the morning, fighters—Spitfires and Lightnings—patrolled above us but no Luftwaffe rose to meet them. At 6:30 a.m. the bombing of the Utah beachhead ceases; our troops start ashore, and land at 7:00. Of this phase we can see little, except that once a small ship was hit near the beach and thrown about 200 feet into the air. Meanwhile there is cannonading on all sides as well as from the shore. Spouts of water rise from near the ships as German long-range batteries try to reach them. The Black Prince is bracketed and hit, and calls for a smoke screen. 2 planes skim the water and interpose a billowing blanket of cloud between it and the shore. One of the planes, however, is hit and seems to skid along the water's surface until it bursts into a glowing ball and then disappears. Closer in, one sees the darting red tongues of the destroyers' guns. Bilious yellow clouds of smoke shoot forth above the mouths of our guns. Aboard the Tuscaloosa, the air is acrid with powder, and a fine spray of disintegrated wadding comes down on us like lava ash. Everywhere there is noise. When we fire, the deck trembles under our feet, and the joints of the ship seem to creak and stretch. When a whole turret is discharged the teeth almost rattle in one's head. At 7:10 a.m. the U.S. Destroyer Corry[25] has been hit and may have to be beached. She had previously been damaged on her way to her station by dropping a depth charge in shallow water against a suspected submarine. At the same time, a periscope was reported seen 1,000 yards from the Tuscaloosa. Some landing craft, having put their troops ashore, are returning—a good sign. A beach fire control party, or parties, has sent conflicting messages to the Shubrite, one that it is firing into our own men, another asking that it maintain its present attack. The Corry has now partially sunk, and will be replaced in her hot spot by the Butler. Communications between the ships are constant, by radio, telephone, by electric lamp signalling, by key, and even by wig-wag. For security reasons, the radio is used as little as possible. At 8:30 a.m. the Tuscaloosa had run out of targets for the time being. Four heavy enemy guns are shelling our troops on the beaches, but a landing has been effected and reinforcements are pouring in. The Hawkins, as well as the Black Prince, received direct hits early in the engagement, but have continued firing, and each has knocked out at least two enemy batteries. The most serious casualty thus far on the Tuscaloosa has been a direct hit by something on General D.'s water closet, adjoining the Admiral's cabin—at any rate, is is completely shattered and in ruins on the floor. When our own guns are discharged the noise is terrific, and without cotton in one's ears would be deafening. We have undergone thus far no attacks by enemy planes, nor have we seen any. There is now, at 9:50 a.m., a complete lull as far as this ship is concerned, and we have not been under enemy fire for some time—the last salvo against us was distant about 2,000 yards. The Tuscaloosa is beginning to look rather forlorn in the officers' quarters. Repeated concussions have driven screws out of their sockets, shattered light bulbs, thrown articles all over the floors, and generally made an awful mess. 10:00 a.m. A Spitfire in trouble lost altitude, gliding down to what seemed a perfect landing but, after a second, nosed under water and disappeared. 10:30 a.m. We are again being fired upon. The first shell was at 2,500 yards and then successively they hit at 2,000, 1,500, 1,000, 500 and 50 yards. After the last, and just in time, for the next shell fell in our anchorage, we shifted position and shelled them back. Our airplane spotters seem somewhat confused. Both the Omaha and Utah landings are so far successful. German radio announced at 7 a.m. the arrival of American paratroops in France, which probably means that some of them were captured. Resistance groups were ordered to await further instructions. Broadcasts have been given by Eisenhower, Churchill, Hull, etc. The Fitch has been hit, and is now picking up survivors of the Corry. 12:30 p.m. Our old enemy, a 3-gun battery which we cannot precisely locate, is keeping after us. It dropped a shell 200 yards away from us, and we got under way. The next shot was exactly correct for range, but off for deflection, which was lucky. When they hit the water near us it feels like depth charges beneath us. 2 p.m. We have fired from the Tuscaloosa over 400 shells. We cannot know how exact we have been except when a hostile battery stops returning our fire, but even so it may come into action again later on, or if it is one of the highly vexatious mobile units, it may reappear unexpectedly at another place entirely. The air spotting system is unsatisfactory. The fighters engaged on it are so far from their targets, and their speed is such that they cannot make very accurate identifications or reports, to say nothing of the many lapses that occur in radio-telephonic contact with them.

There is a decided weakness in the system of air support, and co-operation between it and ground and naval forces, as illustrated in this operation. (It needs much further study, exercises, and coordination.)[26] For instance, there are certain targets—such as mobile artillery and deeply casemated guns—which should be dealt with by bombers, and which the Navy cannot reasonably be expected to

neutralize. In the Utah area alone there are 38 reputed inshore batteries of 75 mm or larger guns which our small U.S. Navy contingent is expected to silence.

Much of the failure of German batteries to cause us greater damage is probably ascribable to the excellent new technical apparatus,
recently brought from Washington and installed on American ships,
which jams the German radio and Radar in a complete manner that
they have been unable to reciprocate. 4 p.m. Desultory fire from all
around us and at us. As General D. has often said, battles mostly
consist of waiting for something to happen. We have not seen Captain Waller for days—he has been constantly on the Bridge. The
Admiral, Commander South and Lieutenant Brooks, our table com-
panions, have been above steadily for the last 24 hours or longer.
The conduct of this ship is admirable—there is no undue bustle or
nervous excitement—everything is disciplined and orderly. We pick
up uncorrelated items of news. Of the destroyers that fired point
blank, at a 2,500-yard range on enemy defenses, only one has been
lost. It is said that no mines or barbed wire were encountered on the
Utah beach, and that advance elements of the U.S. Fourth Division
went ashore almost without loss.

The radio gives us news from outside our little sealed world. President Roosevelt, announcing the invasion, said: "Victory has still
some distance to go," and, speaking of the fall of Rome, expressed
the belief that Italy will again make a contribution to civilization.
Churchill has reported to the House of Commons that the landings
were attended by much less difficulty and with many fewer casualties
than had been apprehended. He stated that advances were being
satisfactorily made, that the paratroop operations, the largest ever
attempted in warfare, had been successful, and that the German
shore batteries had been badly crippled by air bombardment.

Many questions occur to one at this juncture. What happened to
the underwater obstacles so lately photographed, on these same
beaches, why was there no mining, or barbed wire entanglements?
Were the Germans short of troops and of materials, were the
boasted coastal defenses so impressive in photographs and in espionage reports a camouflage or a facade, or had they been seriously
reduced by protracted pre-invasion bombardments? What of the
rocket projectiles that were to blast London, Plymouth and other
cities?[27] Was complete surprise attained in spite of our gloomy
forebodings, or, knowing that they could not adequately defend
the whole coast, are the Germans counting on sucking us inland,
where they hope to destroy us with powerful counter-attacks? Did

the cover plans make them believe we were invading Denmark, Pas de Calais, and the Bay of Biscay? All these questions will soon be answered.

6 p.m. General D. and I have tea, eggs and marmalade. Men are sleeping all over the decks and corridors, collapsed over their guns, doubled up in corners, constrained into curious and uncomfortable postures. We go above to see the officers and hear the latest news. Our indefatigable officers still carry on unperturbed, but looking drawn and tired. Their usually impeccable uniforms are wrinkled or replaced by rougher garments, they are unshaven (in fact the water pressure is cut off), their eyes are red-rimmed, but they are as considerate and courteous as ever. We have the free run of the ship, and going from the CIC to the chart room, etc., is like stopping during the afternoon for gossip in a series of men's clubs—except there is nothing to drink!

7 p.m. Salvoes are occasionally discharged. At the moment we are engaging a battery that is holding up the 4th Division's advance along the beach beside the inundated areas. Dispositions for the night are being made—the larger ships will be in a sort of watery compound screened by destroyers. Attacks by E boats and bombers, as well as possibly by submarines, are expected. The weather has turned, and the sky is now almost entirely blue. This morning it was damp and cold, but this afternoon it is clear and mildly bracing. 8 p.m. The Admiral came down, vastly pleased with the success of the Nevada in breaking up 3 German tank concentrations which were threatening the 4th Division. By using the proper coordination and air spotting, at ranges varying from 26,000 to 28,000 yards, the Nevada's 14″ guns disposed of these groups with a single salvo each, and completely dispersed them. This is astonishing marksmanship. After the first salvo, a call came to Commander South stating the Nevada was firing into our own men and should cease. South said the voice sounded like that of an American, but when, after an inquiry was answered unsatisfactorily, he asked for authentication, there was a hesitation. About that time another burst was fired by the Nevada, and the man on the telephone said there was no use of his giving the authentication as it was now too late. He was undoubtedly a German. His location could not be determined.

10 p.m. More eggs, orange juice and gunfire. Went to bed, or rather lay down, shortly after midnight. Battle stations were manned. However, to everyone's surprise the night was quiet. One enemy raider dropped a bomb near us but we did not open fire, nor was there any activity by shore batteries. The sky was overcast and

the RAF was pounding French airfields, which may be one reason for the lack of initiative by the GAF in this vicinity.

June 7

Up at 7 a.m. Sky again overcast. We have just had delivered to us ten members of C-47 crews who were shot down and fell into the sea after dropping paratroopers inland. I talked to them in the sick bay. They dropped these men at 500 feet during daylight, and came out at 200 feet to avoid AA fire. These two planes were shot down, one by machine guns and the other, the pilot thought, by an automatic pistol. About 8 a.m. a stream of returning C-47's passed alongside us, skimming the sea. There were dozens of them, protected from overhead attack by Spitfires, Lightnings, and Mustangs.

Not much information in CIC this morning. The fascinating Remote Position Plan Indicator shows a continual movement of troops and supplies ashore, although there is still some enfilading fire against Omaha Beach.

The 10 a.m. broadcast announced that, in preparation for the assault, the U.S. Navy had convoyed 7,000 ships across the Atlantic. General de Gaulle arrived in London before the invasion commenced and conferred at once with Eisenhower; the latter stated they were in full agreement on military matters. French civilians have been warned to stay away from northern coast railways and highways. American airmen on Tuesday flew 9,050 sorties, losing 50 planes, and meeting little opposition. American planes newly based on Russian fields have attacked Galatz, in Rumania, and Allied troops have crossed the Tiber at all points.

The Erebus had to retire last night, having split one of her guns.

10:30 a.m. Heard the German radio program which is, as always, excellent. A crisp, optimistic communiqué, claiming the defeat and capture of British paratroop units near Trouville, and the setting on fire last night by E boats of 3 Allied destroyers. Germans claim last night to have shot down 38 American gliders and 51 transport planes carrying paratroops. They state: "The attempt to extend operations in Normandy has now been definitely smashed."

BBC: 1,000 RAF bombers were out last night bombing communications and concentrations behind the invasion forces. Also, American bombers were out this morning.

1 p.m. Commander South says that yesterday afternoon we picked up 3 floating corpses, 2 of sailors, the other a French aviator. A minesweeper was blown up near the beach this morning by a mine, as were several other ships. Few mines were encountered on invasion night, but today, for some unexpected reason, large num-

bers have been discovered and exploded. There have been north-westerly winds since the assault began.

The Quincy is going back to England this afternoon to reload with ammunition. This afternoon at 4 p.m. General D. and myself clambered down a swinging ladder on the Tuscaloosa and boarded a launch. We were accompanied by the aviators who were picked up this morning, by Shadel, and by the 3 corpses. We boarded a De-stroyer Escort vessel (the 695, Captain Michel[28]) which took us near the convoy concentration point. There an LCV (Landing Craft Ve-hicle), conducted by a swarthy boy from Chicago, was persuaded to take us near the Utah beach, where we transshipped to a Duck which took us ashore. As we reached the middle of the beach there was the drone of airplane motors and almost immediately after-wards machine gun fire as they swept immediately over us down the beach. The General, accustomed to such emergencies, rolled nimbly off the hood where we were sitting, onto the sand. I, with slower reflexes, followed, and fell squarely on General D., gashing his chin with my helmet. As the machinegun bullets spattered the Duck's hood, the General grinned happily and said, "Now it will be like this all the time."[29] Two of the 4 German planes involved, ME 109s, were shot down by anti-aircraft fire, and we saw one pilot descend-ing by parachute. This morning there had been a similar attack on the beach by 3 FW 190s, one of which was shot down. Whatever real obstacles had existed on the Utah beach had been removed and piled against the sea wall. Many fake obstacles, mostly wooden poles, still protruded from the sands. There was no barbed wire visible, there had been few mines, and our landing casualties had been very small. The contrary was the case in the Omaha area; there the mines were plentiful, and the troops had been forced to advance up narrow paths between mine fields, clearing their way as they went, against determined enemy opposition. We found our soldiers spread over a considerable area, and trucks passed us containing several German and a number of American wounded. A young American Lieutenant, who commanded a nearby anti-aircraft battery, told us that yesterday afternoon he had driven about 5 miles inland and had encountered some French families. He also pointed out a nearby house which (evidencing the surprise of our attack) was cap-tured on the morning of D-day, and found thoroughly stocked with luxuries such as wine, tobacco, etc. It had evidently served as a com-mand post and officers' Post Exchange.

We met Lieutenant General Bradley and Major General Royce. General Bradley is in command of the U.S. First Army and General Royce is from the 9th Air Force. They seemed well pleased with the

A day after the first D day landings, Bruce and Donovan made their way to Utah Beach on board an amphibious vehicle called a Duck, like the one seen here passing the USS *Arkansas* during the invasion. Courtesy of the National Archives.

progress made to date by the invasion. General D. arranged with General Bradley for me to come out soon and spend some time with the First Army.[30]

Getting away from the beach posed a dilemma, as we had no water transportation. General D. persuaded a young naval officer to send us back on his LCV, which at the moment contained a sailor's corpse, but, owing to the probable delay, we caught a passing Duck and then flagged a cruising LCV, which in turn delivered us to the DE, from which we were transferred to the Tuscaloosa, arriving in time for a later supper at 9 p.m., well content to have touched once more, even if briefly, the soil of France.

We found Bob Thayer[31] here. He is naval intelligence officer on the Bayfield. He said Hitler had just made a speech, boasting that the secret weapon[32] would be used tonight, and that by tomorrow morning there would be no American or British troops left in France, or Allied naval vessels in the Channel. He seemed somewhat vague about exactly what had been asserted, but the above was the gist of his recollection.

During our absence, we found the Tuscaloosa had been engaged in heavy and successful shelling in support of the ground troops. The mischievous old shore battery had come to life again and plumped a salvo between the Tuscaloosa and the Nevada.

Many E boats and submarines were reported to have left St. Nazaire and other Bay of Biscay ports yesterday, headed this way. At 11 p.m. we were told that 52 German bombers had been reported 175 miles away about an hour previously and might be expected here. Shortly afterwards it was stated they were over the Thames estuary.

June 8

12:40 a.m. Up on deck again. 5″ guns manned—E boats and aircraft reported near. From that time on there was plenty of action. Heavy bombing made furnace-like glows on the shore, while AA fire cascaded into the air, sometimes criss-crossing and intertwining beautiful yellow and red colors. We saw at least 3 airplanes shot down. A searchlight on land, supposedly German, made milky pathways fitfully through the sky, miles away. Star shells searched out an area of the sea. Constant reports rolled in, submarines and E boats were suspected of being near, the Radar was probably jammed, and rumors of every description were rampant. Meanwhile, bombing went on all about us and planes, friendly and unfriendly, were constantly overhead. Fires shot up on or near the beaches. We feared that Utah and Omaha were having a bad night of it. Our own ship Enterprise sent word she was being persistently attacked. Although it was believed inadvisable for the naval force to fire their AA guns for fear of betraying their positions, even more than the moonlight had already accomplished, the attacks provoked many of them to reply. Rocket bombs, the radio-controlled missile, on at least two occasions, came whizzing down.[33] Heavy explosions in enemy territory showed the RAF was also at work. The Meredith,[34] namesake of the destroyer lost in the Pacific and herself only newly commissioned, suddenly glowed brightly in the distance. Then a signal came saying she was badly damaged and needed assistance. Another destroyer (they are often affectionately referred to as "cans") went to her. Later 2 large tugs were despatched to try to salvage her. A PT boat crowded with men, some upright, others on stretchers but all cold and miserable and soaking wet, suddenly appeared alongside the Tuscaloosa and unloaded a lot of her survivors. A few minutes later a signal said her condition was hopeless and she would be abandoned. Morning will no doubt disclose other damages to vessels. At 4:15 a.m., things seemed comparatively quiet. We start a bombardment at 5 a.m. so there will be little rest for anyone this night, or what remains of it. 4:45 a.m. After shaving, lay down. No shower for days, as the pipes have burst and the nozzle at the same time split into fragments.

Awakened by our heavy firing but did not get up until 9 a.m. One of our DE's was sunk this morning. It was the Rich, No. 695, on which the General and I made our trip yesterday. Its stern was badly damaged by a mine, and after the crew went forward it ran into another mine; casualties were heavy. The enemy must have sown many mines during the night, and the sweepers are busy. We lost another destroyer this morning, the Glennan. It is down by the stern, and it may not be possible to salvage her. The Tuscaloosa is giving support to American Infantry about 4 miles inland from Utah beach. The Nevada is running out of ammunition. The weather is clear and mild after having been very cold in the early morning hours. We know nothing of what occurred on the beaches last night. Communications between the Army ashore, and its representatives on shipboard via Army channels has been from the beginning of the invasion regrettably poor. There is apparently no way of ascertaining satisfactorily how the overall operations are progressing, which, I should think, would be essential to the Army Commander and his staff on the command ship. We have an artillery officer, Lieutenant Colonel Campbell, with us. He has shore communications, and calls on our batteries for many jobs. However, his own people give him no idea of the general picture on land, and with a limited supply of ammunition it is difficult, though vitally important, to determine relative priorities.

We have been firing off and on all day, but there has been no particular excitement. 7 p.m. Weather has turned rainy and misty. At 9 o'clock left for HQ Ship Bayfield with Commander Mitchell and the Ship's Doctor. Saw Bob Thayer and went over the day's intelligence. Interviewed some wounded soldiers and searched the corpse of a French aviator, but found nothing interesting. On Utah beach salient we have now at the end of the third day reached the objectives set for achievement on D-day. On the whole, things appear to be going well on Utah and less well on Omaha. About 3,000 prisoners have been taken by Utah troops to date; 2,000 of them were sent to England this afternoon together with about 2,000 of our own wounded. Came back in little boat about 11:30 p.m. and found it quite an athletic feat to scramble up the rope ladder in the dark from a bouncing platform.

June 9

12:30 a.m. Usual excursions and alarums. Many planes reported, and reverberations of bombing from all directions. But the principal excitement was the detection of a pack of E boats, and the firing on them by members of our protective screen. Star shells were used to light up the E boats, and there was a great deal of firing, with the results as yet unknown. At any rate none of them penetrated near the big ships. Lay down, fully dressed as usual, at 2:45 a.m. At five o'clock an orderly called me and I turned out on deck, but found only shore shelling was in prospect so went back again.

8 a.m. The sky is very cloudy, and we have been informed there will be no planes from the UK today. We spent a lazy morning and afternoon, although the Tuscaloosa did a lot of shelling at the request of Shore Fire Control Parties. The Tuscaloosa is leaving this afternoon for England to refill with ammunition, so Admiral Deyo and his staff shifted over to the Quincy. At 6 p.m. we weighed anchor and started for Plymouth.

The German radio announced tonight that 200,000 gross tons of Allied invasion craft had been sunk since the invasion started, in addition to the loss of 334 planes and 1300 gliders.

En route to Plymouth, we ran into two submarine attacks, but reached there without any untoward incident at 1:30 a.m. Ira Wolfert,[35] a war correspondent, came back with us. He says the success of the Utah landing was in rather large degree due to our troops having debarked by accident about 1,000 yards to the east of their appointed beach. It turned out that, had they not done so, they would have had to pass over a heavily mined area.

General Donovan commandeered a Navy automobile in Plymouth. The driver was a former automobile racing man, and far more dangerous than any German shells. However, we arrived in London safely at 10 o'clock, having stopped for breakfast at headquarters of Southern Base Section.

5

Today We Have the First
of the Pilotless Aircraft Raids

London, June 10 to 23, 1944

June 10

General Donovan, Ira Wolfert and myself arrived in London about 10 o'clock. I had my first bath in many days, and reported at Claridge's at 1 o'clock, where the General entertained all the Branch heads for lunch, as well as certain other members of the organization.

The General expressed to those present his continued concern that our plans for participation in the war in France had not, whether from our own lack of vision or whether as the result of the reluctance on the part of the American Army to allow a greater scope to our activities, sufficiently taken into account the work our field detachments might do on levels lower than Army. He referred to the fact that during our visit to France he had received confirmation of his prediction that our Army lines would be fluid, and many Frenchmen would be wandering back and forth between our own and enemy territory with comparatively little hindrance. These men, he thought, should be interrogated by our field detachments, and, where found suited to and willing to undertake such work, should be used for intelligence and sabotage purposes, through infiltration and exfiltration. He added that if we could supply such agents with men previously trained by us in W/T communications, so direct contact could be had with these agents by wireless from a field base, it would be important to make such arrangements. In such cases, it would not be necessary for an agent who had penetrated the enemy lines to run the additional risk of coming out and making a personal report.

It was pointed out to General Donovan that Colonel Dickson,[1] G-2 of First Army, had consistently scoffed at the idea that French civilians within the battle zones would enjoy any freedom of movement,

70

and he had consistently refused our request to make provision for such a contingency. In the case of SO, its activities, by direction of G-3 SHAEF were, in conjunction with those of SOE, to engage in strategical, as distinguished from tactical, missions. Since SOE/SO headquarters are directly under the orders of G-3 SHAEF, it might be impracticable to engage in sending saboteurs through the lines without previously having obtained permission from G-3.

The General's instructions were that we should make a renewed attempt, both in the case of SI and SO, and to a lesser degree of X-2, to have the military authorities revise their previous instructions in the light of current conditions, and for us to endeavor to work down to Division level.[2]

He also re-stated his desire that, as quickly as possible, we attempt to arrange with Third Army and later with FUSAG,[3] the attachment to those forces of an over-all OSS officer or officers, who could co-ordinate the work of the various OSS branches of OSS in the field.

The rest of the day was spent in a discussion of a multitude of organizational problems.

June 11

I met the General again at 1 o'clock for lunch. During the afternoon he continued his conferences with members of our staff.

Saw "C,"[4] who was dining with Bill Stephenson. General Donovan came in during our discussion. I pointed out to him a situation which might shortly arise where we would wish to introduce into France agents who had already been trained in the U.K. As he recalled, we had received instructions from the American Theater Commander long ago, and we had since followed them in our operations, that we would despatch no agents from the U.K. without having previously cleared it with SIS. It now seemed impractical to obtain such clearance in emergency cases, because of the time element involved. "C" readily agreed to our suggestion that, in the case of agents sent abroad to operate through enemy lines in an American Army zone, it would not be necessary to obtain such clearance from his organization. Details of this arrangement are set forth in a memorandum in our files under this date.[5]

June 12

General Donovan went out today to the Black station in the country with Armour, Oechsner and Rae Smith. I remained in town and at 11:30 called on Ambassador Winant in company with Russ

Forgan.[6] We brought to Gil's attention the unsatisfactory state of our relations with David Gray, American Minister to Eire. Mr. Gray, of whom I am personally very fond, is exceedingly touchy about his prerogatives, and has long felt that our representative, Spike Marlin, is too pro-Irish, and in addition displays an inclination to discuss with Irish officials matters which lie within the jurisdiction of American diplomacy. After Marlin and Will[7] had reached an agreement with the Eire authorities, shortly before invasion, to tighten Irish security controls over German and Japanese espionage attempts, Gray had felt offended because he considered that neither ourselves nor the American Embassy in London, which latter was a party to these negotiations, had kept him sufficiently informed of the projects. He also felt that, in not so doing, the Ambassador and our office had violated established State Department protocol.

Winant assured me he would smooth Mr. Gray's ruffled feathers. He then went on to say that the murky diplomatic situation relating to General de Gaulle was causing him deep concern, and requested me frankly to express my individual views concerning it. I told him I considered de Gaulle was truly the symbol of French resistance in metropolitan France, that I believed American prestige had gravely suffered from our refusal to accord a more complete measure of recognition to the French Provisional Government, that I had great confidence in the ability of the Resistance groups (which had in some degree already been justified), to assist our invading forces by harassing the enemy's communications lines, by sabotage, by physical subversion of all kinds, and to some extent, by guerilla warfare. I added that since approximately 80 percent of the military and naval intelligence on which the plans for invasion of the Continent were founded had, it is estimated, been supplied by the BCRA,[8] a Gaullist organization, anything completely offensive to General de Gaulle might have repercussions on the services the Resistance groups and the French secret intelligence organization were performing for the Allies. I stated in addition that, having dealt at one time or another with the leaders of practically every Resistance group in France, I felt none of them had an attitude of personal subserviency to General de Gaulle, and in my opinion the supposed State Department fear that he, if accorded full recognition, would, with the assistance of the Resistance groups, set himself up as a dictator, was without adequate foundation to justify the continuation of a policy which at the present time had not only antagonized but alienated the friendly feelings towards America of large and virile portions of the population of France.

Upon General Donovan's return from the country, we discussed the conversations between himself and Messrs. Oechsner and Smith relating to the fundamental differences between these two individuals as to the direction to be followed by the MO organization. Smith wishes to place priority upon the "black" work, which would include not only dissemination of rumors, but also publication of a weekly French and German newspaper and magazine, the furnishing of additional personnel to the PWD black radio stations, the dissemination of subversive leaflets, the employment and training of agents for use behind enemy lines, and the dropping of American officers for psychological warfare purposes amongst Resistance groups. Oechsner, on the other hand, feels the "black" has not clearly justified its usefulness, and priority must be given to the support of MO's role in PWD, where we are furnishing combat propaganda, consolidation and post-occupational personnel, as well as certain equipment and very considerable financial support. Because of the recruiting problem, it is clear that the personnel required by Oechsner and Smith cannot be adequate to meet the needs of both of them. Although Smith is the head of MO branch, London, Oechsner has control over him, since Fred is in charge of MO activities in all of Europe and the Middle East.

The General told them he wanted the black as well as the PWD work continued, but in matters concerning the allocation of personnel, the ultimate decision was to rest with Fred and he should exercise arbitrary power over the assignment of personnel.

Tonight the General had a buffet supper of sandwiches and beer, and left for Prestwick by train at 8:50.

June 13

Commander Kenneth Cohen came to see Russ Forgan and myself this morning to discuss the terms suggested by BCRA for the attachment of French liaison officers to SI and SIS field detachments. The order of mission to these officers, embodying their instructions and sent by General Koenig[9] as C in C of French forces in the UK, would seem to give them authority, on the face of the order, to veto any decisions regarding the use of present or prospective French agents, whether already recruited, or recruited in the field by OSS field commanders. Cohen said SIS had not intended to make an issue of the language of the order of mission, but he would appreciate being informed by us of the further course of conversations with Colonel Roulier[10] on the subject, so that SI and SIS might, if we wished, present a united front in this matter. We decided to leave the order of mission as written, but regard it as an internal French affair, and to work out later any changes which field experience might prove to be desirable. A memorandum of this conversation is in our files.

This afternoon I saw Aaron Brown[11] of the American Legation, Dublin. He had a personal message to me from Gray relating to Marlin. I asked him to arrange with the Minister for Marlin to go to Ireland and introduce his successor, Lawler,[12] to the appropriate Irish officials.

Commander Herbert Agar[13] called to inquire whether it was true we were bringing Paul Hagen[14] to England and if so he would like to discuss the matter before Hagen engaged in any work here. I found that MO was employing a Hagen, who is a statistician, but could obtain no further information regarding Paul Hagen, who was at one time employed by SI, Washington.

Dined with the d'Erlangers.

Today we have the first of the pilotless aircraft raids; the so-called German secret weapon.[15] They commenced at dawn and were on a small scale.

Only four aircraft, all of which exploded, were located on land. The estimated effect of the warhead is comparable to that of a German 2,000-pound bomb. It has minimum penetration and maximum blast, the latter probably effective for a 500-yard radius. The wing span of the craft is supposed to be approximately 16 feet, and its overall length about 25 feet. It is compass-controlled, with an air speed of approximately 280 miles per hour, and is flown at a height of around 2,000 feet.

June 14

We had conference this morning with Colonel Roulier, Colonel de Besse, Captain Guittary,[16] Colonel Forgan and other officers. This followed a conversation with Roulier and confirmed the agreement reached at that former meeting. We now have a definite procedure outlined for the contact of the French liaison officers with our field detachments.

At 11:00 a.m. I saw Lieutenant Colonel Arthur Roseborough on the subject of our working with the 9th Air Force in France.

I lunched with Edwina Mountbatten, who had Mrs. Gubbay, Audrey Bouverie, and David Sarnoff[17] as the other guests.

June 15

At 10:30 a.m. Russell Forgan and I went to see General Sibert and arranged with him for the attachment of a rotating staff with

Within days of returning from Utah Beach to his London office, Bruce began recording in his diary the first attacks of the German V-1s. One of these—called variously pilotless German aircraft, buzz bombs, and doodlebugs—can be seen here falling in the vicinity of Picadilly on June 22, 1944. Courtesy of the National Archives.

FUSAG in the field. In the afternoon I saw Major Hayes, whom General Donovan wishes to transfer to this organization. Later, General Gaffy,[18] Chief of Staff of the 3rd Army, came in to discuss the attachment of Colonel Vanderblue to the 3rd Army. Forgan and I took General Gaffy and Colonel Gus Guenther over to the Operations Room at SF Headquarters.

At the end of the day we discussed with Rae Smith the memorandum to Oeschner as to whether the MO Branch should be continued on the present basis.

Between 2350 hours 15 June and 1800 hours 16 June some 160 PAC (Pilotless Air Craft) were launched, one-half of which made landfall in the U.K.

June 16

I had a long conversation this morning with Rae Smith and Commander Lester Armour regarding the future of the SO Branch.

Went to Bushy Park at 3:30 p.m. to see General Betts[19] and discussed with him the proposal already approved by FUSAG to attach in rotation to G-2, FUSAG, Colonels Forgan, Bruce, and Giblin,[20] and Commander Armour. He approved the idea in principle and will endeavor to clear it with G-3 and PWD before submitting it to the Chief of Staff.

At 5:00 p.m. the matter of priorities in the use of MO personnel as between the Black operations and PWD was thrashed out between Messrs. Oeschner and Rae Smith and Forgan, Armour, Gilbin and Bruce. We were all in agreement that a substantial Black operation was necessary in order, if for no other reason, to justify our participation in PWD, especially from the standpoint of financial support of PWD plans.

In regard to particular personnel, notably Walter Kerr and John Elliott,[21] it was arranged that I should see John Whittaker tomorrow, who will in turn take the question up with Oeschner.

Dined tonight with Bill Stephenson. He was very optimistic about the progress of military operations.

Up to 17 June, 100 people have been killed and 500 seriously wounded in the Greater London area by pilotless plane bombs. In country districts, 10 persons have been killed and 50 seriously wounded. No rockets have so far been launched.[22]

June 17

From 2400 hours to 0500 hours on 17 June, 143 PAC reported by Radar, 70 of which made landfall. Fighters destroyed 8, AA approximately 10.

From 11:30 17 June to 1540 18 June, 138 PAC launched. 94 made landfall, 52 landed Greater London, 30 outside—rest undiscovered. 5 destroyed by fighters. No report yet on AA results. Between 0540 and 0900, 15 more landed. Photo Reconnaissance shows two new sites ready between the Seine and the Somme and three new sites in Pas de Calais area. Gus Guenther was killed (Sunday, June 18) by a pilotless plane explosion in the Guard's Chapel at the Wellington Barracks.[23]

Saw John Whittaker and Stacy Lloyd[24] this morning and further discussed MO operations. Whittaker ascribes very little importance to the Black, but feels it should not be a difficult task for a small number of competent men to publish a Black or Gray paper in German and French.

Lunched with Arthur Goldberg and George Pratt.[25]

At 3:00 p.m. decorated Lieutenant John R. North and Lieutenant Burke with the Silver Star, which had been awarded to them for their exploits in the Mediterranean last summer.

Conferred with Cassady[26] and Forgan on the future of the Medusa Plan.

There were pilotless air raids all afternoon. After today, it is likely that AA fire will no longer be directed against these pilotless planes but, if they are not shot down by fighters, they will be permitted to fall wherever the end of their flight may place them.

June 18

Went to the office in the morning and read cables. More raids today. Dined with Chester Beatty.[27]

Yesterday, and so far today, there has been no anti-aircraft fire in the London area against PAC. I think there are two main reasons for the discontinuance in this area of AA fire:

(a) Because they were rarely able to hit PAC; and

(b) Unless the PAC were exploded in the air by hitting the warhead, it did no good to bring them down as they naturally explode upon impact.

June 19

At 10:00 a.m. saw Majors Gaskell and Scaife regarding the status of the French liaison officer, Colonel Bilbane, attached to SI detachment at 3rd Army. 2:15 p.m. Called on General Roy Lord,[28] Deputy Chief of Staff, to make a general agreement on the issuance of Army orders to members of our organization who may visit the continent.

4:00 p.m. Further conferences with Major Gaskell, Colonels Forgan and Vanderblue, Roulier and de Besse on the relationship between ourselves and BCRA in the field. It was settled that Colonel Bilbane

A team of "Jedburgh" agents intended to be dropped into Occupied France receives radio instructions before departure. Courtesy of the National Archives.

would be under the orders of Major Gaskell, and Major Gaskell would make all payments to French agents. Such payments, with names of agents, would be reported to this headquarters, which in turn would settle the allocation of expenses with BCRA, probably on a fifty-fifty basis.

4:30 p.m. The Executive Committee discussed plans for a move by part of this headquarters to the continent when the zone of communications[29] headquarters staff begins to operate there.

Colonel Joseph Haskell,[30] Lieutenant Colonel Van der Strict and others met to consider the problem of whether, for the purpose of gathering intelligence in specific areas, SOE/SO Headquarters could not instruct its field agents, Jedburghs,[31] and organizers to perform such tasks. It was pointed out that such a procedure would be very difficult because of the understanding between SOE and SIS that SOE would not give instructions of an intelligence nature to SOE agents. It was decided to present this matter to G-2, SHAEF and seek his assistance in bringing about the desired result.

Tonight Bill Stephenson gave a dinner for the top personnel of Baker Street to which he invited Colonels Forgan, Haskell, Giblin, Commander Armour, and myself.

June 20

At 10:00 a.m.—Staff Meeting. Colonel Reutershan reported for duty this morning and will be assigned to SI Branch. It was settled that Colonel Palmer[32] will serve, at least temporarily, as assistant to Colonel Forgan. Bunny Carter came in from 3rd Army and said part of our lift for the SI detachment had been set back but he was trying to persuade General Gaffy to send over the detachments as a unit.

Lunched with Colonel Giblin and George Brewer,[33] who has just returned from Sweden, at the American Club.

I saw Ambassador Winant this morning. He informed me the Irish situation vis-à-vis Minister Gray is in such shape that we can now send our X-2 personnel there.

3:00 p.m.—Meeting of the American Intelligence Committee. Colonel Forgan presented at this meeting an interesting paper on the accomplishments of SF headquarters thus far in the management of resistance forces in France.

When I returned to the office, I found Minister Gray had tried to reach me by telephone from Dublin. He then telephoned the Embassy and stated he was unwilling to have Marlin come to Ireland tomorrow. I am, therefore, sending a personal letter to Mr. Gray by Will, setting forth my feeling that Marlin has been a loyal member of this organization and has done an efficient intelligence job in Eire.

Commander Graveson[34] wanted some Mark 21 sets from Broadway. I discussed this with Commander Cohen, who agreed to furnish them but pointed out that, since they were to be used by agents dropped into Brittany, he felt this matter should have been cleared with his office.

June 21

Arranged with Maddox[35] to see Cohen on the subject of Brittany agents. We also have before us this morning a letter from Cohen regarding the request to us from Algiers to send an intelligence team into Czechoslovakia. This was first referred by me to General Ingry of the Czechoslovakian Government, who replied in effect that he would appreciate our taking it up with the British. The British oppose our sending such a team. Since this presents the same type of problem which has frequently arisen in the past, we expect to make representations to Broadway regarding our intention of preserving an independent secret intelligence contact with all foreign governments or secret services.

Commander John Ford,[36] who has just come back from the beaches, reports that his Field Photographic group did a very fine job. One of his men was on the destroyer, Corry, which was sunk.

Lunched today at the Waldorf with Major Murray Gurfein.[37] We saw Roulier there, and as a result of his intervention with the Chef, had a wonderful lunch of smoked salmon, steak and strawberries. The Chef, Ruette, has relatives in Passy's service.

Lester and I had a long talk this afternoon with Major John Elliott, who has agreed to continue his efforts with Rae Smith to publish a weekly German newspaper.

Wally Booth came in from Area B to discuss his ideas of tying up the Northern chain of Medusa by dropping W/T operators of the Proust[38] group in the Paris and the Loire areas. Booth is still anxious to be commissioned in the Army. He has failed his physical examinations to date on account of deafness. Usually, before taking the examination, he blows his nose vigorously, which improves his hearing, but the last time he forgot to do this and received a very bad medical report. We are now trying to obtain a waiver for him.

Saw Bill Stephenson at Claridge's at 6:00 p.m.

General Bedell Smith, Chief of Staff, telephoned this afternoon and reprimanded me for a despatch sent via U.S. Naval Communications by Colonel John Haskell to General Donovan in Washington, an information copy of which was received in London. Admiral Stark had sent it to General Smith, who said that, since it contained reports on military and political matters, it should only have been sent to Washington after having been cleared through General Eisenhower's Headquarters. We immediately instructed Haskell in this sense.

June 22

Four Proust men who are to be dropped in Brittany in a few days are lacking the proper French clothes. SI called SO for help in furnishing these, and the delay of SO in so doing has caused some inter-branch animosity. However, Joe Haskell has undertaken to straighten the matter out.

We were informed this morning that Gaskell, head of SI field detachment at 3rd Army, is in the hospital with an aggravated case of malaria and will not be able to return to duty for a month or longer. We have made arrangements therefore to shift Colonel Coster from 21st Army Group to take Gaskell's place.

At lunchtime, Forgan and I picked up Colonel Passy and all went down to Berry Bros. There, we had three bottles of champagne and some armagnac with Major Rudd and Mr. Warner Allen. The champagne was Krug 1929, Krug 1926 and Pommery and Greno 1892— the last practically a still wine, but excellent. They have promised to have us again for a Burgundy lunch. Passy talked very interestingly

Admiral Harold R. Stark, seated at desk, the commander of U.S. naval personnel in the European theater, confers with Hollywood film director John Ford, head of the OSS photographic branch. Courtesy of the National Archives.

about the Resistance Group movement and its success. Approximately eight German divisions are believed to have been immobilized by the activities of this movement.

On the morning of 6 June, every telephone and telegraph line from Paris to major concentration points such as Calais, Creil, Lyons and Marseilles was cut.

They remained so for four days, and when the Germans repaired them they were cut again.

Sabotage began instantly on railways radiating from the capital, so that the Germans were compelled to arrest 36 chief executives of the railways and appoint their own men to these vital positions.

Bridges were blown between Paris, Normandy and Brittany. Several of the most important war factories in the Paris district were closed down by the Germans because of large-scale sabotage.

This activity around Paris has put the German Command in a quandary, whether to employ thousands of German troops in hunting down the saboteurs, or to save manpower and allow the sabotage to go on.

Militarily, the most serious threat to the Germans comes from organized resistance in the Jura Alps, Massif Central, around the Lower Rhone Valley, and great stretches of the Dordogne River.

Here, German troops have had to be used to isolate whole departments, and to take over executive powers to immobilize Patriot forces.

Shortly after invasion day, in the Massif Central, a large combination of Patriot forces was attacked by a whole German division. About 1200 Patriots were killed. Orders were immediately given to all Resistance groups to avoid concentrating in large numbers and to split up into small guerilla bands.

Ambassador Phillips came to see me this afternoon to obtain any information we have on the strength of de Gaulleism in Normandy.

Since Normandy, and particularly the region around Isigny, is the great center of milk production in France, and since the Normans have always been famous for being well fed, the conditions of life there under German occupation have probably been better from a food standpoint than in almost any other portion of France. In addition, the behavior of the German troops has been very correct. The Norman is a conservative politically. For these and other reasons, especially the close control exercised over the seacoast areas by the Germans, the strength of De Gaulle in Normandy has apparently to date not proved to be impressive.

We received today a copy of a cable from the War Department to Eisenhower stating that the OSS request for an additional 600 officers and 2,000 enlisted men could only be met, if at all, by taking this allotment out of the troop T/O of ETO. There will, of course, be great opposition to this procedure. At a meeting of Branch Chiefs, it was decided that this subject would be discussed by Joe Haskell with General Bull,[39] and by Forgan and myself with Generals Betts and Barker before we approach the Chief of Staff.

I have had considerable difficulty in getting orders from 21st Army Group and 1st American Army to go to France and meet John Haskell there. Tonight permission came through.

A cable arrived this morning from John Haskell stating that General Bradley, commanding the 1st American Army, had ordered all OSS activities, except PWD, with 1st Army to be grouped together in a separate camp for unified administration purposes under the senior officer present. Operationally, each detachment remains under G-2 or G-3.

Saw Colonel Guy Westmacott,[40] of British SIS. He has just returned from France, and had a stormy channel crossing. Because of conditions in the channel during the past few days, all travel has been behind time, and there is serious difficulty in supplying the British and Canadian Army with sufficient munitions and stores.

At 3:30 p.m. Forgan, Maddox and I went to see General Betts about having SF instruct its networks to make intelligence reports. He will take up this matter with the proper authorities. Because of the touchy relationship between SIS and SOE, it is a delicate problem to approach.

Later, we had a long conversation with Graveson and Joe Haskell about General Gubbins' letter to me demanding that the British radio operators at Station Charles[41] be immediately replaced by Americans. We decided to send 36 of our newly arrived operators to replace the male British personnel there, and refer to Washington for a possible substitution of 60 WACs for the 60 British FANYs.[42]

6

The Scene of Bitter Fighting

Normandy, June 24 to July 1, 1944

June 24

Further conferences with Joe Haskell, Graveson and Canfield regarding the situation at Station Charles.

10:30 a.m. George Pratt and Arthur Goldberg are very anxious to have Jolis and some of the "Faust" (German) agents sent abroad as soon as possible.

Commander Turnbull[1] gave me a list of document and clothing requirements he wished me to secure from France.

We discussed Commander Cohen's letter on the limitation of WT communications from PROUST agents to Station Victor.[2] Since this is connected with the old prohibition against our sending abroad agents from the UK without express clearance from SIS, it was decided that Forgan would take the matter up with C.

After innumerable last-moment conferences at the office, I motored out beyond Reading to the 9th Air Force field at Grove, near Wantage, and boarded a C-47. It was filled with mail and cargo, and the only other passengers were a supply sergeant and a not over-feminine Army nurse. We lay on the sacks, and an hour and a quarter after leaving the airport landed in France on a metal runway near Omaha Beach. It was a beautiful flight. We were unescorted by fighters but saw no enemy planes.

I was fortunate enough to meet John Haskell on the beach about 5:30 p.m., and he took me at once to the Norman Manor house which is the headquarters of the OSS detachments.

The original part of this building was constructed in the early 17th Century. It is of stone and forms part of a large square, two sides of which, in addition to the side occupied by the main building, are composed of long, solid stone stables, cowbarns, and granaries; along the other part runs a wall about ten feet high. Within this enclosure, the exact center of which is occupied by a manure

After the D day landings, Bruce made several visits to OSS units with the Allied armies in Normandy. Here soldiers and equipment move out from the beaches toward the front in July 1944. Courtesy of the National Archives.

pit, there are varied and ever-shifting contingents of ducks, geese, chickens, donkeys, turkeys and pigeons, to say nothing of groups of children so numerous that they seem to have been spontaneously generated from the soil.

The Manor house and the farm are rented from the absent proprietor by a typical family of Norman peasants; that is to say, somewhat dour, substantial, conservative, apparently unemotional, well-fed, healthy-looking individuals, devoted to the practical and little given to the aesthetic. I was given the ample nuptial bed in a room with John Haskell, Bill Jackson and Lieutenant Colonel Colby. Across the hall were Ken Downs[3] and Captain Guittary, our French Liaison Officer from BCRA. In a neighboring field is our encampment, with camouflaged tents, motor equipment, telephones, and other operational impedimenta, while our radio center is across the fields some distance from us.

John Haskell has done an excellent and difficult job in bringing our scattered units together and concentrating them under a central administrative control.

I was taken at once to call on Major General Keane, Chief of Staff to General Bradley, and Colonel Myers,[4] the Deputy Chief of Staff. There, as elsewhere, thanks to John Haskell's previous friendships and his engaging personality, I was courteously received, and made to feel that OSS is welcome in this area.

John and I had supper at headquarters, and set out afterwards, with Bill Jackson, in a jeep. Stopping at Isigny, once the center of the French dairying industry and now a sadly battered village, we called on Monsieur Duhamel to try to persuade him to be head cook for our establishment. He had worked in New York for many years as chef for old Ogden Mills[5] and later for Hal Phipps. He was deaf to our importunities, excusing himself on the grounds of age—62— and family responsibilities. However, he recommended that we call on Monsieur Fleuri, the Mayor of Isigny, where we might hope to buy some wine which the Germans had overlooked. We have lost a chef, but at least we may gain some brandy as a result of our visit.

Quitting Isigny, we went through Carentan, where our trip might well have come to an untimely end. Just as we were about to pass a shattered building, a German shell descended in the middle of the débris about twenty-five yards away, but, aside from throwing up a shower of dust and rubble, did no harm. It was followed by two others, uncomfortably close, as we sped by. Carentan is completely messed up, since it is close to a bulge in the German lines. The day of its capture, the X-2 men picked up a clandestine German radio set there, but the operator had beaten a successful retreat.

We passed through Montebourg, the scene of recent fighting. It is sad to see how ruined and devastated it is. The amazing thing in this trip was the lack of congestion of traffic on the beautiful, straight road to Cherbourg, in spite of the bitter struggle there. We went to within five miles of Cherbourg, and stopped at the Command Post of the 79th Division, a unit which is distinguishing itself. There was a good deal of gunfire to be heard and smoke to be seen over the port.

We turned around and, before reaching Carentan, branched off the main road and visited a farmhouse where Captain Guittary and some of the Proust men are collected. They all seem delighted to be back in France and the men eager to do work in enemy territory.

We motored back in fine, clear, cold weather to our base, which we reached about midnight.

In many fields along the road we saw the mangled remains of American gliders that had transported parachute troops. As the fields are small and heavily staked, landing losses, aside from enemy action, must have been very great. Some American parachutists are said to have had their throats cut, others to have been hanged, when captured by the Germans. It is reported that their comrades retaliated by taking no prisoners.

June 25

Had a good breakfast of café au lait and a fried egg at the farmhouse. Although we are in a great fruit country, there is none in season at this time of year. In spite of this being Sunday, one would only suspect it by noticing the attire of the peasants as they go to and from their churches. The usual neat, black Sabbath clothes are much in evidence. As we drive along, most of the children make the V sign and wave their hands, as do many of their elders. The natives seem to accept stoically the destruction of their homes. We have seen many refugees, sheltered by their neighbors, and all of them have expressed their relief, in spite of their own losses, at being rid of the Germans.

The larger towns and villages, especially those situated at crossroads or on railways, have been tragically damaged by shelling and bombing. However, as one moves about the country, one is impressed not so much by what has gone but how much, under the circumstances, remains.

We have passed numerous trucks loaded with enemy prisoners, and are struck by their sorry appearances. They seem of all ages, most of them shabby and dejected, with occasionally a fine, strapping, arrogant-looking blond youngster amongst them. In fact, I would believe that a considerable percentage of them are non-Germanic, probably Poles and Russians.

John Haskell and I found a farmhouse which we can use when Army Headquarters move within a few days. It has been ordered that the OSS contingent shall be billeted or bivouacked not less than 500 yards or more than two miles from the new headquarters.

One is pleasantly surprised by the abundance of food here, with the exception of bread, which is in small supply. Today we had delicious steak from a local cow for lunch, and an equally satisfactory roast beef tonight. Butter, formerly requisitioned by the Germans, is everywhere for sale in great golden blocks. Camembert cheese can be bought for 22 cents a box; with the exception of butter and cheese, prices are, however, high. Civil Affairs officers, under the

Army Command, have very wisely barred most of our soldiers from frequenting the neighboring villages and restaurants—otherwise we would probably devour the inhabitants' provisions and merchandise like a plague of locusts.

We went to two of the American Corps today and made arrangements to furnish them personnel and also French liaison officers from BCRA.

Did a great deal of motoring over this beautiful countryside and went to bed about midnight.

Everywhere there are trucks, troops, and tents. The fields are filled with ammunition, gasoline, and supplies. During the day there is an incessant buzzing of friendly airplanes—at night all is quiet except for occasional shell fire. Many of the roads along which one travels are within range of enemy artillery, but few of them appear to have been much damaged.

The inhabitants do not seem to be as strongly Gaullist as they are said to be in many other parts of France. The photograph of Marshal Petain is still in a place of honor in some houses we have visited. The population does, however, welcome with open arms and kisses officers in French uniforms. Our liaison officer, Captain Guittary, is overjoyed by this type of reception.

June 26

Not up until 8:30, which is the same as the existing double summer time in England. The sun is shining, and the birds are being very cheerful. Toombs,[6] our MO intelligence officer, with PW, came to see us at breakfast time.

Later, John Haskell and I went to Bayeux, and found it almost unscathed by war. We lunched at the Hotel Lion d'Or, once a famous hostelry. The dining room contained a mixed bag of British, Canadians, and Americans. The food was naturally meager in variety but substantial and well-cooked—hors d'oeuvres, stewed lamb and cheese. There was no wine or spirits on sale. We had to do some shopping, and obtained plywood boards for map backing, and other things. There was a surprising abundance of miscellanous articles for sale in the shops—for instance, plastic tableware and an array of porcelain and furniture such as one would not find in London.

We motored to General Montgomery's headquarters, which was under canvas outside of Bayeux and there found Major Mills, the SF British representative, but Colonel Henderson,[7] the SIS man, has not yet arrived. From there, we visited the American Ground Forces salvage dump, where all the flotsam and jetsam of military paraphernalia is gathered and sorted. Most of it is picked up and trucked from the battlefront, and includes thousands of mess tins, helmets, gas masks, clothing, etc., lost, abandoned, or left by our soldiers. Much of it, of course, belonged to dead or wounded men. We selected what we thought might be of use at our camp. At Isigny we bought from the Mayor, who is also a wine dealer, some Calvados, Cognac, Champagne, Sauterne, White and Red Burgundy. There were 12 bottles in all, at 2,080 francs, or $41.60. None of these brands were of high quality, but we were fortunate to get anything, since during the German occupation their troops took the major portion of the vintners' stocks everywhere in France.

John and I did other errands and returned in time for supper to find the X-2 boys had some British and French CE officers eating and spending the night with us.

During my stay I have seen a great number of our Army Staff officers, amongst others General Keane, Chief of Staff, Colonel Sam Myers, Deputy Chief of Staff, Colonel Dickson, G-2, and Colonel Thorsen,[8] G-3, and Colonel Page, P&PW, of 1st Army.

At V Corps, we saw Colonel Ford, G-2, and Lieutenant Colonel Adams, Assistant G-3 (Colonel Hill, the G-3, was out).

At 19 Corps, Colonel Washington Platt, G-2, Lt. Colonel Tom Crystal, Assistant G-2, and Colonel Maguire, Chief of Staff, and Colonel West, G-3.

At Bayeux we had a long talk with Monsieur Mercader,[9] leader of the local French intelligence organization.

Since the invasion, he has been through the enemy lines nine times. He is a bicycle dealer and was at one time racing bicycle champion of France—a resourceful, brave and agreeable young fellow. He has just put three agents through the lines for the British, and two for ourselves.

As always in warfare, one is impressed by the calm of field staff officers as compared with their tension and preoccupation with paper work and details in such places as Washington, London, or training camps. Here there is no great bustle around them. The atmosphere in their tents is quiet and orderly. There is little telephoning, and a minimum of files, and therefore more time for deliberation and conversation.

The feeling of the people here toward the Americans and British was, I am told, in the beginning somewhat lukewarm. The Norman is by nature undemonstrative. The German troops had behaved very correctly. The homes of many of the inhabitants had been blown to pieces by us. Would these new victors, against whom they had been warned by the Vichy radio, treat them any better than had their Teuton conquerors?

Soon the Normans thawed out. Everywhere we go French civilians, especially the children, give the victory sign or wave their hands or blow kisses. The Americans fraternize everywhere with the French and, with their usual generosity, share their tobacco, food, chocolate and chewing gum (of which the children have become inordinately fond).

One of the priests at Bayeux, who speaks English, greeted us with tears in his eyes.

In Caen, which is still held by the Germans, it is estimated that between three and four thousand French civilians have perished from our bombing and artillery.

June 27

This morning John Haskell, Ken Downs and myself motored in a jeep to Cherbourg.

We passed through Carentan, which is still under German artillery fire, through ruined Montebourg and shattered Valognes. We stopped at the 7th Corps Headquarters, where we were kindly received by General Collins and where we explained some of our plans to Colonel Carter and Lieutenant Colonel O'Malley of G-2. Carter had just replaced Colonel King, who was captured by the Germans a few days ago. General Collins told us that on the previous evening he had accepted the surrender of the German Commanding General and of the German Admiral at Cherbourg.[10] When Collins asked the General why he did not have all his men cease fighting, and follow his example by surrendering, the German answered that he had given them orders to resist to the end and, after all, the determined action of small numbers of men could delay the projects of large armies. At any rate, early this morning the Germans, entrenched in the Arsenal, were still holding out against our naval gunfire, air and land attacks. Later this morning it was announced that the Arsenal had been surrendered, and four thousand prisoners taken in it.[11]

After lunching with Joe O'Malley, we continued into Cherbourg. There was surprisingly little traffic. As we approached the city we found the surrounding countryside strongly fortified with great tank ditches, pill boxes, wire entanglements, heavy guns, etc. Except for dwellings along the road, the surrounding farm buildings were not badly battered. A few dead horses and cows, bloated into obscenely grotesque postures, were to be seen here and there. Many fields, recently the scene of bitter fighting, were filled with the beautiful red and white cows which are so pleasant a feature throughout

On June 27, 1944, Bruce conferred in Cherbourg with Maj. Gen. Joseph L. Collins who had accepted the surrender of the German commander, Gen. Karl von Schlieben (left) the previous evening. Here Collins meets with von Schlieben at the time of the surrender. Courtesy of the National Archives.

the Cotentin peninsula. Cherbourg, which has a normal population of about 30,000, had been largely evacuated some days ago. Its outskirts were in a shocking condition of ruin and devastation, but the center of the city was only moderately harmed. As one approached the docks, however, one had a conception of how complete skillfully managed demolition can be. All cranes were destroyed and great temple-like masses of concrete had been tossed about as if a giant had thrown them petulantly away. The Quais, alongside which trans-Atlantic liners had once discharged so many carefree passengers, looked as if a tornado had struck them. Everywhere girders were twisted and bent, and whatever remained upright seemed to be bordering on an imminent collapse. The harbor itself contained many wrecks of ships, and from time to time, from various parts of the city, one heard the explosion of land mines or delayed bombs. Corpses of soldiers, both German and American, surprised one in

Touring Cherbourg soon after its capture, Bruce remarked on the strong German fortifications, like this bomb-scarred artillery emplacement over-looking the harbor. Courtesy of the National Archives.

unlikely places. In a corner of one garage a dead German lay where he had been shot, but looked as if he were alive and ready to throw a grenade.

As we drove into a parking lot, a group of thirty or more German officers and soldiers who had just been discovered by our soldiers and rooted out of their hiding place, were being searched. At the conclusion, the young Southern lieutenant in charge told his men some of the captives had complained because the searchers had taken away their medals. The lieutenant announced that unless they were promptly restored he would search his own men, which quickly brought about their restitution.

Being short of transport, we bent our energies toward acquiring German or German-commandeered vehicles. In the course of our pursuit, we picked up half a dozen French and Spanish mechanics. They said for days they had been sabotaging German motors, and some of these left behind were capable of being repaired. Every-

During his visit to Cherbourg just after its fall to the Allies, Bruce witnessed many such scenes as this of German prisoners of war marching through the city's streets. Courtesy of the National Archives.

thing that could roll on wheels had been taken along by the Germans as they had retired from the town. In this way, we finally secured one Citroen passenger car which runs after a fashion, and left behind our squad of mechanics who, during the next forty-eight hours, are going to try to restore two trucks to mobility.

As we drove around the city, we saw quite a few corpses of American soldiers recently picked off by snipers. John and I went to the Mayor's office and induced that functionary to give us complete sets of all types of identification cards and the other documents we need for our future activities.

At four o'clock there was a gala celebration on the steps of the Mairie. The building itself was festooned with huge French, American and British flags.

An American band played the Marseillaise, God Save the King, and the Star Spangled Banner. General Collins drove up in his armored car, and addressed a microphone in French. The Mayor replied. Everyone shook hands and adjourned upstairs, where we drank warm champagne.

We drove through the Arsenal. How 4,000 soldiers ever stayed alive in it, in view of the severity with which it had been bombed and shelled, is a matter for wonder.

Coming back home, we stopped at a German prison camp. There seemed few prisoners between the ages of 20 and 30 except those belonging to Luftwaffe units, who had an appearance far superior to the others. Many of the prisoners looked as if they were sixteen or seventeen, or over forty. They were dusty, unshaven, and stolid. Considerable numbers of them were Poles and Russians who would, we were told, have been glad to have surrendered long ago, except for fear of being shot by their German officers.

We had supper at the Carentan base, washed down with some refreshing flagons of cider.

Last night about 11:30 there was the first German air raid since my arrival here. German planes dropped flares, bombed and machine-gunned, were greeted with Ack-Ack and went on home. They were in small numbers.

The weather here has seldom been good. Just before I arrived, channel conditions were such that more craft were lost from weather complications than were destroyed during the assault landings by enemy attack. Last Friday, however, they had a good day and put ashore 20,000 tons of supplies on the beaches. Since then the regular flow has continued.

June 28

Captains Guittary and Lambert have just returned from a trip. At St. Sauveur-le-Viconte yesterday the inhabitants had shaved the heads of twelve women who had been sleeping with German officers and soldiers, and who must henceforth slink about the village. It sounded like the Scarlet Letter. The Frenchmen with us think it is a very fitting and salutary punishment.

The German General Von Schlieber, who commanded in the Peninsula, was sent off to England last night. He is a great brute of a man, about 6 feet four inches in height, and his arrogance has incurred the dislike of everyone who has met him. He made endless difficulties about boarding a small ship. Finally one of the MPs, at the end of his patience, booted him vigorously in the behind and told him to get the Hell aboard. The General meekly obeyed.

This has been an idle day. I did paper work all morning and discussed at length the proper set-up for our operations.

After lunch, Downs and I went to Army Headquarters where I called on General Bradley and his Chief of Staff, General Keane. We obtained permission for our personnel, which numbers about ninety officers and men (exclusive of agents) to wear the 1st Army shoulder emblem "A."

All day long our aircraft fly above and around us. A new air strip is being dynamited and cleared about half a mile away. Many air strips have sprung up in the vicinity almost as quickly as if they had been brought into being by rubbing Aladdin's lamp. Our fighter planes are active at night as well as by day. Yesterday, by mistake, a flight of Spitfires attacked a column of American troops and four Allied planes were shot down by our men. Such incidents have been very few here, although they were unfortunately not uncommon in the Sicilian campaign where identification was more difficult on account of the presence of numbers of enemy planes.

John Haskell was to return to London this afternoon, but just before his departure we had word that Joe Haskell is arriving in the morning, so his trip is postponed.

General Sibert and Bill Jackson (Fusag G-2) came to supper with us tonight.

June 29

After breakfast, Ken Downs, Sergeant Sweeney and myself set out for Cherbourg. We stopped at the Carentan base, and had a pitcher of cider with the French proprietor there. The cross roads at Carentan are still under enemy fire. At Cherbourg we found the mechanics whom we had left there to work on our German cars. We then went to the Hotel Atlantique to see General Roosevelt. The whole courtyard was filled with troops attending the Decoration ceremony of some of the men who had especially distinguished themselves in the early stages of the invasion. General Barton conducted it, and it was very impressive. Many of those who have been awarded decorations for their gallantry during the first ten days are no longer alive to receive them. Ted Roosevelt was in very good form. He has been constantly engaged in leading assault forces, sometimes as small as platoons, into action. He has during this war been very fortunate in only having once been wounded, and then very slightly. He is brave as a lion and has been recommended for the Congressional Medal, which everyone who has served under him thinks he has richly deserved.

The Atlantique was the headquarters for many of the German Military and Naval officers as well as for the Todt organization.[12] It afforded a fertile field for our spoliation. Ted Roosevelt very kindly gave us carte blanche to take away what we considered absolutely necessary to our operations. We picked out quantities of clothing and documents for use by agents, typewriters, paper, ink, pens, and other supplies of which we were in great need. Our greatest lack is transportation. The Provost Marshal proposed to remedy this shortage by commandeering some civilian cars for our use—the first one that his MPs picked up was our own!

At the Atlantique there was every evidence that the Germans had departed in a hurry. Clothing and equipment were strewn pêle-mêle all over the place, and in the headquarters of the Todt organization there were great piles of shoes, socks, and other workers' garments.

There were frequent loud explosions in the city, no doubt from delayed-action mines or bombs. Probably, too, there were German agents left behind. In Carentan last night about fifteen men in civilian clothes were picked up who were supposed to have been sniping or directing artillery fire. They were reported to have been sheltered by women with whom they were living.

We went from Cherbourg to the Corps Ordnance Park about 10 miles outside Cherbourg where captured enemy automotive equipment is concentrated. Most of the vehicles were no longer mobile, but we selected two Citroens and two Mercedes Benz and requested they be turned over to us. This request involved our going to the Ordnance officer many miles away at VII Corps, and thereafter our return to the parking center. I drove a German Mercedes Staff car back to the camp, where we arrived about midnight, having had nothing to eat since breakfast, but well satisfied with the results of our scrounging. We found Joe Haskell there.

June 30

Colonel Roulier, Monsieur Mercarder, and some French officers arrived this morning and were closely followed by Major Arnold Baker[13] and Major Feiser of SIS, who are here in a liaison capacity. This house is simply crawling with people of many nationalities, including Algerians and Spaniards. The dog which attached itself to Ken yesterday in Cherbourg and whom we have named "Das Reich" is cavorting about the courtyard, where a goat is eating the legs off someone's trousers hanging from the laundry line. Our other cars have arrived and altogether this is a busy spot.

John Haskell left for the UK this afternoon, and Ken Downs and I went down through Bayeux to visit the First Division. We had quite a long talk with the Commanding General, the Chief of Staff (Colonel Mason)[14] and various officers. Many people consider this the best division in the American Army, although little of its original personnel remains. Its spirit is wonderful, and even around Headquarters there is a great air of military efficiency, meticulous courtesy, and discipline.

After supper, went over to Army Headquarters.

July 1

Spent the morning at our own and at Army Headquarters. It has rained all morning, as it has intermittently for the past four days, and the roads are boggy.

I went over to see Colonel Dickson (G-2) at Headquarters, and also saw John McLean and others. After lunch we had a call from Army Ordnance which indicated that we might lose our captured vehicles. Ken and I visited Lieutenant Colonel Taylor and discussed the subject with him. He is from Greenwood, South Carolina, and is a passionate bird-shooter and dog-trainer. After an hour's conversation on American field sports, he very kindly confirmed the allocation to us of the vehicles in question.

Today it has rained hard. Only one transport plane has arrived on the Omaha beach strip. When Joe Haskell, Bill Jackson and myself went down to board it, we found a long queue of prospective passengers clamoring for places. Fortunately, Byron Foy was in charge of traffic arrangements, and we all secured places. There were twenty passengers and a heavy load of baggage, amongst which were Haskell's and Jackson's three cases of brandy, collected from the German General's tunnel at Cherbourg. Other passengers were taking back cheeses and miscellaneous wines in quantity. The C-47, after a couple of skips and a jump, lumbered into the air, and an hour and a half later we touched ground at Hendon airport.

7

The Sinister, Droning Noise of German Pilotless Planes

London, July 2 to 20, 1944

July 2

After a night of sirens and all clears, and the sinister, droning noise of German pilotless planes, I went to the office and discussed various matters with Walter Giblin and others. The robot bombs have now descended on London every day and night for over two weeks. Although the weight of bombs dropped is comparatively small, they have induced considerable fear in the population. Each day, forty to one hundred and fifty persons are killed by them, and a considerably greater number gravely injured. These people are tired, and the mechanical, uncanny nature of this device seems to have affected the nerves of many of them. Countermeasures are relatively ineffective, so it is to be presumed that the nuisance will continue until the sites · in the Dieppe and Pas de Calais area, from which they are chiefly propelled, are overrun by our troops. On account of this menace, there has been a considerable exodus of people from London.

Eating places, such as Claridge's or the Connaught restaurants, to which access was once almost as difficult as that to heaven for a rich man, are now uncrowded, and even the streets have an air of partial desertion.

None of our organization has yet met with a serious mishap. Some of the R&A men have been hit by slivers of flying glass. John Hayes and Henry Proctor[1] were knocked down on the street by blast, and others have been blown from their beds, but that is all. One of the doodlebugs fell on Sloane Street in front of billets which our men had left five minutes before and killed 50 or 60 American soldiers belonging to another unit.

July 3

Spencer Phenix[2] came in this morning en route to Spain. I had a talk with George Brewer, who is leaving in a few days for Stockholm.

At 11:15, Fred Oechsner, Rae Smith, and others from MO discussed various plans they had under consideration. John Haskell and I considered an assortment of matters and then lunched at Claridge's with Lieutenant Colonel Manuel,[3] Chief of the BCRAL. He wants to take up with General Koenig the issuance of an order by the latter forbidding French liaison officers with British and American Armies to engage in Secret Intelligence work. With this proposal we were in accord. In the afternoon, Vanderblue, Gaskell and Louie Timmerman,[4] who are leaving tomorrow with the Third Army for the Continent, talked over the last minute complications that invariably arise in this type of work. Later, we had an Executive Committee Meeting.

July 4

Regular Staff meeting at 10:00 a.m. Hazel Cropsey, who is working with Harold Coolidge on the Reporting Board, came to see me with a letter of introduction from Vincent Sheean.[5] Like almost all the other girls, she wants to go to France as soon as possible. I gave her the sage advice that she should brush up her languages at the Berlitz School or elsewhere. Hubert Will told me about his trip to Ireland and Minister Gray's obduracy regarding Marlin. I have written to Whitney Shepardson laying the situation before him. Forgan, Giblin and I lunched at Bucks with Sir Findletter-Stewart,[6] of British Security, and one of his assistants.

Manuel came over in the afternoon with the draft of a proposal letter from General Koenig to SHAEF on the duties of French liaison officers. We suggested certain changes in the draft. Following that, I talked to Ken Cohen on the same subject, and we also promised to give him 150 .45 automatic pistols.

Dined with a very pleasant company at Gertie Legendre's[7] new house, where we stayed up late listening to Tommy Stone[8] (Canadian SIS, SOE, etc.) being engaging and charming at the piano.

July 5

Chandler Morse and Russ Forgan brought in a draft of a letter replying to General McClure's[9] request for the assignment of three more R&A men to PWD. Owing to the scarcity of personnel, we decided to offer him only one of our staff. Brigadier General Miller, U.S.M.C., Operations officer from OSS Washington, arrived today, and I am routing him around the Operations branches. He was shortly followed by Lieutenant Colonel Davis, Chief of SO Algiers for France, and I had an interesting talk with him.

Bruce mentioned the "fine work" done by OSS Major Peter J. Ortiz, a veteran of the French Foreign Legion and the U.S. Marine Corps. Ortiz (third from right) is seen here on a mission conferring with maquis in Occupied France. Courtesy of the National Archives.

Major Ortiz, U.S.M.C.,[10] who has been one of our SO men in France with Resistance Groups, is to be decorated this afternoon by Admiral Stark with the Navy Cross for gallantry. He has been in Southeastern France for months with the Maquis and Patriots there, and has done fine work.

Lunched today with Ronnie Tree[11] at Bucks. Hope to arrange to put his house—Dytchley—under earmark for possible use by OSS.

Tonight, I am dining with Chester Beatty, who is having Brendan Bracken, Major Churchill[12] (the PM's brother) and Desmond Morton (PM's political secretary). I have sent CB three Camembert cheeses which I brought with me from France and, though I fear they are immature, they may be improved by his excellent Krug 1928, Château Cheval Blanc 1934, Port and Brandy.

July 6
Walter Giblin very kindly gave me a half dozen eggs, and Polly Howe's Virginia ham was restored to me, having been cooked by the Chef at Bucks.

Last night, Major Churchill and Bracken both expressed the view that the British public would never stand for indiscriminate bombing of German cities by the RAF as a retaliation for pilotless plane attacks on London. This view must be shared by the PM, who today, in a lengthy speech on the subject, at last swept aside the fiction that the bombs were dropping only on Southern England, and detailed the damage done by them not only there but in London.[13] To date, there have been 2,754 such planes despatched and 2,752 persons— mostly civilians—have been killed by them and 8,000 others seriously enough injured to be hospitalized. There was a sad incident yesterday when one of them fell on a rest house in the country sheltering 40 or 50 babies under two years old, and killed almost all of them. Intermittently during the day and night sirens and all clears blow, bells ring in the buildings, indicating a raider directly overhead, and generally they are a confounded nuisance.

One of our SI men, Byfield,[14] returned yesterday with a slight hand wound. Being on the point of boarding a transport for France, he was taking a photograph of the proceedings when a fellow soldier or officer accidently discharged his weapon and shot both camera and hand.

Had a talk this morning with Joe Haskell about the new set-up that will have to be made at SF Joint Headquarters[15] as a result of General Koenig assuming control there. The British are, I believe, trying to make this control almost a fictional one. General Koenig is aware of this, and is insisting on exercising real authority. As the essence of Resistance is French, and almost all those actively engaged in the work are French, Joe and I feel we should, from an American standpoint, strengthen Koenig's hand. The whole problem will immediately be taken to General Eisenhower and General Smith for decision.

Lunched at Bucks with General Miller, and endeavored to present to him briefly the OSS position in this theater. Saw Lieutenant Lawler about his recent trip to Ireland, and his conversations there with the Minister, Joe Walshe[16] (Minister External Affairs), Dan Bryan (Irish Army G-2), and Paddy Carroll[17] (Irish Police Chief). He is to go there from now on as occasion warrants it, and collect intelligence and counter-espionage information.

Bill Maddox has been ordered to the Mediterranean Theatre as Chief Intelligence Officer there. He came in to say he would greatly prefer to stay here, and to ask he be allowed to make a quick trip to Washington.

A cable was received authorizing Joe Haskell to return to Washington to make a personal report to General Marshall on French Resistance Groups.

Discussed Gerry Miller's future with him. Ditto later with Russ D'Oench.[18]

Ronnie Tree came in, and we have settled the matter of procedure in applying for the use of Dytchley.

Harold Coolidge's display of Air-Sea Rescue Equipment is fascinating, and makes it appear that, with shark repellent, salt water transmuters, a burning glass, a multitude of signaling devices, fishing kit, heated suits, sun shades, concentrated foods, etc., one should be quite happy and comfortable in a little rubber boat indefinitely.

July 7

Most of the morning was spent at General McClure's office with Oechsner, Smith and Armour all present. We advised General McClure that we now had about 80 men working with PWD, and we proposed eventually to increase the figure by fifty percent, but could not go further. As to MO purely black activities, we have forty men now working under Rae Smith and intend to obtain about 12 additional. We asked for permission to have MO conduct any field agent operations if the pending plan is approved by SHAEF. General McClure had no objections to this, or to our supplying up to six officers to be dropped into Resistance Groups. He also approved our request to have Stacy Lloyd and a French liaison officer go to France immediately to investigate the possibility of MO agent operations there.

Lester and I had lunch with George Brewer at Bucks. He seemed to have built up a creditable show in Denmark and elsewhere. He is returning to Stockholm this weekend, and we are budgeting him for $50,000 for the next three months.

Joe Haskell came in to report on a meeting called by Lieutenant General Smith regarding General Koenig's status in the Resistance operations. The question is now involved in political considerations and the final decision is undetermined.

Colonel Roulier arrived from France with some important captured documents. They had been dredged out of a duck pond by two of our Proust agents. They were unharmed, having been enclosed in a tin box. The Proust agents had been told by a French farmer with whom German officers had been billeted that, upon their departure, he had noticed they did not have with them a tin box which they had always guarded with especial care. Having searched everywhere else, they had the initiative and imagination to examine the pond. Amongst other documents, were detailed maps of the German mine fields in the Cotentin Peninsula which may prove of great value. We turned these spoils over to G-2 SHAEF.

At four o'clock Commander Cohen and other Broadway representatives, together with Colonels Manuel, de Besse and Roulier, met with us to try to evolve some method of introducing order into the disorganized agent situation in Normandy. It was generally felt that Koenig should issue an order forbidding French "tactical liaison" officers from engaging in secret intelligence work, which should, as far as French representatives were concerned, be left to BCRAL officers attached to SI or SIS units.

Before we could finish this meeting, Forgan, John Haskell and I had to adjourn downstairs to see General Betts, who told us that General Kenneth Strong[19] (G-2 SHAEF) wished to form a small staff section at SHAEF to deal with secret intelligence matters, and would like to have it composed of four officers from SI and four from SIS. General Betts wished to have our opinion of this contemplated procedure. We agreed that General Strong's ideas should be put into writing so that we might have an opportunity to study them. We expressed the view that we could not consent, unless ordered by the Theatre Commander, to any arrangement which would impair the independence of the American Secret Intelligence Service.

I dined tonight at the Connaught with Hanson Baldwin, Francis Miller[20] and John Haskell. Hanson had spent the first eleven days of the invasion aboard the Augusta and ashore. As usual, he was interesting and attractive.

July 8

I notice by a cable this morning that Washington has only just learned of the death of one of our ETO underwater swimmers, who died as a result of strangulation because of a failure of oxygen in his diving mask. It was apparently an unavoidable accident.

Had a long talk with General Smith, USMC, of the Washington office. Bob Alcorn and Cady[21] are both very concerned as to the possible fate of their relatives in the Ringling Bros. Barnum & Bailey fire at Hartford, Connecticut, just reported in the paper.[22] Shortly afterwards Alan Scaife brought in Jim Bovard,[23] the latter of whom, knowing that his wife was on the train, fears she may have been killed in the terrible Santa Fe wreck also just reported.

Talked with Lieutenant Hodgkinson[24] of Alcorn's office, who is going out next week to First Army to handle unvouched funds. Also Dr. Jahn, just returned from ten months of SI work in Stockholm, where his cover was that of a pulp and timber expert. If the SI service is made permanent, he wishes, like so many others, to stay with it as a representative of the Department of Agriculture.

Discussed with Reutershan his proposed activities as Chief Administrative Officer at First Army.

Lunched at Bucks with Bill Jackson (Fusag). Saw General Sibert and Jonny Castles there. The former told me that our paper asking for the attachment of Forgan, Giblin, Armour and myself at Fusag, although approved by him and by SHAEF, had been turned down by G-3 Fusag. This is a great blow, and means a multitude of red tape to be unwound.

Left this afternoon on the 4:45 train to spend tonight and tomorrow at Dytchley.

All the trains are jammed, since, in addition to the normal British urge to spend the weekends in the country, there is now superadded on the part of many persons the desire to escape the bombing of London. In fact, the Government very wisely encourages such evacuation by non-essential workers, and is reviving its 1940 effort to induce this type of migration, especially as it affects children.

At Dytchley, I found that Ronnie was housing 30 or 40 London children. Some of the officers camped in his park came in before dinner. They are in the American Medical Corps, and the CO, Captain Lyon, says they are shortly, after almost three years in base camps, to go to France. They are all delighted at the prospect.

David Beatty and Mrs. Bragg[25] were also staying there. Lord Beatty is concerned over the bad feeling which is increasing between the British and American Navies, and the display of jealousy toward each other. He thinks on the American side that Admiral King has taken no steps to alleviate this situation.

It rained all day Sunday, to our great chagrin.

July 10

I started the morning by calling General Sibert regarding the dilemma into which we have been plunged by the rejection of the request attaching Forgan, Giblin, Armour and myself to Fusag.

We received word that Vanderblue and our detachments with Third Army have arrived on the other side of the channel.

General Betts called to say General Strong and himself had been unable to embody in writing their views on the Secret Intelligence Staff at SHAEF, and were now asking us to send four of our SI officers to form part of an advisory staff section there. I am to discuss the subject with "C."

Katek[26] is deep in Czechoslovakian problems. We are having trouble with the British, who claim that American-Czech intelligence teams will further confuse an already mixed situation. We have also been asked by the Algiers office to do something in Czechoslovakia on the sabotage side. This has been referred by the Czechs to General Gubbins.

We are, with the exception of SO, behind in our War Diary work. None of the Branches has a qualified individual assigned to this task, and this condition will have to be remedied.

At the Executive Committee Meeting at 4:00 p.m., we talked over the merits of the establishment of an overall OSS headquarters base on the Continent for recruitment and training of agents versus that of bases at each Army and at Fusag.

We decided, especially in view of reported low morale, due to bombing and to a long period of non-combat duties, amongst our enlisted men, to have a dance on August sixth.

Three PT boats have now been assigned to OSS for use in connection with clandestine operations. We can use them also for the transportation of our personnel to and from the Continent.

Two hours of conversation between the Executive Committee and Messrs. Rae Smith, Whittaker and Stacy Lloyd on proposed MO agents to be used behind enemy lines. Paper submitted by them to be redrafted tomorrow.

Tonight Walter Giblin and I went to a party at the Officers' Mess, Park Lane, for the heads of sections connected with Central Base Section—Brigadier General Pleas Rogers[27] was the senior officer present, and we had a very enjoyable evening, despite the retailing by all hands of his particular favorite story about the "Buzz Bomb." American Army losses from its effects have been very low. The worst incident caused the death of sixty-four soldiers and officers in Sloane Square. Soldiers billeted in London have now been ordered, where possible, not to sleep on any floor higher than the second.

The weather continues wretched.

July 11

Telephoned General Betts this morning to inform him that I had talked to Stewart Menzies last night about the proposition that SIS and SI would each furnish four officers for a Special Staff Section at SHAEF to deal with Secret Intelligence matters. Stewart wants to postpone any decision on this until he sees General Strong and General Bedell Smith. We share this view, since the need for these officers is difficult to comprehend.

John Whittaker returned this morning with a redraft of the MO Agent paper.

We had a long meeting with representatives of every Branch to agree upon final plans for the establishment of our Headquarters at Communications Zone. The rest of the day passed in conferences on miscellaneous matters.

July 12

General Sibert took me to see General Kibler[28]—G-3 of Fusag—who had objected to our request to attach our senior officers to G-2 Fusag. We discussed the matter for an hour, but arrived at no favorable conclusion, since General Kibler felt that such attachment should be at SHAEF, and not at Fusag level. He expressed himself emphatically as wishing no OSS officer to be interposed, with operational authority, between himself and the head of the SF detachment.

Had a long talk with Commander William Ladd,[29] ONI representative at CE, about the X-2 prospects in the Far East. He had been in Washington during Colonel Cowgill's trip there. From an American standpoint, the question of the jurisdiction of the various organizations in that type of work in the Far East still remains to be settled.

Russ Forgan and I lunched at the Waldorf Hotel with General Koenig and Colonel Passy. The General expressed himself as being very discontented with his position as head of SFHQ, where he felt his authority was merely nominal. He expects to see General Smith, Chief of Staff, SHAEF, on Thursday, and either be accorded a full measure of control over SFHQ activities or resign. We told him, as far as the American OSS representation there was concerned, its members would loyally obey any orders given to them by SHAEF. We had a delicious lunch: soup, sole, steak, vegetables, Camembert cheese, gin and Vermouth, 1934 Burgundy and Calvados.

At 3:00 p.m., Francis Miller reported to John Haskell and myself on certain intelligence developments at SHAEF, to which he was lately transferred. We met with Canfield, Van der Stricht and Bross[30] to go over various points raised at General Koenig's luncheon.

At 6:30, Bill Maddox had a cocktail party, preparatory to his leaving for Washington. The guests were all men and women who had been with OSS London for more than six months. Now that we have a personnel of over 2,900, it is difficult to realize how few we were not long ago. There was general sorrow at Bill's leaving, especially since he is uncertain as to whether he will return. Some of his admirers drowned their grief in mixed concoctions with gin bases.

Up to July 11, there have been 3,200 pilotless planes launched, of which 2,392 made landfall in England and 1,237 penetrated to the Greater London area. 658 of them were shot down by day fighters,

259 by night fighters, 345 were destroyed by AA fire, and 74 by barrage balloons. This covers the period since June 15th.

At ten tonight I went to General Koenig's office at 21 Upper Grosvenor Street, where he had assembled General Gubbins, Brigadier Mockler-Ferryman,[31] Colonel Passy and myself, to hear an exposition of his proposals for the handling of French Resistance. There was a great deal of conversation as to how complete command over these activities could be turned over to the French. We adjourned about 2 a.m. with nothing definitely settled.

July 13

Taylor Cole[32] came to see me this morning to advise me of further developments in the relationship of SI Stockholm with the Swedish Secret Service. I have arranged for him to meet Felix Cowgill (head of British CE) and Hubert Will this afternoon.

Van der Stricht, Canfield and Bross reappeared this morning for a further talk about General Koenig's position. It was agreed that, regardless of what stand SOE might take, I should write General Koenig explaining that OSS was organized as a military detachment of ETOUSA, and that whatever orders on the subject of French Resistance Groups were issued to us by SHAEF would be loyally obeyed. Pending receipt from SHAEF of orders on the subject, I felt it would be improper for me to take any position in regard to the affairs under consideration.

John Haskell came in with Lieutenant Colonel Reddick[33] and Commander Turnbull, the one head of the Research and Development Branch and the other in charge of Censorship and Documents. We agreed informally to have the approach by SI to these two divisions canalized through Reddick, the senior officer.

Russ Forgan and I lunched at Bucks.

Hubert Will came to see me at 2:30. He has under consideration the acceptance of a commission as an Ensign in the Navy. Although his work as Acting Chief of the X-2 Branch should carry a considerably higher rank, and although he had been strongly counselled by some of his associates to remain a civilian, I urged the contrary view. He is a young man, he has passed most of his life in Government service, and he intends to remain in it after the war. Undoubtedly, there will be in Government circles a post-war discrimination in favor of members of the armed forces, and I feel he should recognize this fact and accept a commission. If he fails to do so, I am afraid he will later reproach himself for his decision.

Gerry Miller brought Colonel Heflin[34] to see me at 3:30. Heflin is in command of the four Liberator squadrons designated for our use for clandestine operations by the Eighth Air Force. He returned yesterday from a trip to France in a Dakota (C-47). This was a daring expedition to a point near Lake Geneva in a passenger plane without self-sealing tanks, armor, or guns. It passed without incident. He landed on an airfield, next to one bombed by the Germans the preceding night, where he found about 200 French patriots assembled, and was also met by our OSS officer, Owen Johnson.[35] He and his crew were led away in the darkness, while a body of men remained behind to camouflage the plane. He stayed two and a half days, moving in uniform around the neighborhood. He reviewed a number of Maquis troops, and commented favorably on their appearance, morale and military discipline. He stated that the journey back and forth was very exhausting, since they felt, as indeed they were, completely helpless if they should encounter either flak or enemy fighters.

Henry de Vries[36] told me he had argued with Bill Maddox until three o'clock this morning, laying before him the reasons why he felt Maddox should return to his work here after his present trip to Washington. Bill came in to say goodbye, but his night vigil and the arguments of Henry had not visibly affected him.

Arthur Goldberg talked to me about the suspicions some members of OSS seem to entertain regarding the Labor Division of SI.[37] He assured me these suspicions were entirely unfounded, and their determination and purpose was to gather military intelligence, and not to concern themselves with the post-war restoration of European trade unions.

I dined with Tony and Margaret Biddle.[38] They had King Peter of Yugoslavia,[39] Princess Alexandra,[40] Princess Aspasia,[41] Ed Murrow, Patricia Burke, Oscar Solbert,[42] Rose Fiske, Anna Orr-Lewis, Julian Allen and others. The King asked me to notify General D. it was most important that Ambassador Fotich[43] be somehow—if possible—tactfully ejected from the Embassy building in Washington. In London, trouble is also brewing for the King and the Subasic[44] government. Some of the malcontent Serbian faction here, such as Gabrilovitch,[45] Stodj, et al, are hopeful of proclaiming a Serbian Republic. The Queen Mother (according to Tony) is probably involved in this intrigue, hoping it will eventually lead to a monarchical restoration with Peter's brother replacing him on the throne.

July 14[46]

Captain Garnone Williams[47] (RN) of the Southeast Asia Command came to see me this morning to tell me how his coordination of clandestine operations in that theatre is progressing.

Commander Graveson has just given me a new piece of WT apparatus developed by his people to take out to Widewing,[48] where I am to attempt to secure priority for the use of planes to test it. It would permit the use of plain English with good security, and enable agents behind enemy lines to talk at a distance of at least thirty miles with an airplane. It is believed to be a great improvement on the SIS Ascension apparatus.

Lunched today at PARK House, General Spaatz' house near Wimbledon. General Spaatz, General MacDonald, General Anderson, Sally Bagby,[49] General Curtis, and Colonel Heflin. They were all much interested in Heflin's account of his recent Dakota trip. This morning they had despatched 350 bombers for their second daylight delivery to Resistance Groups, and the results so far reported were excellent.

I presented various problems, such as dissemination of intelligence items, our desire to use light planes (they will probably give us the use of some Stinsons shortly to be received), Graveson's request to have a top priority to test his new invention, etc. As has always been the case with the 8th Air Force, these questions were viewed deliberately, sympathetically, and helpfully.

Upon my return, Taylor Cole, Forgan, John Haskell and myself met to consider the proposal emanating from Washington that SI Stockholm be placed under operational control of SI London. We are opposed to accepting it, since it might reduce the independence now enjoyed by SI Stockholm, which is presently responsible to Washington headquarters, and make it, under our control, subject, as we are, to the orders of the Theatre Commander, ETOUSA.

Forgan and I saw Horton[50] to determine on how to distribute Wood cable material[51] so that it might prove most useful to the American Air Forces.

Captain Loxtercamp,[52] of the Security Branch, asked me to permit him to make a trip to Algiers to study our security setup there and in Italy. The matter has been taken under advisement.

Harold Coolidge stopped in to express his sorrow at Ted Roosevelt's death, which was announced today. According to the papers, he died in Normandy of heart failure.

July 15

The quietest day I have spent in the office for a long time. Not a single conversation on a controversial topic! So far as I can remember, this is unprecedented.

I left this afternoon for Lavington Park to stay with Barbie Wallace.

July 16
Spent the day and night at "Beechwood."

July 17
Went after an early breakfast to Freehold, where I saw the installation and the remaining Proust agents. I then came into London on a majestic 1-½ ton truck. The first person I saw upon arrival was Atherton Richards,[53] who had reached here from Washington last night. Giblin, Richards and myself lunched at Bucks.

At twelve noon yesterday, a buzz-bomb fell just back of Conduit Street, and disposed of what little window glass still remained in that vicinity. The radius of blast seemed to be about five hundred yards.

This afternoon, Ensign Tarry, the son of Mr. Tarry of Staunton Hill, came to see me. He was in good fettle, and had been on an LST for the last year. He participated in the Sicilian and, latterly, in the Normandy landings.

A letter from Helen Clark[54] asking about little Tommy. I have no cheerful news for her, but there is still hope; when last seen, his fighter plane was very low, in trouble, but over rather flat country. Young Avy has now shot down eighteen German planes. I wrote to the Ambassador last week to try to stir up the question of awarding a DSM posthumously to Tommy Hitchcock.

I had a letter from General Gubbins today suggesting we approach jointly the matter of supplying Resistance Groups in Czechoslovakia because of the delicate situation there.[55]

Executive Committee Meeting. We went over the revised allotment figures, which total an approximate increase of 570 officers and 1,360 enlisted men, practially doubling our existing allotment. The Poles are selecting 40 German prisoners of war (impressed Poles) and are going to train them for our SI work. Raymond Guest has just returned from seeing Admiral Wilks,[56] who is indignant because a British Colonel (whom he says represents OSS!) gave, a few days ago, a party at Cherbourg to which he did not initially invite any British or American officers. When the Colonel rectified this error, he committed another one by seating his guests improperly without due distinction of rank. Guest is to notify the Admiral that OSS does not employ any British Colonels! We have obtained permission to take our PT boats hereafter into Cherbourg Harbor.

John Haskell had a superb dinner at Claridge's tonight for Colonels Passy, Manuel, Roulier, and two of their French associates. From SI he had de Vries, Colonel Palmer and Major O'Brien[57] as well as

Colonels Forgan, Giblin and myself. Almost everyone made a little speech, and it was a most sympathetic gathering. Our relations with the French Secret Intelligence Service are on a very satisfactory basis.

July 18

Staff meeting at which Mr. Williams outlined clearly and logically the need to deal with personnel problems on a more efficient basis. Immediately afterwards, General Miller, Armour, Vanderblue, Timmerman and Downs (all of whom returned from France last night) met with Colonel Palmer, Colonel John Haskell and myself to go over again the question of appointing an OSS officer exercising all the functions of command for the various field detachments.

Hubert Will is agitating because he feels his orders to visit the Continent are being unduly, and perhaps deliberately, delayed by our own people. This I believe is a misapprehension on his part and springs from his lack of acquaintance with the slowness of Army procedure. It is, however, typical of endless questions of a somewhat like nature which arise here frequently and are time consuming.

Lunched at Lester's flat with him, Forgan and Downs.

A long discussion between Will, Captain Erdwurm,[58] Giblin and myself concerning alleged discrimination in air priorities, travel orders, etc., against the X-2 Branch.

Fred Oeschner came in at 6 p.m. to tell me he had heard privately that the European Advisory Commission has just decided, during the German occupation period, to have PWD cease its functions as a joint Anglo-American enterprise. Propaganda will consequently be conducted separately by the Americans, British and Russians. Fred feels this to be a terrible political mistake, and fears the Russians, since British and American counsels will be divided, will completely dominate this field. At that juncture, he will probably resign from OSS and resume his activities as a publicist and expert on Germany.

July 19

Forgan, Giblin, Commander Turnbull and others left this morning for the Continent.

Henry de Vries and I had a long talk about a certain delicate internal SI matter.

Talks with Atherton Richards, General Miller, and Alcorn.

Joe Haskell returned yesterday from Washington, and I talked to Gerry Miller and him about the question of having an overall OSS man in command of all OSS detachments at Armies and Army Group.

Quentin Roosevelt[59] and his wife came in at noon. He has now been transferred to OSS and will be sent from here to Washington, with Chungking as his ultimate destination.

Lunched at Bucks with Stacy Lloyd. Afterwards, I went to see Tony Biddle and discussed the French situation with him. He gave me a message from King Peter requesting me to ask General Donovan to return Yarrow here at once.

Major Andrews called me to say he had just had a violent altercation on the telephone with Major Stearns[60] and he was going to ask to be transferred out of the organization if he was to be placed under Stearns' orders.

After flying around most of the day and being unable, because of bad weather on the French coast, to land, Forgan and Giblin returned late this afternoon.

Guest is now organizing a ferry service with his PT boats.

Trafford Klotz called me on the telephone from the Far Shore.[61] It was a most unsatisfactory conversation because of the limitations imposed on the manner of asking questions and making answers.

Had a long conversation with John Haskell about transferring responsibility for supervision of SI from G-2 ETOUSA to G-2 SHAEF.

Dined with Ken Lindsay, Dan Grant,[62] a French officer, and a British banker at Ken's delightful house on Brook Street.

July 20

Gerry Miller has suggested that Paul Van der Stricht be made Coordinator, reporting to the Director, of OSS activities directed against Germany.

Colonel Cowgill, British CE, came to see me this morning regarding the supposed attempts of Huntington Harris, an OSS representative in the Union of South Africa, to investigate the personnel and operations of OSSWA Brandvag, an anti-Smuts[63] organization. This, in Cowgill's opinion, is bound to lead Harris into a field of complicated political and social problems which the British have found too hot to handle. Mr. White[64] of MI-5 is to inform me further on this matter.

I also talked to him about Murphy's orders to Will to report as head of X-2 operations centered at Algiers.

Long talk with Timmerman, who is going back to Third Army for another week and will then return home.

Talk with Forgan about streamlining our organization here, and inquiring into size and efficiency of our field detachments. Feel no decision can be reached on these matters until we have all visited the Continent.

Bruce noted approvingly the number of parachute jumps made by former tsarist officer Serge Obolensky, whose OSS Operational Groups helped liberate Sardinia. Here Obolensky (left) is shown with some of his OSS colleagues. Courtesy of the National Archives.

8th Air Force wishes us to decorate Kindleberger and Rostow[65] for their outstanding achievements.

Lunched with Alan Scaife at the Connaught. He is very pleased at the progress being made by SI. SI now has introduced onto the Continent from the UK forty-four Sussex agents, half of whom are wireless operators, five Pathfinders (over whom the British exercise, with us, joint control), four Proust men (with four more immediately to follow), and three Desk agents.

Stopped to see 24 Grosvenor Street, into which SI has just moved some of its personnel. Not counting billets, we now have nine houses in London being used as offices, and quite a number of country establishments.

Beverly Byrd[66] came to see me. He is the son of Harry Byrd, and a Private in the 82nd Airborne Division. An attractive young man.

He was wounded in the arm on his fourth day in France, and although some of his nerves are still paralyzed, he is recovering rapidly and expects to rejoin his unit within a month.

Serge Obolensky[67] told me he had just completed his fourteenth parachute jump. He has about 120 men and 20 officers, all qualified parachutists, in his Operational Groups, and they are anxious to get into action.

8

The Reverberation of the Bombs

France, July 21 to 25, 1944

July 21

Forgan, Giblin and myself left London by automobile at 9:30 this morning and arrived at Portsmouth about 11:00, where we boarded PT boat No. 99. Timmerman, Vanderblue, Brigadier General Hoag[1] of ATC and his Aide, Lieutenant Colonel Boy, were already there. We had scarcely left the dock when we ran into a choppy sea, and the crew afterwards said it was the second roughest trip they had ever made. This did not, however, influence them to abate their speed, and the craft bounded and slapped the waves at a steady thirty knots. We all clung to the few handy bits of wood or steel on the deck. The boat itself is really a huge surf board propelled by powerful engines, and except for its various guns, there is little on deck to prevent one from being swept overboard. It rained throughout, but that mattered little for, within fifteen minutes of our casting off, we were all drenched to the skin by the salt spray which swept over us, sometimes in showers and at other times in almost solid sheets of water.

After about an hour, I went below to meditate on the vicissitudes of sea travel and to smoke a cigarette. Before I could do either, I was suddenly propelled, from my seat on a kit bag, by a shock that might as well have been caused by a fast-moving vessel hitting a particularly solid iceberg, upward toward the ceiling of the cabin. As I was inertly falling from this expedition into space, another shock turned me around in midair, and deposited me, twisted and crumpled, on a pile of baggage. I thought for a moment my back was broken, as I could not stand up and walk. Two sailors picked me up and lay me on a bunk, and told me to stay quietly there. I had no inclination to do otherwise, so there I remained in considerable pain until the crossing was completed. I stuck a pin into each leg, could not feel anything, and assumed I was paralyzed. Meanwhile, Russ

Forgan, who had been sitting next to me, had been similarly projected upward, and feared he had cracked a bone in his neck, a surmise which a later X-ray happily demonstrated to be incorrect, but he was left very stiff and sore.

In about three hours after leaving Portsmouth, we were told to land, but it then appeared that, through some miscalculation, we had arrived at the wrong beach, so we got under way again and made a twenty-five mile rush to Omaha Beach. There we transshiped to a Duck, the marvelous amphibious truck that is the greatest vehicular invention of the war. Stopping to inquire our way to where we hoped our transport awaited us, Colonel Sadler, who was connected with the Port Command, must have been touched by our waterlogged appearance. He invited us into the Château where his unit was quartered. There we changed our clothes and had supper before starting off again. Meanwhile, three OSS cars had arrived, as had Ken Downs. General Hoag, Forgan, Giblin and myself set out in one of them, conducted by Sergeant Kirouac.[2] As we were proceeding through the Norman mist, there was tremendous excitement in the convoy ahead of us. Cars began to turn around and dash in the opposite direction, and those of their occupants who had gas masks were feverishly adjusting them. I stopped a captain riding an onrushing truck and asked him what was happening. He stated that the MP at the next crossroads had ordered all movement to reverse itself as quickly as possible, since there was a gas attack actually taking place at that point. We had no masks, and became engulfed in a mad rush of traffic down the road. General Hoag took us to a supply dump and drew gas masks for all of us. Taking advantage of a General's companionship, I drew for myself a map case I had long coveted.

While we were at the supply depot, the alarm was sounded there, and the soldiers precipitated themselves upon the available masks like hungry lions on raw meat.

The spectacle was most unedifying, and would not have occurred amongst combat troops. It did, however, point up the fact that if the Germans had actually used gas (which, since we were at least fifteen miles from their lines, was obviously unlikely) and it had permeated the air in the territory we traversed, there would have been thousands of soldiers who had lost, discarded, or forgotten their masks, in spite of there being a fine for not having them on hand.

General Hoag, anxious to try the facilities of a PT boat, had expected to return with it. We dissuaded him from that course, and he decided to wait until tomorrow and go back to the UK in his own favorite element—the air. Accordingly, we left him with the attractive Colonel Wertenbaker (from Charlottesville, Virginia, a nephew of the historian) and made our way to the OSS headquarters. Russ and I were billeted tonight in two comfortable rooms in a nearby village. Having expected to spend the night under canvas, it was quite a surprise to be bedded down in deep mattresses and spotless sheets.

July 22

When we returned to headquarters for breakfast, we found we had luckily been spared an incident that had robbed those at the base of most of their night's sleep. About two in the morning a gas alert had been sounded and they had been ordered to wear their masks.

What the cause was of the second alert, I never discovered, but the first was occasioned by a smoke screen that some amateur alarmist mistook for gas. Once the news spread, there were numbers of people who smelt gas, saw it, and claimed to have been poisoned by it!

After an excellent breakfast, Russ and Walter accompanied Dana Durand[3] to Cherbourg to seek out a château for our complement of personnel in Communications Zone. I stayed behind, visited our various detachments, and discussed administrative matters with Colonel Reutershan. In the afternoon, after interrogating an American paratrooper, who had just escaped from the Germans and been brought through our lines by members of a Resistance Group, Ken Downs and I went down to the First Division, stopping on the way to see Joe O'Malley at 7th Corps. Lieutenant Colonel Evans and Major Gale, of 1st Division G-2, declared SI had furnished them their best intelligence, which was most gratifying and a great tribute to Ken. As always before, I was tremendously impressed by the morale and discipline of that Division. They are, however, aggrieved at the meager manner in which decorations have been awarded their members, as contrasted with the bemedalled condition of many headquarters officers who have never even smelt powder except at safe field exercises. I personally think their sense of an injustice having been done them, as well as that felt by numerous other combat troops, is completely justified.

July 23

Commander Quirk[4] and I went to Cherbourg, driven by the inimitable Kirouac, who delighted me by saying he was going to give me a silk parachute from which I could cut out the neckerchiefs so useful—and even decorative—against dust and sun.

We lunched at the house taken on Rue Hlain by the SCI Detachment. Charlie Neave was there, as well as McCandless, Oakes,[5] Durand and others. We had gin and Pernod before lunch, claret with it, and Calvados afterwards, to say nothing of lots of chit-chat.

After lunch I went down to Third Army. Gaskell had broken his ankle in a motorcycle crash, and, being immobile, I found him at the mercy of Colonel de Besse's conversation, which, upon my entrance, was diverted at me and flowed in an inextinguishable torrent for an hour and a half. Colonel Bilbane also appeared, and told me he was not being treated by the members of our SI Detachment with the deference due to his rank and his twenty-seven years of service as a professional officer in the French Army. We propose to salvage his injured amour propre by giving him a tent of his own in which, Achilles-like, he can sulk when he so desires.

I found things on the whole in good shape with our people. Lieutenant Colonel Powell, in charge of the SF Detachment, has been displaying an excessive zeal in trying to contact G-2 directly on intelligence matters, thereby short-circuiting SI. I hope the words of admonishment I addressed to him will have a salutary effect.

Vanderblue and Timmerman were comfortably situated in a large tent with a field to themselves. In Charlie's habitual fashion, he had provided himself, like a good soldier, with every necessity and comfort, including a stock of excellent cider. I saw Paul Mellon,[6] who was happy to have escaped from London to the field.

I returned to Cherbourg at 8:00 p.m., and dined and spent the night at Rue Hélain. After dinner, Forgan, Giblin and I walked down to the harbor. Although it has not yet been put in order, a few small vessels, tugs, and barges are passing into it and unloading on what remains of the quais. What seems miraculous is that the railroad is now functioning between Cherbourg and Bayeux.

July 24

Left early this morning for Third Army. Vanderblue and Timmerman took me to lunch at the 8th Division (8th Corps) CP near La Haye du Puits. While there, I was fortunate enough to get a new bandage wound around my ribs at the Division first aid station. My back is still giving me almost ceaseless pain.

After lunch, we motored to a ridge overlooking Gerville. The sun came out, our artillery from behind us was shelling the enemy, the enemy was shelling our positions, and yet it all seemed peaceful except for the overpowering stench given off by bloated dead horses and cows which were lying in ditches, fields, barnyards, and elsewhere. Actually, there is little live livestock left in this countryside.

An OSS field detachment with American forces sometime after the Normandy invasion. Courtesy of the National Archives.

La Haye du Puits is badly wrecked. I fear our high command has mistakenly insisted on possessing each crossroads and village, instead of speedily by-passing them, and mopping up afterwards. Time after time, French villages have been persistently shelled and bombed after the enemy had evacuated them. Moreover, in many instances the enemy had only small patrols in them, and had erected their main defences in the fields and hedgerows.

We went around the Forêt Mont-Castre. I left Tim and Charlie and returned to our Headquarters at First Army.

After supper, Ken and I called on General Sibert, Tommy Tompkins and Bill Jackson at First Army Group. While there, I saw Captain Pat Dolan[7] (MO officer attached to PWD), dressed more as if for comic opera than field service.

We stopped at Press Headquarters and saw Bob Casey, of the Chicago Daily News, Larry Lesueur,[8] of Columbia Broadcasting, and others.

Ken told me that after I left last time they tried once again to get some of General Von Schlieben's cognac at Cherbourg. Since the entrance of the tunnel was closely guarded by our MPs, Klotz and others of our men managed to enter it through a rear entrance. They were unable to reach the brandy in cases, but managed to siphon off from casks enough to fill about twenty five-gallon tins with which they started towards their waiting truck. All their efforts were, however, thwarted, and they were lucky to escape court-martial when they ran into a wandering Major from the Provost Marshal's office who made them leave their loot behind.

Speaking of villages wrecked by American attacks, an old Norman was asked the other day what he thought of them as soldiers. He answered: "I know nothing about their military qualities, but they are the greatest 'démenageurs' I have ever heard of."

There are lots of stories about the Russian General who has been visiting here. He likes to interrogate prisoners in Russian and German. He is very tough, and frightens them. He asked a German prisoner the other day, who had previously served on the Eastern Front, if he had ever seen one of the gas vans that were used to asphyxiate Russian prisoners. The German incautiously replied they had been seldom used, and then only to dispose of lunatics. The General gave his sinister belly-laugh and answered: "We are going to find lots of lunatics in Germany." Another prisoner ventured to say to the General that he had heard, when the war was over, the Soviets would carve Germany into little bits. The General answered: "Not Germany but Germans, Ha! Ha! Ha!"

Tonight what sounded like a lone German plane came over and the whole neighborhood burst out with anti-aircraft fire.

The great American attack was due to start this afternoon. The bombers started to work but visibility was so poor it was again called off. Unfortunately, some of the bombs dropped fell amongst the infantry of the 9th Division and killed quite a few men. This attack, scheduled for last Thursday, has been postponed time and again on account of the weather, which has been unprecedently bad for this season.

July 25

The attack commenced at ten o'clock this morning. Wave after wave of four-engined bombers in seemingly endless procession flew over us, and, as we stood in the farmyard, we could see the German Ack Ack rising to meet them, and occasionally bring one down in a spiral of gray smoke. The reverberation of the bombs

Bruce observed firsthand the slow progress of the Allies in the Normandy hedgerows. Here American soldiers take cover from German fire in the countryside near St. Lo. Courtesy of the National Archives.

caused a tremor as if a minor earthquake was occurring. Flocks of fighters darted in and around, above and below the big ships, but no Luftwaffe challenged them. We motored to another farm where the view was better, and must have seen altogether over 1,000 heavies pass beyond the German lines. The thunder of the engines and of their bombs continued for an hour. Toward the end of that period the dive-bombers and mediums joined in the affray. At eleven o'clock the American artillery opened up, some of it booming like heavy surf, some of it sharp like the noise of firecrackers. Thereafter, the infantry moved forward. Actually, the results achieved by nightfall were very disappointing, in that one of our two divisions committed to this offensive gained about 2,500 meters, and the other scarcely advanced at all.

I spent the rest of the morning at Army Ordnance clearing a truck that our two mechanics had brought down from Cherbourg. It was a Matford once captured or requisitioned by the Germans, and where it was procured by our French civilian mechanics, it is better not to inquire. The procedure for requisitioning captured vehicles is becoming more and more involved, but Lieutenant Colonel Taylor and Captain Buchanan have let us keep our trophy.

Lunched at Headquarters, and afterwards talked to Neave about his position at 12th Army Group and to Durand regarding X-2 matters. Trafford and I went to call on Colonel Wertenbaker, who said he would send me to England tomorrow on a Cessna. From this air field, we motored to Quettehue. There is an XI Century Norman church there, the interior of which is well worth seeing, being lithe, delicate and graceful.

The weather, which had started today in a promising fashion, had now turned rainy, so Trafford and I waited in the Inn of Three Hundred Men for Ken Downs and Bud North, who were to join us for dinner. The country through which we had driven to Quettehue struck me as being even more full of flowers than similar country in England. Rambler roses were everywhere, huge hydrangeas were in blossom and, to my great surprise, I saw two magnolia Grandiflora in bloom. The apple orchards are so numerous that they must in springtime present a glorious sight.

The Inn of Three Hundred Men is considered to have one of the finest cuisines in France, and it did not belie its reputation this evening. It is run by three middle-aged women, who come from three separate parts of France, who had three fox terriers, and who have maintained this charming hostelry for the past twenty-seven years. Why it is named as it is I did not inquire, but is it not for the reason one immediately conjectures.

We had soup, grilled plaice, filet mignon, peas, carrots and potatoes, brown bread and butter, salad and cheese, and stewed cherries with the thickest of cream. No less important, we had a noteworthy bottle of 1937 Meursault, a bottle of red Meursault, and a fine champagne of the highest merit. The bill for ourselves and our two chauffeurs was about $50, which is another instance that food—and especially wine—is by no means cheap.

When we started to motor back, we found one car without any lights and could not start it. We left North and a driver to bring it on in the morning.

We did not get back to camp until one o'clock. The night was black and there were many convoys on the road. There was quite a bit of artillery in action, and gun flashes streaked the sky. As we drove into the courtyard, the stars came out and a tiny crescent moon appeared.

9

Troubles and Conversations Tumble Over Each Other

London, July 26 to August 5, 1944

July 26

Up at seven. Lively bombing and artillery in the distance this morning.

I breakfasted at Colonel Wertenbaker's camp, and left in the Cessna, with a pilot and two other passengers, at 9:15. We passed over Cherbourg, the Isle of Wight, Bournemouth and Southampton, and arrived at Heston Airport, near London, at 10:45. I spent the afternoon in various conferences, and heard that Henry de Vries had had a complete nervous breakdown and that Russell d'Oench had gone home.

July 27

This is like old times. Troubles and conversations tumble over each other: We arranged definitely to have a dance for the enlisted men next Saturday. General McClure has asked for Crane Brinton's services. Chandler Morse has raised the complicated issue of what role R&A is to play in Germany. Quentin Roosevelt came in to say goodbye. Sporborg called and said SOE would loan Hackett[1] to MO. Stearns informed me that besides nine billets in London, we have twenty other buildings here in the capital, when I had supposed we had only nine in all!

Lane Rehm[2] reported in. Atherton Richards has been viewing our establishments and is pleased with their management. Chandler Morse is not willing to release Brinton to PWD—this I have explained to Murray Gurfein, who is now Acting Chief of PWD Intelligence section, where his rank handicaps him. Joe Haskell explained the most recent developments in SFHQ as a consequence of General Koenig's demands. It is expected that a directive on the subject will issue next week. The Field Photographic men have arranged with the U.S. Navy, following the telegram Downs and I sent from France, to send some teams to the Continent to photograph captured fixed military installations there for future reference before a ban is imposed on such photography. Conferred with John Haskell and Colonel Palmer. Louise Hepburn[3] gave me some background on de Vries' breakdown—he had a similar collapse about twelve years ago. It is especially sad, since he had such a brilliant mind. He is a superb linguist, being equally at ease in German, French, English, Spanish and Dutch, and fluent in Portuguese and Italian.

Bill Casey[4] reported on his Washington trip and certain plans he has for the future.

The Flying Bomb continues to be an irritation and a menace. For instance, from July 24 to July 25, 52 persons were killed and 218 seriously injured in the Greater London area. During that period 62 PAC were launched, 47 made landfall, and 26 landed in the Greater London area. Fighters destroyed 12 of them, AA four and a balloon barrage three.

Many people are becoming tired because of the interruptions of their sleep, and complain that even when there is no bombing they are unable any longer to sleep soundly.

We have recently had only two persons injured amongst our three thousand—both of them were cut by flying glass, but not badly.

July 28

Lunched with Colonel Passy at Bucks. He is shortly going to Brittany in connection with Maquis activities there. He has strongly recommended Joe Haskell as American Deputy to General Koenig in the new Resistance Group setup, and wished to ascertain my views as to how this will function from an American standpoint.

Before going to lunch, I had seen Walter Bell[5] from Broadway. He brought with him a short report on the insurrection in Germany.[6] This resulted from John Haskell's demand that Broadway give us any of their information on the subject in return for our valuable "Breakers"[7] material. The truth is that, on the positive intelligence side, Broadway is lamentably weak—especially as regards Germany— and most of the reports they send us are duplicates of those already received by us from foreign secret intelligence services. C has requested that Colonel Palmer, who is now deputy to John Haskell and who is to be our SI liaison with Broadway, be introduced to him.

Paul Van der Stricht has told me of the latest developments in the SFHQ-French situation. It is assumed now that SHAEF will give

General Koenig complete command over activities of Resistance Groups in France. In that event, our policy should be loyally and faithfully to support Koenig.

Fred Oechsner, Rae Smith and Lester came in to try to settle jurisdictional differences in MO. They arise chiefly out of the fact that, although Smith is head of MO Etousa, Oechsner is the over-all head of MO in Europe and the Mediterranean. I have suggested to Oechsner that he resign as such, revert to his position as Special Assistant to General Donovan, and serve here in that capacity, continuing his attachment as deputy to PWD, SHAEF. He is going to consider this proposition.

Long talk with John Haskell and Will about telegram received tonight from Forgan and Giblin, stating that Colonel Dickson has recommended to General Sibert that SI and SCI detachments at First Army be, in effect, removed to 12th Army Group. This involves so many collateral policy decisions that I have wired them to take no action but to await the arrival of John Haskell and Will.

Dine tonight at the Dorchester. Admiral Wilson was giving on Admiral Stark's behalf a farewell dinner for Admiral Kirk, who is returning to Washington. With the exception of Lieutenant General Lee, Major General Laycock[8] (head of Combined Operations) and myself, all of the guests were British or American Admirals, Commodores and Captains.

Admiral Hall told me that when the plan was presented in writing he would give serious consideration to our request for the use of PT boats for operations into Denmark.

July 29

Jimmy Murphy[9] and Hugh Will came in this morning. The former has just arrived from the North African Theatre. He recounted the difficulties of OSS, due to lack of organization, inefficient officers, and general incompetence in such terms that the whole show sounded chaotic and dangerous. He states that OSS possesses no prestige whatever there, and is regarded as a menace to the military effort. He says General Donovan is unaware of this condition, and nobody dares call it to his attention.

Colonel Palmer saw Henry de Vries yesterday. The poor fellow has dementia praecox and is to be sent home. Russ d'Oench very generously left me a cheque for $1,000 to take care of any of his expenses.

Alex Griswold,[10] the son of my old friend Ben Griswold of Baltimore, reported to me with letters from his father and from

Alice Garrett. He was always considered a brilliant individual. He is now a Major in the Army assigned to SO Branch.

Timmerman returned last night from the Third Army and has reported to me and applied for transportation home. Kirkpatrick came in to apply for an SI job in Chungking. He is due to leave tonight in a PT boat to deliver some French agents on the coast between Avranches and Granville, to gather intelligence for the First Army. This is the last night of the moon in which a PT can operate in that locality—the operation has already been postponed for the past three days because of bad weather.

Gerry Miller showed me his paper on a consolidated Berlin-OSS mission which will be considered at a Staff Meeting next week.

John Hayes inquired what should be done about Henry de Vries' personal effects, which are scattered about in several places.

I received a top secret note, dated yesterday, from General Rogers of CBS,[11] saying that a long range rocket attack on London might take place, and advising the evacuation of all personnel that does not need to remain here. The text of it follows:

"1. Based on the best information available to this headquarters, it is considered entirely within the realm of possibility that the Germans may soon employ a long range rocket in desultory bombing attacks against this country, particularly the London area.

"2. It is recommended that all personnel and activities whose operation in this area is not vitally essential to be moved to some other location as expeditiously as possible."

I have decided to take no action on this. It is in the form of a recommendation, not an order. The use of this rocket has long been feared but it has not yet come to pass.[12] We could only move at this time a very small number of our personnel without entirely disrupting our normal activities. If the menace becomes an actuality, we can then take appropriate steps.

Lunched at Bucks with Joe Haskell.

Joe went to see Major General Bull yesterday about the SFHQ situation, and General Bull has advised him that he should become General Koenig's Deputy. This changeover will present many complications from an OSS standpoint. Joe and I are agreed that SO operations outside of France and Scandinavia should be conducted along lines independent from those of British SOE.

After lunch, Colonel Rehm and Major Alcorn talked to me regarding unvouchered funds. The situation in this theatre appears to be in proper order—in North Africa it sounds utterly confused and unsatisfactory.

Jack Pratt and his wife called. They have been here with SI for about two months and have been kept under cover in the country. They now want to give up their connection with OSS and go home. They claim the stories circulating against them (in the case of Mrs. Pratt that she was suspected of being a German agent) by Ambassador Hayes[13] in Madrid have been repeated in London and have plagued them. They are thoroughly discontented, and I think the best thing is to let them go. They had been under the tutelage of de Vries.

John Haskell and Lester returned from SHAEF, where they had attended a meeting on the OSS-ETO application for an additional allotment of officers and men. Since the JCS has ruled that any allotment granted must come out of the ETO troop allotment, our chances of securing help from this source are not good.

July 31

From 0600 July 27 to 0600 July 28, 151 PAC were launched; 110 made landfall, and 57 landed in the Greater London Area. Forty were destroyed by fighters, 23 by A.A., and three by balloon barrage. In the Greater London Area 77 were killed and 294 seriously injured during this twenty-four hours.

I had a letter yesterday from Billy Delano about Major Van der Graacht,[14] who was associated with his architectural firm, and also is a great friend of his. He has been here a short time in SI and is doing liaison work with SHAEF. His parents are Dutch, and he speaks Dutch, German and French. He is an excellent officer and should prove useful to SI.

Doctor (now Major) Murray[15] of the Student Assessment Board reported in this morning, having just arrived from Washington. He has no definite instructions, so I have attached him to this office on temporary duty.

Alan Scaife brought me John Haskell's letter to Whitney Shepardson about the reasons for sending Russ d'Oench home. It seemed to me a reasonable and complete statement of the facts. John, Lieutenant Colonel Sutherland,[16] and Hugh Will got off to the Continent yesterday. On Saturday the Twenty Grand trip by PT boat to deliver French agents on the coast below Granville was cancelled because of the rapid advance of the American troops in that vicinity.

Lieutenant Brittenham[17] wants to go to Normandy and take with him an officer of the Belgian Secret Intelligence Service, so that the latter can contact some of the members of his chains in the area occupied by our armies. I told him that, without SHAEF's approval, we could not at this time make such arrangements.

Major Dasher[18] is greatly exercised over Soviet-Polish relations, and has given me various interesting memoranda founded on his conversations with high Polish officials. These matters so closely concern the American Embassy and the State Department that we must tread warily in reporting them for fear of being accused of trespassing on the preserve of those august agencies.

Atherton Richards is alarmed about the OSS position in the Mediterranean Theatre. We are to discuss his views further.

Almost every day I sign numbers of promotion papers, court martial proceedings, etc. Lately, marriage applications have been increasing in number. I always approve them on principle, but do not see the prospective parties. An American soldier or officer marrying abroad must first secure the approval of his Commanding Officer. In spite of—or perhaps because of—Buzz Bombs, Cupid is doing a thriving business. It was the same during the Blitz of 1940—people under such conditions seem to form more rapid attachments than they would under normal conditions.

Mr. White of MI-5 came to see me about Huntington Harris' work in the Union of South Africa. He is to take the case up with Jimmy Murphy, since it has a strong X-2 flavor.

Dick Mazzerini,[19] who has done an excellent job here on Italian and Albanian affairs, as well as being instrumental in setting up the Document Section, came to say goodbye. He is going to Washington, whence he hopes to visit Rome, where he served with me as Vice Consul many years ago.[20]

Raymond Guest reports he has on hand for the PT boats a number of projects for August, including one that Captain Slocum,[21] the British DDODI (Deputy Director Operations Division Irregular), wishes to lay on for Norway.

Lieutenant Colonel Bilbane, French liaison officer with SI Detachment, Third Army, came in just before lunch to say that Third Army was about to become operational, and there is confusion between action and intelligence activities in Normandy that must be straightened out. I am to see him and Colonel Manuel this afternoon.

Bill Casey is anxious to comply with General Donovan's wish that he go to the Mediterranean Theatre for a month. I have cabled General Donovan asking that he not confine Casey to Secretariat work but let him have a real opportunity to see what is going on in that Theatre, regarding which we have had here disquieting reports.

Dr. Briscoe, Scientific Adviser to all British clandestine organizations in the UK, accompanied Colonel George Taylor[22] of SOE and Commander Gibbs, of SIS, to offer OSS participation in a joint scientific laboratory to be established in Calcutta to manufacture secret inks, to carry on secret photography, to fake passports, and to finish documents. I have asked Washington for its decision. Garnons-Williams, the Coordinator of Clandestine Operations in the South East Asia Command, is now in Washington, and can supply the General with further information on the subject.

A long meeting at four o'clock with Colonels Manuel, Bilbane, and the SI group. The French wish the status of their BCRAL liaison officers at American Armies to be more regularized. This is impossible at present and will remain so until Third Army and Twelfth Army Group become operational. They went away quite happily.

From five until seven we had a meeting of Branch Chiefs. Amongst other propositions, we discussed one emanating from SO advocating the appointment of a Chief of Staff under the CO, OSS, Etousa, to control and coordinate all activities directed against Germany not only from this theatre but from the Mediterranean Iberian Peninsula, Stockholm, Bern and elsewhere. Lieutenant Casey is to make a study and report on this proposal.

Drank gin, ate lobster, and talked shop with Lester at 39 Upper Grosvenor Street.

August 1
Staff meeting this morning. Subject of sending personnel to the Château at Faymonville was deliberated. Outside the château grounds there was heavy mining by the Germans, and they have not yet been cleared. Twenty Rangers, whose outfit is now billeted at the Château, have thus far been killed or injured by mines. We propose not to let any of our personnel wander outside prescribed limits.

Ensign Forney,[23] from Security, arrived with a dossier about Hatch, who works for X-2. It is a highly confidential and unsavory affair. His wife has just killed their two young children in New York, and blames her action on the fact that she claims Hatch is a homosexual. The press has not yet metioned the fact that he is in OSS. Forney is to pursue his inquiries with Jimmy Murphy.

Hadley-Dent[24] brought Bunny Phillips of SOE to see me. The latter, after serving in SEAC, has been in the U.S.A. with Bill Stephenson, and is returning there in ten days to replace Bart Bouverie.[25]

Mr. Edwards of G-2 Etousa, left with me some papers abandoned at the Red Cross Mayflower Club by a man whose initials would appear to be G. V. A.

This dereliction is a minor breach of security, and the individual's identity must be checked with Commander Vetlesen.[26]

I lunched with Francis Miller in a private room at Brown's. He is enjoying his assignment at SHAEF, and is going to arrange for me to see General Wickersham,[27] and talk to him about the possible use of OSS personnel in the post-surrender period.

At 4:30 p.m. I went to Baker Street, where Mockler-Ferryman, one of his assistants, Joe Haskell and myself discussed the impending changes in handling French Resistance brought about by a broader grant of command authority to General Koenig. Both SOE and OSS have told Joe they have complete confidence in him and will back him as Koenig's Deputy in every respect. The one step I advised him against was his suggestion that he would continue to function as Koenig's Deputy as well as in his present capacity at SFHQ. Continuance in the last position would, I feel, eventually subject him to criticism since he would owe allegiance to two masters.

Dined tonight at Gertie Legendre's. A large group was there, including Vice Admiral Glassford,[28] who took the first American Naval mission to Dakar, and who had once served on the China Station.

August 2

Gerry Miller and I left at 9:30 a.m. this morning and motored out to lunch with Colonel Heflin at Harrington airfield. He has 61 Liberators and one Dakota (C-47) engaged in clandestine operations, conducted for us by the 8th Air Force. The rate of loss on these missions is thus far a little less than 1%. Last month they made over 550 sorties.

We returned to the office about 6 p.m., where Lester, Rehm, Atherton Richards and I had a long conversation about cutting down the allocation of unvouchered funds to our officers for rent, entertainment, etc., and also about drawing personnel from NATO[29] into ETO.

Commander Cohen called me about our Lieutenant Burke accompanying Passy on his forthcoming trip. SIS is sending an officer and a W/T operator. They will handle communications and make any intelligence available to us. Generally, they conceive that this expedition will possess the same elements of mutuality as the SUSSEX plan.

August 3

Colonel Bill Jackson of SO came in this morning to tell us the latest developments regarding Colonel Dickson's (1st American Army) request that SI and SCI units now at First Army be removed to Twelfth Army Group. We now find that G-3 at First Army has made the same request affecting SF Detachments there. We are to

confer on the matter this afternoon with Joe Haskell. Russ Forgan
sent me a letter by Jackson on the same subject.

I had made an engagement to go to Portsmouth today to see
Major General Bull about our allotment but, because of the above
and other business, have been obliged to cancel it.

Colonel Parker talked to me concerning his views on the establishment of a permanent secret intelligence service. Harry Proctor and
Major Dups[30] want to send four Midiron men into France to tie up
communications for the Medusa Chain. To do this they need lift
and reception parties which must be furnished by SFHQ. They say
Paul Van der Stricht has turned down the proposition. I have telephoned him and hope it will be straightened out.

Chandler Morse and I discussed General Bissell's[31] request to
General Donovan for the transfer of Kindleberger to G-2. I am to take
it up next week in France with General Sibert. General Donovan
cabled last night asking whether we had taken steps to establish an
OSS Mission representative of all branches for the occupation phase
in Germany. This is a matter to which we have devoted considerable
attention, but regarding which we have not evolved any definite plans
since the American Government and Army have not formalized the
structure to be established there. Chandler thinks I should discuss
this with General Wickersham, which I propose to do tomorrow.

Mr. Lovitt, from the Embassy, arrived with a cable from Hallett
Johnson[32] of the State Department asking that his daughter
Priscilla, who works for Gorman in the Security Office, be returned
to the State at once or sent on a long vacation "far North." He cabled that the parents of Miss Norris,[33] whom I do not know, were
making the same request. I assume this is on account of his reading
about the flying bombs. I consider the request disgraceful—as well
as placing the girls in an invidious position—but assume, unless
there are Civil Service rules to the contrary, it must be complied
with. With our hundreds of civilian employees here, this is the first
request of the kind made to us.

Colonel Kehm of PWD called to say our civilians operating for
PWD in France had OSS on their Adjutant General's office identification cards. He fears if any of these men are picked up by the
Germans, they may be executed as spies. He wants these cards recalled and new ones issued. Major Andrews is to care for this.

I have received a personal cable from Allen Dulles[34] about an un-
pleasant reference in a BBC broadcast to a German who is covertly
supplying him with valuable intelligence. He wants such references
discontinued. Phil Horton is to handle this.

At 5:45 p.m. had a long meeting with Joe Haskell and Bill Jackson about the situation vis-à-vis First Army and Twelfth Army Group of our Field Detachments. SF is going to stand pat for the present, since their detachments are now under the direct orders of General Koenig, and no disposition can be made of them by OSS without his concurrence. Jimmy Murphy saw Colonel Sheen today and decided to withdraw his 1st Army Detachment to Twelfth Army Group. The SI situation remains undetermined. Jackson made a suggestion which I said must be passed upon by John Haskell. It was that the possibility be explored of forming a joint SF and SI detachment at First Army which would report to the Chief of Staff and not to the Gs. This proposal obviously involves many policy and jurisdictional questions.

Dined with Lady Reading. Pauldie Fenno, Margaret Colt, Ambassador Winant and Amory Houghton[35] were there. The Ambassador, talking of bomb blast, told of a case where a man literally had his eyes torn from their sockets by it.

The PM stated yesterday that 800,000 buildings (about 40% of all buildings in the Greater London Area) had so far been damaged by flying bombs.

August 4

Spoke to Alan Scaife about Mrs. Homan's (landlady of Henry de Vries) case. She thinks she and her house are under surveillance. I have told him to caution members of his Branch to say nothing about de Vries except that he has had a nervous breakdown and is being sent home.

Jimmy Murphy tells me the Hatch affair is a very sad one. Hatch denies the charges made by his wife against him, and privately states his wife is a neurotic and nymphomaniac. He does not want to go home, and says his family doctor can give any necessary testimony. He is a brilliant linguist and has done very well in X-2.

Spent an hour with Colonel Palmer, Dr. Macleod[36] and Alcorn talking about unvouchered funds payments for SI purposes, and the question of Area B PX accounts.

I saw Mary Norris, of the Security office, whose return home, according to Hallett Johnson's cable, is desired by her parents. She is 22 years old, and says she wants and intends to stay here.

Air Commodore Huskinson of the Ministry of Aircraft Production came to see me at noon as a result of a letter to me from Charlie Winn,[37] who is still with the British Air Commission in Washington. He talked to me about Mrs. Page-Morris, an OSS Washington employee, who speaks fluent Russian, and who wants to come over here. Huskinson was completely blinded in 1942 during a bombing of London, and was blown out of bed the night before last but not injured.

A letter arrived today from Commander Gibbs (Broadway) asking for a speedy answer to our Washington cable regarding the establishment of a Joint Scientific Laboratory at Calcutta, and enclosing copy of the proposed directive to Dr. Higgins, who will head it. Have sent a follow-up cable to General Donovan on the subject, requesting an immediate reply.

Commander Vetlesen tells me Colonel Bernt Balchen[38] has just brought back from Sweden a rocket shot there (probably experimentally) by the Germans. It is about 35 feet long and has a warhead of ten tons. It is expected here that such rockets will shortly be used against London, and are the V-2 weapon of which the Germans hopefully boast. Meanwhile, V-1 continues to be used, especially in cloudy weather. On the night before last, the largest attack thus far launched put seventy or more into the Greater London Area. For some reason, Mayfair has been only slightly damaged, but in some parts of London the destruction is widespread and will, if continued, be responsible for an acute housing problem, especially this winter.

Lunched at Bucks with Russ Forgan, who is very interesting about his experiences with our problems on the Far Shore, where he has done a fine job.

Russ and I went to see General Wickersham at Norfolk House this afternoon. He is General Eisenhower's Deputy for matters affecting the occupation of Germany. He proposed that the three OSS Intelligence Branches should be formed into an OSS Mission to be attached not to any Staff Section but directly to his Deputy or to his Executive, who are above all Staff Sections. On many matters they would have direct contact with Wickersham. We discussed this later with Chandler Morse and all think that, if it can be worked out, it will be an admirable arrangement.

Later, Russ and I had a talk with Tony Biddle about General Koenig's position and about Polish affairs.

King Peter is still pressing to have Yarrow sent here. The General has notified us that the State Department is delaying his trip. Bob Alcorn is handling this through Princess Aspasia and Princess Alexandra.

August 5

Saw Lieutenant Bucky of SI. When he was lately at a replacement camp, he attended a welcoming lecture, in the course of which the

American officer in charge delivered a diatribe against the British and the negroes in the American Army. He said there was intense dissatisfaction amongst the listeners over this talk and he felt it was his duty to bring it to the attention of the Army authorities, but he did not know how to do so. I told him to give me a memorandum on the incident without signing his name to it. I will call it to Ambassador Winant's attention.

Saw Priscilla Johnson about her father's (Hallett Johnson of the State Department) cable. She does not want to go home and does not intend to leave. I told her to settle the matter directly with her parents.

Mary Pallister wishes to resume driving for the Motor Pool. Major Stearns has this under consideration.

Ulius Amoss[39] came in. General Brereton has been shifted from his present command, and Ulius is not as optimistic as he was about being made a Brigadier General.

Lieutenant Colonel Missal,[40] our Washington Medical Officer, talked to me about establishing an OSS Medical Unit here. I asked him to place his suggestions in memorandum form and the matter would be referred to Colonel Giblin upon his return.

Colonel Palmer called to say Lieutenant Fossel[41] had been involved in an automobile accident last night and had broken his arm and suffered a brain concussion. He has also punctured a lung. His condition is serious but not critical.

C called to say he could not see Colonel Palmer today. When he can see him he will, if I am away, arrange through Walter Bell for Forgan to introduce him.

A conference with Alcorn and others over the Area B PX situation. Captain Vinciguerra[42] is to see the PX people about it today.

Said goodbye to Louis Timmerman, who is leaving for home tonight.

Lunched at Bucks with Frank Canfield. Long discussion on General Koenig and associated matters.

Gravey came in, having arrived from France last night. He wished to be advised of our future plans insofar as they might affect Communications requirements.

Francis Miller called, rather angry that Jimmy Murphy had refused to attach an X-2 officer whose presence at SHAEF Miller had arranged with Will. Section V of MI6 is sending SHAEF such an officer. Jimmy states to me he has no officer available for this assignment. He will try to smooth over any ill feeling that may have arisen in this connection.

Gerry Miller talked to Colonel Forgan and myself about the SO setup for countries other than France. He is to consider General

Donovan's recent cable to Herschel Johnson,[43] go over the matter with Joe Haskell, and come to us for further deliberation.

Fred Oechsner saw Lester and myself to tell us OWI and PWE expect to break away from PWD when Germany is occupied. If this is accomplished, Fred feels the position of MO will be somewhat vague—this will be no novelty.

Went for a short time to the dance for all OSS personnel and their guests at Porchester Hall, Paddington, which commenced at 1900 hours and ended at 2230 hours.

10

The Soil of Continental France
With OSS in the Field, August 7 to 19, 1944

August 7

Lester Armour and I motored out to Northolt this morning, where Ulius Amoss had arranged for us to take a Ninth Air Force Mail Courier plane. The last time I had been at Northolt was with Tommy Hitchcock last year when we spent the day with the Polish fighter squadrons then stationed there. Amongst others, there was the Kosciusko Squadron, to which friends of mine, including Fauntleroy, Merian Cooper, John Speaks[1] and Buck Crawford—all of whom I first met in Warsaw in 1920—had belonged during the Soviet-Polish War. The members of this present squadron had a most interesting scrap book that had been kept from its inception, and contained photographs and accounts of the exploits of the Americans who had once belonged to it.

We left Northolt at 12:30 p.m., but, having learned that the weather was bad in France although it was the most beautiful morning in England I have seen this summer, we stopped at the airport outside Portsmouth to make further inquiries. We finally got off at 3:00 p.m. and landed near Grandcamp an hour later.

There was nobody to meet us, but fortunately we saw Jack Harris and Bill Casey bound for England by the next plane. They had one of our jeeps, so we clambered into it. We stopped at Twelfth Army Group to visit Ken Downs, and then went on to St. Pair Sur Mer near Granville, where Walter Giblin had located our Continental base. We found him, Colonel Reutershan and others there, and stayed up talking until one in the morning.

We have here a hotel and casino, both somewhat battered, to house the bulk of our personnel. We also have five villas, only one of which is now inhabited. There is running water but no electricity. St. Malo, across the bay, is still held by 3,000 Germans, and the shellfire and bombing is heavy. The port of Granville must have been heavily mined, since there are comparatively frequent explosions there, and geysers of water rising high in the air.

Tonight, after dark, several German bombers flew over and dropped their loads several miles away.

The view from here is superb, and the countryside is full of flowers—hydrangeas, rambler roses, and some superb dahlias. As we came down the road today to this base, we found all the French along the way smiling, waving, and giving the V sign. The young French children are charming. The GIs and officers give them chocolate and portions of their rations. There is a constant demand from the children for chewing gum, and we passed one jeep today on which was emblazoned in white paint "No Gum Chum."

At Twelfth Army Group this afternoon, Winston Churchill appeared, to make a call on General Bradley. As he left, in a small limousine, we all lined up along the road and saluted. He was dressed in a Royal Air Force uniform, and returned our salute with one of the inevitable long cigars clenched in his teeth.

The officers' mess here is good. The Army food is supplemented with local meat, butter, and a pleasant red Bordeaux, which costs about $1.25 a bottle. The beach in front of the villa is long and shelving, and in the afternoon is thronged with children. St. Pair was occupied by the Germans, but is unshattered since no fighting took place in it. In its environs, there are barbed wire entanglements and some of the fields are mined.

August 8

Awoke to a morning of brilliant sunshine. Lester and I started off to Rennes in a jeep. Along the road to Avranches, we saw numbers of German tanks and vehicles which had been destroyed, and equipment such as gas masks, mess tins, etc., which had been abandoned. So great was the destruction of transport that, if it continues at such a rate, the enemy's supply problem will rapidly become insoluble. Nothing could testify more strongly to our ovewhelming mastery of the skies than the freedom and insouciance with which our armadas of trucks, bulldozers, and other automotive equipment of every kind roll in their thousands along the roads.

After passing through Avranches, which is badly damaged, we soon emerged into a country that presented almost no evidence of ever having been threatened with war. A beautiful, almost straight road led us into Rennes. There was little traffic on this route, and very few American troops to be seen, although yesterday the enemy attacked us at Mortain—which they retook—with four Panzer

Divisions, with the intention of penetrating to Avranches and cutting off the American forces in Brittany. The attack was repulsed, over a hundred tanks were destroyed by Allied planes, and Mortain was recaptured.

When we arrived at Rennes we went to the old Gestapo headquarters, now occupied by our SCI men. Finding our contingent had gone out to lunch, we followed its example, and, under the guidance of a genial sergeant, were led to a small bistro where the only other customer was a Senegalese Corporal, black as the Ace of Spades, wearing a French Red Cross brassard. Our first course was charcuterie of which the best Paris restaurant need not have been ashamed. Then we had steak, tough it is true, but at least veritable beef. French fried potatoes, Camembert cheese and salad completed the meal, which was painlessly washed down with a bottle of pinard. The whole repast for the three of us (our driver, Mac, completing the trio), cost about four dollars.

When we returned to headquarters, we found Major Tom Lee, Dana Durand, Ben Welles,[2] and others there. They gave me a rubber truncheon with a coiled spring inside which had been used by the Gestapo on it prisoners. They had grisly tales, backed by documentation, to relate about German methods of extracting information.

On our way back we stopped at Mont St. Michel, which is unravaged by war. I think it is quite the most dramatic and, at least from a distance, the most beautiful place I have ever seen. The doors of the Cathedral were locked, so we had no opportunity to view the interior, which a vague recollection of Henry Adams' book[3] made me greatly regret. When we reached our base we had a late dinner, and at nightfall John Haskell and Trafford Klotz appeared, freshly arrived from the latter's Château at Rochefort, Brittany. It appears that Trafford, who had been absent from there during the war, was rapturously greeted by everyone in the neighborhood. The local resistance people guarded their seigneur during his stay from enemy encroachments, since the Germans who had just quitted the Château were still nearby. John said he had never seen a greater love for anyone displayed than that expressed for Trafford—it is not surprising, for he is in every respect a very superior individual.

August 9

We went this morning to Twelfth Army Group, where we saw General Sibert, Bill Jackson, our own people, and at a distance, Secretary of the Treasury Morgenthau,[4] who looked rather gross and sweaty in his town clothes.

General Sibert assigned SI a pressing intelligence mission, and we tried to straighten out with him the imbroglio which has arisen as a result of General Bradley's orders to recall the SI and SCI detachments from Armies and assign them to Army Group. Lester and John are going down to Third Army tonight and effect their immediate removal.

We lunched at Twelfth Army Group and then went back to St. Pair. On the way up, we had passed Commander Graveson and Captain Conway, who thereafter joined us. Gravey pointed out to me a lovely Château, originally requisitioned for our use, but taken away from us by General Crawford,[5] representing SHAEF.

It seemed it had been a German headquarters. Abandoning it in haste, amongst other records left behind by them was a list of local women who had worked for them in various ways. Annexed to the list were Wassermann tests[6] affecting some of them. These papers having fallen into the hands of local patriots, the usual penalty of hair cropping was applied to these unhappy creatures.

August 10

It was cloudy this morning, but later it became hot and sunny. As usual, the roads were dusty and churning with traffic. We spent a couple of hours with Gravey discussing communications problems. Then John Haskell set out to see Neave and others. He expects to leave for London tonight or tomorrow morning. Lester and John had returned late last night from Third Army to report that the removal of the two detachments had been cancelled that very afternoon, and so we have reverted to the status quo ante. It seems General Gaffy, the Chief of Staff, at about the time we were seeing General Sibert, had placed Captain Byfield on a special plane and sent him to General Allen, Chief of Staff of Twelfth Army Group, with the request that OSS at Third Army remain undisturbed.

Lester and I took Jimmy Murphy and Bob Blum, who had arrived last night, with us to Third Army, whence they expected to go on to Rennes. We met Rip Powell, Commanding the SF Detachment, on the road. He was much gratified over Resistance results in Brittany. He told us a French officer named Passy[7] had come through the American lines a couple of days before and that he, Powell, had promptly despatched him on another mission!

He was somewhat surprised to hear that Passy was General Koenig's Chief of Staff and had formerly been head of both Intelligence and Resistance for de Gaulle.

Comdr. George L. "Gravey" Graveson, OSS Communications branch, accompanied Bruce during the days leading up to the liberation of Paris. Courtesy of the National Archives.

We called on Charlie Vanderblue. Eight French officers sent out by BCRAL for attachment to SI at Third Army had just arrived and were reporting to de Besse and Bilbane. The latter was in one of his offended moods, and once again thought Gaskell was not treating him with due deference.

We went to see Bunny Carter, who stated the Army was most pleased with the work being done by our detachments. A few days ago he had been sent by General Patton, in Bilbane's company, with a small task force to Angers. They had run into ambushes and other troubles, and finally made their way back. Bunny spoke of the terrible things the Germans were now doing to French civilians. He had personally seen, in a ditch near where they had been seated eating their lunch, the bodies of three French boys age about fourteen, each of whom had a couple of hours before been shot through the neck by German soldiers. But, worse than that, he had gone to the morgue in a village where Bilbane and he spent the night, and seen the bodies of twelve French boys between the ages of fourteen and sixteen who had been killed by members of the 17th SS Panzer. The Germans had torn out their testicles, gouged out their eyes, and pulled their teeth before finally despatching them.

Such stories as these explain why the Germans are so willing to surrender to American troops and so afraid of being captured by the French. Incidentally, I read yesterday a paper captured by our men at the Rennes Gestapo headquarters which recounted the results of a great Gestapo conference in Paris in 1943, in which the Chief frankly told his colleagues that 99% of all French people must be recognized as sincerely hating the Germans.[8]

We came back via St. Ouen to St. Pair, where we arrived about seven. Soon afterwards, Stacy Lloyd and Count Paul Munster[9] appeared and stayed for dinner. It was strange hearing Munster, who is working for Stacy in his MO team, talk about ways of inducing Nazi soldiers to revolt or to surrender. He had served as an officer in the German Army for four years during the last war, but since had lived almost exclusively in England, and is married to an Englishwoman.

August 11

A beautiful day. Tremendous explosions in Granville, where they are clearing the harbor of mines and the streets of huge concrete obstructions. The detonations almost but not quite break the windows of this villa. Mark Armistead[10] and Buddy North (the Black-Bearded One) came this morning to report satisfactory progress on the photography of fixed military and naval installations. The Air Corps has given them every assistance, and they have completed the takes of Brest and the neighboring coast.

We then went—Graveson, Armour, Conway and myself—to Neave's Château where we lunched admirably on fresh fish, calf's liver, and cheese. Lieutenant Colonel de Besse and Captain Dutet produced first a very good bottle of Moulin à Vent and then a bottle of red Bordeaux, while Charlie made a generous contribution of cognac. Following this, we went on to Twelfth Army Group, and, after talking to Kirkpatrick about the military situation, called on Colonel Fitzpatrick, the P and PW officer. Thence we went to the P and PW centre, several miles away, and called on Colonel Powell, in whose tent we found Colonel Blakeney[11] and our own irrepressible Pat Dolan. Powell seemed pleased over the work done by the OSS men attached to PWD.

The constant waving of hands and returning the V Sign gestures made by the natives during these trips is giving us all a sort of finger palsy. One exuberant lass almost felled Gravey yesterday by throwing at him, as the car passed, a bunch of carrots, and another smacked us squarely with an enormous dahlia. As the GIs pass through villages in their trucks, they shower gifts on the children and, for the moment, the Americans are enjoying a honeymoon of popularity.

We reached St. Pair at seven, and found Arthur Goldberg and Pat Warburg of the Labor Desk, and Charlie Vanderblue and Ed Gaskell of Third Army there. The Chief of Staff at Third had hauled Charlie over the coals this morning because of the unauthorized visits in his area of OSS personnel. We propose to remedy any recurrence of this type of departure from established military channels by the issuance of strict orders here and in London.

It looks as if a great battle were now joined roughly in the areas bounded by Flers, Argentan, Laval and Le Mans. Further to the South, the Americans have occupied Angers, but the bulk of German forces in the West is concentrated in the rectangle bounded by those four towns, of which Le Mans is firmly in our hands. Optimism prevails everywhere. The pockets of Germans remaining in the Brittany Peninsula are being mopped up, although Lorient, Brest, Nantes and St. Nazaire have not yet fallen. However, they are doomed, and several thousand prisoners are being taken each day.[12]

August 12

Sunny and clear. This morning we talked to Vanderblue and Gaskell about an increase in SI personnel at Third Army, and sent off a long cable to John Haskell on the subject. Then we settled various administrative and finance matters with Colonel Reutershan and Lieutenant Hodkinson respectively. We all lunched together, and immediately afterwards, Lester, Graveson and myself set off in a jeep with Mac for St. Malo. The road from Pontorson onwards was in fine condition except for a few bomb craters near bridges. When one considers the speed of an airplane and the height at which bombs are released, it is wonderful to me that they ever hit a target or come near it. Much of our bombing is not, of course, famous for its accuracy. A few days ago, some American bombers were requested to support the British on their front. Several miscarriages resulted which did not tend to strengthen Anglo-American amity. About a hundred British were said to have been killed, including a Divisional General.

As we drew near St. Malo along a road which for miles had been all but deserted, we found ourselves in advance of a considerable number of units of American artillery firing industriously away. One of their targets was Dinard, where we could see the points of impact fairly clearly. We stopped at a crossroads where a signal party told us the Citadel was still held by the Germans, and that American troops in the city were having a difficult time dislodging them. They advised us not to continue along the road we were following without a guide, as they stated there were still some snipers nearby. We went to a command post located about 3,000 yards from the Citadel as the crow flies, and were told to stay away unless we had real business to transact in St. Malo. We retraced our steps to a nearby village, where we had a mixture of Calvados and gossip. An ancient in the bar told us there had been many Russians quartered in the village and that their conduct had been very bad. He described them as being ignorant and brutish, unaware of what the fighting was all about. On our way, we had passed two truckloads of German prisoners. To a hasty glimpse, they appeared to be young and sullen. Meanwhile, heavy German guns from the little island de Cèzembre had been shelling our forces in and around St. Malo.

Speaking of the conduct of soldiers, Charlie Vanderblue reports that in the Third Army area the French in certain respects entertain a very low opinion of our troops. He says he had heard from the Judge Advocate of twelve rape cases in that area involving American soldiers.

On my last visit I saw a little French girl of about twelve appeal to Joe O'Malley, when I was visiting his Corps, to afford her and her family protection against some negro soldiers who had terrorized them for two days. Discipline in the American Army is far too lax except in the fighting divisions.

August 13

Lester, Gravey, Mac and I left St. Pair this morning and, after swallowing a great deal of dust, stopped near Fougères, where we had an excellent lunch with cider, red wine, an omelette, veal,

Bruce made repeated notes in his diary on the efficient American supply service during the campaign for France. Here trucks assemble at a depot to load ammunition, food, and gasoline before rolling to the front on the Red Ball Express highway. Courtesy of the National Archives.

French fried potatoes and salad. From there, we went on to Laval and to Le Mans, which we reached about 6:00 p.m. We found Ken Downs, Russell, Mowinckel, Major Brault[13] and others at the Hotel du Saumon. All along the route we were impressed by the miraculous organization of the American Army Service of Supply. With a regularity and order that appears almost mechanically arranged, they cruise relentlessly toward their destinations, carrying their freight of gasoline, ammunition, rations, and what not. Engineers accompany them to repair bridges and major damage and to keep the roads in order. Signalmen install permanent communications along the main routes that the American Telephone and Telegraph Company would consider creditable work.

Le Mans is almost undamaged. There is an abundance of merchandise in the shops. The inhabitants are in high good humor, and there is a quantity of food and wine—at least for the present. Since transportation for export to Paris is non-existent, a rich agricultural country such as surrounds Le Mans has an abundance of wheat eggs, and fowls. The beautiful red and white cattle of Normandy seem to be replaced here by cows of a darker color and, although there are not many horses, such as there are appear sturdy and well-fed.

We had a bottle of wine at the Hotel de Paris, and then went to a restaurant, seething with soldiers and civilians, for dinner.

There are several agents being held here by Downs for infiltration through the enemy lines. We have also overrun here one of the Sussex agents, a woman who was parachuted. Her companion was captured by the Gestapo on July 31, and was tortured in the most horrible manner before he died. Six other Sussex agents who were near here left just before the capture of Le Mans by the Americans to try to reach Paris and set up communications from there. Taking with them their radios, they made the fatal mistake of proceeding in a stolen German Army truck. They were dressed as Todt workers, and one of them was a woman. They were stopped last Wednesday at a road block by a German patrol, and the first thing uncovered was a radio set. On their way to headquarters, one man jumped out of the car and, although fired at, managed to escape. The others were interrogated and executed the same day. The survivor went to the town where they had been killed, verified their fate, and then reported to Downs here. He is a young man of about twenty-five, quiet and reserved, but obviously deeply distressed by the loss of his comrades.[14]

August 14

After a night of noise due to the unceasing flow of military traffic through Le Mans, we started off for Alençon. Mistaking the road, we went to Bonnetable, and then came back and made a fresh attempt. The bridge was blown at Beaumont, so, after a detour there, we resumed the fine high road. Alençon had suffered little until it was bombed by about thirty German planes the night before last. The Place d'Armes, with its fine Hotel de Ville and Palais de Justice, is very handsome. Around the corner from it, we lunched at the Hotel de la Victoire on charcuterie, steak, salad, red and white wine, and a bottle of champagne. There were a number of young resistance group men, as well as several soldiers from General Le Clerc's Second Armored Division (the members of which are dressed in American uniforms) having lunch in the small restaurant with some of their local friends. Singing commenced, the Marseillaise was shouted with the usual excitement and all hands drank champagne.

The low casualty rate among the many agents that OSS dispatched to France was no consolation to Bruce as he contemplated the brutal fate of these five members of a Sussex team who were shot by the Germans. Courtesy of the National Archives.

We then went with Ken to see the G-2 at the Fifteenth Corps. He had very little information we did not already possess. For some reason almost inexplicable to us here, the British and Canadian Armies have made little headway from the North. The result is that the Americans have made a huge sweep and have enfolded most of the German forces, but, because of the lack of progress by the British, a corridor of perhaps 20 miles between Falaise and Argentan affords the Germans a possible avenue of escape. The Boches are breaking up into small formations; one crossed the road a few miles out of Alençon this morning. It consisted of ten heavy tanks and about 20 light armored vehicles. After basting six jeeps, they happened to encounter this formation moving off toward the Forêt de Perseigne.[15] The Air Corps claims to have annihilated it before it could join up with other German units.

The number of prisoners taken since the invasion started is said to be about 150,000. The morale of all soldiers, except the SS, has greatly deteriorated, and there is a steady flow of voluntary captives. This large pocket should be cleaned out rather quickly, and there would appear to be little to arrest our rapid progress toward Paris, if we have the wisdom to keep pushing and give the enemy no respite.

I went with Michel Brault to the Hotel de Ville to see the head of the local resistance. His boys are in great form, swaggering about with sten guns and grenades. The Germans are thoroughly frightened of them, and with good reason. The Resistance partisans are not lenient to their prisoners, and do not encumber themselves with many of them. They are adroit at using the small amount of materiel at their disposition to the best advantage. One group of them yesterday surrounded a small forest held by a vastly greater number of Germans. They poured gasoline around its fringes, set it afire, and, as the Germans emerged, in broken ranks, killed most of them.

General Le Clerc,[16] of North African fame, has command of the only French Division at present on the soil of Continental France. Everywhere his tanks go his men are welcomed with almost hysterical enthusiasm. They have fought very bravely and, although they have lost a good many tanks, they seem almost as likely to be destroyed by the embracements of their countrymen and country-women as by enemy action.

On the way back to Le Mans tonight, we stopped for supper at a small hamlet named Le Boulay, which is on the Sarthe River. A member of the local Resistance gave us cider, and we drank many healths. In the local billiard room we had an omelette and fried potatoes, with large slabs of delicious coarse brown bread.

The other side: German soldiers near Limoges burying comrades killed by the Resistance. Courtesy of the National Archives.

Major Brault is a famous Paris international lawyer. I had met him in London about a year ago, where he was known as "Gérome." He had just come out of France and was an important figure in the Maquis.

One is much struck by the general excellence of German soldiers' personal equipment as contrasted with the poor quality of their automotive equipment. Their uniforms do not appear to be shoddy, their clothes and boots are in good condition, and such articles as canteens and messkits are at least equal to our own. The first thing all soldiers abandon when in flight is the gas mask, and the countryside is littered with them. Few armies in history could have attained such a consumption of wines and spirits per capita as has the German Army in France. Everywhere they have been posted they have left behind masses, almost mountains, of bottles—all empty. The French, although a most agreeable and attractive race, and in many respects an admirable one, are often, even to their friends, somewhat irritating; when they deliberately seek to annoy—as they have done during the German occupation—they must be absolutely maddening. They are masters of passive as well as of active sabotage. The courage and recklessness of the civilians who constantly volunteer to pass back and forth through the enemy lines, where the penalty of apprehension is torture and death, is surprising and invigorating.

August 15

We went out this morning towards Angers. We passed the Le Mans airport on the edge of the city. It has been almost completely perforated with bombs, but already our engineers are laying strips across it. The properties in the neighborhood are wrecked. Across the road from it, the great Gnome-Rhone motor works are blasted. We could obtain no information about conditions along the highway to Angers until we arrived at a Gendarmerie in a little village about 10 miles from Le Mans. The Gendarmes there all seemed to be part of the local resistance movement. They advised us to attach ourselves to a convoy, since there were still small bands of Germans operating along the road. No convoys being available, we were forced to ignore this sound advice, and we sped down this magnificent highway, much of which was lined with great poplars and locusts, into La Flèche. Today is the Assumption. Church bells are ringing, and all the cities and villages are en fête. The streets are lined with men, women and children waving hands and flags, and occasionally throwing bunches of flowers. At La Flèche, having had no breakfast, we repaired to the Hotel de l'Image, where we were accosted kindly by the entire kitchen staff. Gravey set up his radio in the courtyard in an attempt to pick some news off the air. Then we had a marvelous lunch—first cold eggs, then an omelette, beef, potatoes, cheese and pudding. The white Anjou wine was cool and refreshing.

The country between Le Flèche and Angers is part of the so-called "Garden of France." It well deserves the name. Great expanses of wheat fields, orchards, pastures and forests stretch on either side of us. The country is well watered. The apples are just beginning to acquire a pinkish tinge, and the wheat stubble and sheaves are a mellow gold. Chickens, ducks, geese, and, occasionally, turkeys are to be seen. Many peasant families keep large Belgian hares in little cages where they fatten for the table. The first indications that we are approaching a vineyard country are manifest. Here and there vines grow, usually in rows within well-tended vegetable patches. Under the sun it is a smiling countryside, and the people seem more cheerful of countenance than the inhabitants further North. Here and there along the road is a destroyed house or hamlet, or a burnt-out tank or truck.

From La Flèche to Angers, the road continued to be perfect. Along it we met only one jeep and one hospital automobile, but there were many cyclists. We passed through the city and followed another car into a battered suburb where there were signs of fierce and recent fighting. Here we found ourselves at an Army salvage depot. Stacks of abandoned enemy rifles, machine guns, and small cannon had been collected, and one had to be wary of walking because of possible mines. Potato-mashers and other grenades were still lying around, and there was a good bit of blood, although all but a few corpses in the vicinity had been disposed of. The Germans were a couple of miles away and were still shelling the city at night.

We returned to Angers, visited CIC headquarters, and called on the G-2 of the 80th Division. The Germans had blown the main bridge leading to the South bank of the Loire, and held the territory between Angers and Saumur in inconsiderable force. The night before, one of their raiding parties had crossed over to our side and cut some of our communications.

We interviewed several resistance people who were drifting about, one of them a quaint little bald-headed Count, who said he was a direct descendant of Lafayette. He spoke English well, and was introduced to us by a Canadian and a Norwegian, both of whom had been prisoners of war and had been brought by him into our lines this morning.

We also saw Colonel Bilbane and Captain Jacques Beau.[17] They were checking up on five agents who were sent across the river two days before to gather intelligence. It is feared they have all been picked up by the Germans.

We returned from Angers and went through Le Mans directly to the new command post of the Third Army. General Gaffy, the Chief of Staff, had told Charlie Vanderblue he wanted to talk to me about the coordination of our units there. The taking over of command of SF Field Detachments by General Koenig had complicated the situation, but General Gaffy wants SF at Third Army under Army Command, and Vanderblue as Coordinator between it and other OSS units. He instructed us to cable Joe Haskell to come out and discuss the matter with him. We also talked to Colonel Gay,[18] Deputy Chief of Staff, and to Bunny Carter, arriving back at the Hotel de Saumon after dark. We had news tonight of the successful landing of Allied troops this morning at Marseilles.[19]

August 16

We spent a long time this morning trying to discover Stacy Lloyd and his MO villa. When we reached it our bird had flown, so we went out to Third Army CP and lunched with Vanderblue. Mowinckel, Beau and others discussed various details with us, and we sent a message by Alan Conway to Reutershan asking the latter to come here immediately with services personnel, clothing for overrun agents, cots and blankets, etc., to take over the administration of three houses in which we will collect agents.

When we returned to Le Mans in the afternoon we sat on the terrace of the Café du Commerce and had a bottle of white Anjou wine from the district of Layon. The girls and young women in this city are very pretty and attractive. Neither men nor women seem ill-fed or shoddily dressed. It is true the fashions in clothes one sees on the street are not the latest thing in chic, but there is much more smartness in everyone's appearance than I had anticipated.

The shops display a greater variety of things for sale than one would see in London. Silk and rayon handkerchiefs, perfumes, lipsticks, a variety of toilet articles, quantities of recently published books, tableware, glassware, kitchen utensils are all available, although some of them are on ration points.

We went out to Stacy's villa for dinner. Stacy did not arrive, but Paul Munster entertained us with an omelette and beefsteak meal. Vanderblue, Gaskell and Wendell Gibbs[20] were also there.

At midnight Stacy came to our hotel, and we drafted a telegram asking that an Austrian, who had formerly worked at Hambro's Bank, be sent out immediately to help in the Black German work. They are delivering, by an agent, into Paris today some leaflets, one of them purportedly signed by Rommel[21] saying the German cause is hopeless and advising surrender. General Quesada[22] has undertaken to drop others of these leaflets from the air onto German troops.

This afternoon we saw two of the overrun Sussex agents. They are keen as mustard and wish again to be dropped behind the enemy lines and resume their dangerous work.

August 17

Lester, Gravey, and I went to a nearby Bistro this morning and, with the aid of the buxom patronne contrived to breakfast satisfactorily on our K rations. We then went toward Chartres. At Lucè, about three kilometers from Chartres, we were stopped at the bridge by a Captain of Engineers who told us there were snipers in

Lucè as well as in Chartres, and we should proceed no further at that time in a jeep. A colonel proceeding there had been killed a short time before. We crossed the bridge on foot and met up with a squad of engineers in a ditch. They were literally lying in a welter of unused German grenades, with a bazooka on the bank, and a perfectly good German artillery piece with plenty of ammunition nearby. As we were crossing the bridge, the American artillery opened up behind us and set a couple of large oil dumps on fire a mile away from us. The Boches replied, and fired a haystack about five hundred yards on our right. Ahead of us, there were occasional bursts from machine guns and rifles. The Corporal from Georgia who commanded our ditch party told us the French Resistance people were trying to clean Chartres of the enemy, and were firing indiscriminately in the process. At one point, they suspected that the two steeples of the famous cathedral were harboring snipers, and cut loose on it.

After a time we left our position and went back to lunch in a village about seven miles away. While we were there, Joe Driscoll,[23] of the New York Herald Tribune, came in with two other correspondents. They had been in Chartres during the morning and said that German artillery had, just before they left, damaged one of the spires of the cathedral. Mowinckel came along, and we decided to have another go at Chartres. We crossed the bridge and a sniper fired twice (or two snipers fired once), just missing us, as we entered the city. We halted at the main square, and joined a small group of soldiers on the corner. The Germans were firing again near the cathedral, which is behind the square, and some American artillery was crashing away about a quarter of a mile ahead of us. Behind us, the Germans were throwing shells for awhile, and judging it an unwise time to visit the interior of the cathedral, we went on back and stopped at the now-familiar bridge to borrow gasoline. While we were waiting, everyone around flung themselves on their faces, about twenty soldiers erupted from a halted truck, we all cocked rifles and pistols, and nothing appeared! It transpired that the Germans were shelling a machine gun post about a hundred yards from the bridge.

After we returned to Le Mans, Mowinckel came in. He had tried to get through Chartres and had been stopped. He then returned to look for us, as a couple of Americans had just been killed on the square where we had been standing, and, not finding us, had proceeded home.

August 18

We decided this morning to move to Chartres, and take all our equipment with us. We went to see Vanderblue at Third Army, and became so entwined in conferences we did not get away until afternoon. Amongst other things, General Gaffy had charged me with the task of clearing with Twelfth Army Group, SHAEF, and General Koenig the further arming of Resistance Groups by the Third Army to support its operations. I sent a wire to Bill Jackson, asking him, if possible, to come down tomorrow morning so I could advise him of General Gaffy's wishes. Meanwhile, we must remain here until the matter is settled.

I also saw General Wood, whose son is serving with us, and General Patton, who was very genial, and talked to me of long-ago fox hunts in Baltimore. I saw Charlie Codman (General Patton's aide), George Murnane, Jr. (General Gay's aid) and Bunny Carter. I discussed the SI situation with Lieutenant Colonel Allen[24] (of Pearson and Allen Merry-Go-Round fame), and Major Schmuc. We then told the SI men what we had heard and left them. On the way back, we went to the house at Rue L'Huisnes, and found it bulging with French agents. The five Sussex agents who were killed by the Germans had been photographed where their bodies fell. I saw the photographs and they were horrible. They had all, including the woman, been shot through the groin and the stomach. One of the men in the village where they were killed had taken the pictures after the Germans evacuated it, and brought them to us so we could identify the dead.

We went out to Stacy Lloyd's villa, and saw some new leaflets which Paul Munster wanted to distribute. On the way back we met Stacy, who was just returning from shepherding his wood-burning seven-ton truck, with three French agents in it, and sacks of potatoes and vegetables. He had accompanied them to a point about sixty miles from Paris. The black leaflets had been tucked away in their extra tire. Unfortunately, just as they entered enemy territory they had a blowout, so a hasty transfer had to be made which, it is hoped, escaped unfriendly notice.

There is now quite a flow of civilians along the roads in the direction of Paris, many of them on bicycles but many on foot, trudging along with knapsacks on their backs. There is also an exodus from Paris of people from whom valuable intelligence can be obtained. The city is desperately short of food, the supply of coal is so low that the services of electricity and water are almost suspended, and the Germans have, it is said, withdrawn considerable members of their troops and supplies, and almost all their secret archives.

We went back to Rue L'Huisne to send a wireless message, and found Trafford Klotz and Ben Welles there, as well as still more newly-arrived agents. So many persons turn up saying they have just come from Paris that Lester says he wishes someone would arrive fresh from Chicago.

Colonel de Besse wandered in tonight, as did Major Brault. Monsieur Mouthard[25] (an assumed name), one of the established intelligence men of BCRA, trickled into our gathering. He has been running an intelligence chain for three and a half years, and is an old friend of General Haskell, the father of our two Colonels.

Trafford, Lester, Gravey and I had dinner at the Hotel de Paris. An omelette, a navarin of lamb, tomato salad, and three bottles of Alsatian Riesling were very satisfactory at a price of eighteen dollars. It will be interesting in later years to compare prices in these abnormal times to those that will finally prevail. The official exchange rate is two cents for a franc.

During this great offensive, the British and Canadians, reinforced by a Polish Division, have made very little progress. The most the ebullient General Montgomery can say of them is "they are holding firm." Their officers, however, are to be seen in numbers in the American Sector, although it is very difficult for American officers to obtain access to the British Sector. This is provocative of some ill-feeling, especially since many of the American officers and men are disdainful of what they consider the lethargy of their British allies.

Mowinckel came back tonight from Orleans, which he reports as being entirely in our hands. He had a swim in the River Loire, a pleasure of which I have not partaken for twenty-four years. The Russians are said to be three miles from the East Prussian border, to be regrouping their armies and to be bringing up supplies for a great offensive. The Southern France landing of American-French forces is successful, and a satisfactory beachhead has been established. As a sidenote, General Patton travels everywhere with a white bull terrier, and when I saw him today he was not wearing the two pearl-handled pistols which rumor has declared to be inseparable from his person, but only carried a single shoulder holster.

The Germans are reported to be collecting large forces in the Forest of Fontainbleau, perhaps in preparation for a counter-attack. V-1 continues to be directed against England, and prisoners of war declare that V-2 will shortly appear and will scatter virulent germs.

One of the most encouraging aspects of the campaign was seeing two American Diesel locomotives at the railroad crossing near Stacy's. The sergeant in charge said they had put ashore at Cherbourg ten locomotives and ten trains of forty or fifty cars each. The track was very rough, and the journey from Cherbourg to Le Mans had taken them three days, but soon they would have it in condition for fast travel. The supply problem is the only thing now limiting the speed of our advance, and getting the railroads back into working order and importing rolling stock, partially to replace the vast amounts destroyed or taken away, is of vast importance.

August 19

Bill Jackson appeared this morning, and it was arranged that he would deal with the matters discussed with General Gaffy. We then started off and lunched at Nogent-le-Rotrou, arriving at Chartres in the afternoon. We found the town quiet, and all the hotels closed. All was not quiet, however, at the Prefecture where a constant drama took place in the courtyard. When we arrived there, a row of women, with their faces pressed to a wall, presented their backs to the crowd. They were individually interrogated and taken away to an upstairs room. I went there and found them in process of having their heads shorn—first with scissors and then with clippers. Most of them were very unattractive, but there was one good-looking girl of about twenty, who faced the situation almost gaily.

Members of the French Forces of the Interior were much in evidence, and very careless with their weapons. They, like some of our own soldiers, are "trigger happy," and while we were standing there at least one piece was discharged by accident, an occurrence that has become familiar to us. We went to the cathedral, which is essentially undamaged. Its wonderful stained glass windows were placed in storage long ago, so the interior had lost its pristine soft luminosity. Leaning over the parapet of the cathedral Close, and looking into the terraced gardens and shrubbery below, we witnessed what seemed to be a rabbit hunt. A Senegalese, a Gendarme, and several civilians, carrying an assortment of weapons, were poking about in the weeds, vegetables, and underbrush, looking for German soldiers. They could not have anticipated that any German they might encounter would offer fight, for from time to time they would turn their backs on as yet unexplored terrain to smoke and chat together. At the Prefecture, prisoners were being brought in from time to time, tired, dusty and apathetic.

We decided to spend the night in the country, and drove out toward the Command Post of the Fifth American Infantry Division beyond Leves. Near Leves we found a large field, at the foot of a hill, surmounted by a large and hideous Château. The gatekeeper

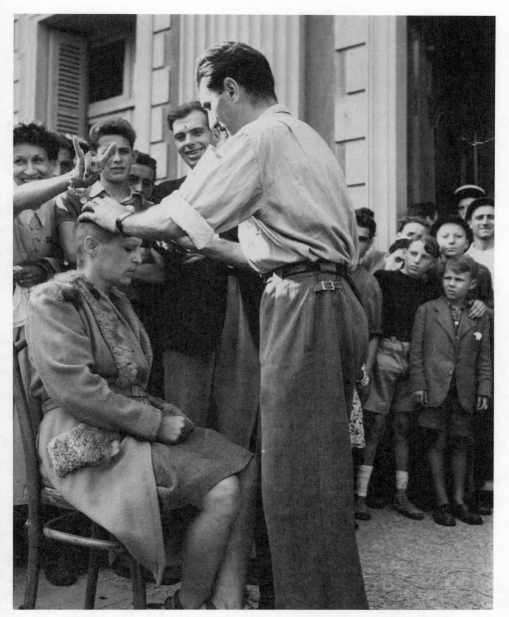

At Chartres Bruce observed an incident, like this one photographed in front of the city hall at Merton, in which women accused of consorting with Germans during the Occupation had their hair shorn as an emblem of their shame. Courtesy of the National Archives.

told us we were free to use the field, and presented us with two bottles of red wine. We sent his son off to purchase eggs, and enjoyed an excellent omelette. We went across the road, at no great distance, to inspect a Château that had been occupied by the Gestapo. The evacuants had left behind them a mass of filth, broken furniture, and litter of every description. In the charming river, flowing through the garden, a huge gas-inflated hog floated belly upwards, his four legs sticking stiffly out like fat antennae.

Shortly after we had crawled into our sleeping bags, there was a deluge of rain. Lester and Gravey became soaking wet; Mac and I were luckier, but at daybreak we were a bedraggled looking quartet. However, some nescafé and another omelette soon remedied the situation.

11

The Frenzied Joy of the Crowds Is Impossible to Describe

Paris Liberated, August 20 to 29, 1944

August 20

We climbed the hill this morning to investigate what we almost considered our own Château. It was completely deserted, and seemed to have been the headquarters of an important German staff. There were numbers of new machine guns, rifles, mines, grenades, signal equipment, and clothing scattered about, and the usual heaps of empty wine bottles. We proceeded through it carefully, for fear it had been booby-trapped, for we had found a lot of such contraptions packed outside. Nothing happened. We decided to report, which we later did, the presence of these arms to Commandant St. Clair, the Chief of the Chartres Resistance Group. They should prove very useful to his men who are cleaning out German soldiers by-passed by the American forces.

It was then decided that I should go to the Fifth Division C.P. and try to ascertain what the military situation might be. On the way there, we passed about a dozen dead German soldiers, and three or four Americans. They were all bloated, stiffened, and their skins black. At the C.P., I saw Colonel Thackeray, and afterwards had a long talk with Major General Irwin and his Chief of Staff, both of whom General Donovan and I had met in Northern Ireland. Mowinckel came in, and said he needed permission to obtain access to the huge German warehouse at Chartres, where he hoped to obtain clothing, sheets, blankets, cutlery, etc., to furnish a house he had taken for the SI Staff and agents. This was readily granted, and we started off for Chartres. Ernest Hemingway[1] was also at the C.P., and I arranged to meet him tonight at Rambouillet.

In Chartres we received a message from Le Mans saying General Donovan was expected there today, and that I had better return at once. Having so many fish to fry, it was decided that Lester would meet him and try to persuade him to come on to Rambouillet.

Bruce (left) and Hemingway (third from left) at Rambouillet helping liberate the local wine stores just before the drive on Paris. Courtesy of R. Harris Smith, *OSS* (Berkeley: University of California Press, 1972).

The German warehouses were amazing. There were tens of thousands of plates, cups and saucers, boxes of contraceptives, and
empty wine bottles. Less numerous, but still in enormous quantities,
were tooth brushes, shaving cream, toilet water, sun-tan oil, razor
blades, combs, brushes, boots and shoes, uniforms and underwear,
blankets, goggles, cutlery and kitchen utensils, seemingly sufficient
to stock all the hotels on the Riviera. It was a staggering sight.

Mowinckel, Gravey and I drove from Chartres to Rambouillet.
The road was almost deserted, and presents many good points for
ambushes. Near the Château, we found the Hotel du Grand Veneur,
where we promptly plunged into a bath of excitement. Hemingway
had a room in the hotel, and at his beck and call an American private known as "Red,"[2] whose name was Archie, as well as about ten
Resistance men. We were enchanted to see him. Agents and patrols
kept rushing in with reports, some of them contradictory, but all
indicating that the Germans were laying mines down the road toward us about eight miles away, with a force of approximately 150

men. As there were no American troops in Rambouillet, Hemingway
and the French had become more or less convinced the Germans
would retake the town tonight. We grilled the only Boche prisoner
we could find. He either knew nothing or was a good actor, so we
turned him back to the French, whom he was firmly convinced intended to execute him.

Finding myself the senior officer in town, I was persuaded to report the latest intelligence to the Second Regiment of the Fifth
Division back at Maintenon, and try to obtain some arms from
them. Gravey and I drove through Epernon to Maintenon and
called on Colonel Rolfe. All he could spare us was two boxes of
German hand grenades which we piled into the jeep.

I stopped to see the Resistance leader at Maintenon, who promised to send a reinforcement of his men to Rambouillet—he hoped
to have thirty or forty of them available.

When we got back to La Grand Veneur, it was like being in Bedlam.
Monsieur Mouthard (Michel Pasteau) had arrived to join us, and
Mowinckel had left with some urgent intelligence for Le Mans.
Agents were nipping in and out, and everyone, including a stray
American woman resident in France, was buttonholing me, asking
questions and giving the answers at the same time. Newspaper cor-
respondents had sprouted out of the ground, and the world and his
wife were eating and uncorking champagne.

The forces at our disposition were about thirty Americans—officers
and men—including two very drunken AWOL paratroopers, ten
Resistance people, fourteen gendarmes, and a few machine guns.
Major Thornton, of IS 9 SHAEF, was most helpful and, with the
French and Major Neave[3] (a British officer), arranged to patrol the
roads leading toward Paris and report back any German movement.
Between Hemingway, Thornton, Neave, Gravey and myself there
was constant contact.

When Gravey and I left about 11:30 p.m., the scene in the Grand
Veneur dining room was something to behold. Most of the armed
forces of the Allied Nations at Rambouillet had during the course of
the evening eaten there, but at this hour it was the French who really displayed their stamina. Champagne in quantity was produced,
and toasts were freely given and exchanged. Couriers reported with
messages from table to table as well as from further afield.

Groping our way in the dark, Gravey and I went to the house
of the Comtesse d'Aymery, on Place du Gouvernement, where
Mowinckel had arranged for us to sleep the night. Having located
our lodging, we returned to the Grand Veneur for a last look. Colonel

de Chevigné, head of the French Forces in Northern France, had arrived and injected some of his views into our military strategy. Meanwhile, the sharpshooters from Maintenon had crawled up in a circus truck, thirsty and hungry, and were being feasted in the dark in that incredibly genial dining room. People purporting to have just arrived from Versailles and Paris were popping in and out.

After midnight, finding most of our forces disposed in an orderly way around the Grand Veneur, although some of them were still fighting a rearguard action in the kitchen, Gravey and I finally went to bed and, except for a few rifle shots, heard no fracas during the night. We had arranged a password "France-Orléans" that all our people hissed at each other. I tremble to think what would have happened to any unwary patriot who had ventured on the street after midnight without knowing this word. Actually, if there had been any German agent in the town to spy out the number of our forces, he would have been utterly confused. At the hotel so constant was the influx and reflux of the Captains and the Kings, the self-appointed messengers, our regular scouts, and so great was the fanfare that any onlooker would have fancied we were in Rambouillet in great strength.

August 21

It rained heavily last night, and this morning all is quiet. In the garden of the Grand Veneur a Frenchman has just made the mistake of taking a German grenade apart and the patriots are now firing their pistols at it, trying to explode it about twenty yards away from where Gravey is tenaciously attempting to reach London on his radio.

Monsieur Mouthard, Gravey and myself had coffee together, after which I despatched our now weary cohorts from Maintenon back home, having promised the hotel-keeper to be responsible for the food they had consumed—the liquor, we hope, having been the contribution of a grateful town to its liberators and safe-keepers!

I had expressed to Mouthard my desire to buy a small French flag to put on our jeep. In the forenoon a delegation, including an Archbishop, waited on me in the garden, and I was presented with a flag adorned with gold fringe and a metal standard, as well as with an engrossed document expressing "the gratitude of the population of Rambouillet."[4]

The imagination staggers at the thought of what Mouthard must have said to the donors!

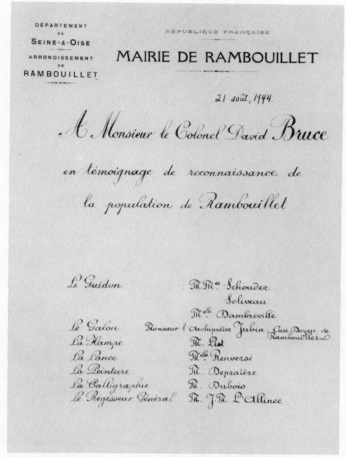

On August 21 a delegation of civic and religious officials from Rambouillet
presented this certificate to Bruce for his part in liberating their town. He
managed to keep the document throughout the wild dash into Paris that
followed several days later. Courtesy of the Virginia Historical Society.

Our local Army disintegrated rapidly today. Having decided that
the American troops were not going directly to Paris by this route,
the correspondents and specialists are haring off in all directions.
Hemingway and ourselves are holding this position, and sending out
small patrols along all the roads. It is maddening to be only thirty

American forces taking Fontainebleau about the time Bruce was with Hemingway at Rambouillet. Courtesy of the National Archives.

miles from Paris, to interrogate every hour some Frenchman who has just come from there and who reports that even a very small task force could easily move in, and to know that our Army is being forced to wait—and for what reason? Yesterday, the Resistance people, hearing we were in Versailles and were moving onto Paris, rose prematurely and are said to have suffered considerable losses.

The Seventh Armored Division crossed behind us this afternoon, and has been cannonading a few miles away in the direction of Chevreuse. It is assumed to be proceeding towards Fontainbleau, where forces of Germans are reported to be assembling in the Forest.

We moved into a room at the hotel this afternoon and, with Ernest and Mouthard, engaged in a series of interrogations. One man had the exact location of a minefield he had seen the Germans lay last night. Another had taken part in yesterday's insurrection in Paris.

While at Rambouillet awaiting the final Allied push on the French capital, Bruce learned that gendarmes and members of the French underground, like those shown here, already had risen against the German garrison in Paris. Courtesy of the National Archives.

Another had spent the preceding night at Trappe, and so on. Two women were brought in who had been living just within the present German lines on the road to Paris. They were Alsatians, and were accused by the people in their little village of sleeping with Germans. One of them had three children and a husband who had, until May, worked in the French War Ministry at Vichy and later at Paris. We sent a patrol out, which arranged for a neighbor to shelter the children and brought the husband back here. His arrival precipitated the sort of conversation in which the French delight and excel. The Resistance Chief asked me gravely whether I thought the husband had the face of a classical *mari cocu* or was it not rather of the music-hall type. Before the poor man could be interrogated, at least fifteen people were ardently discussing his connubial status. The tireless and resourceful Mouthard undertook to take charge of this now frightened little family, and to question them at length.

During the afternoon, someone denounced to me a woman walking in the hotel garden who is alleged to have been the mistress of an important Gestapo officer at Paris. I have sent for her dossier and we will interrogate her tomorrow. As I was walking down the street this morning, a car stopped and out stepped a Frenchman and his wife. They opened the back door of their car, and asked me to take over three German prisoners who were sitting stiffly in a row while a youngster with a sten gun watched them from the rumble seat.

I had to decline their custody, but we will interview them later. Today, we had a deserter from the Wehrmacht brought to us. He is a Pole, very young, and dressed in civilian clothes. We are keeping him in our private cooler for further interrogation.

We have been busy as bees all day, and tonight enjoyed a wonderful dinner. The proprietor is from Périgord, and presented us with a Paté de Foie Gras stuffed abundantly with truffles.

As usual here, a minor crisis occurred at nightfall. Word came in that SF Headquarters was to make parachute drops of munitions in the neighborhood this evening, so we decided we ought to warn any American patrols, and to place Frenchmen with them to identify any friendly transport that might have to pass through in this connection. Ernest, Mouthard, Gravey, "Red," and the Resistance Adjutant sallied forth with us into the blackness for this purpose. There was the usual comedy of errors, but when we finally returned we had added a number of bazookas, rifles, and other grenades to our stocks—I know, because I had to sit on them in our crowded jeep on the way home.

Mac returned today. Lester had thoughtfully sent him back with the jeep and with badly-needed money.

August 22

Mouthard has just made a report to Ernest and myself, and has asked and been granted permission to go away for fifteen minutes to kill a civilian traitor. We lent him a .32 automatic.

Couriers are pouring in. Chevreuse is empty, Etampes was captured this morning.

Yesterday was cloudy and rainy. Today is clear and beautiful.

Nobody can understand the present Allied strategy. General Patton's Third American Army has been in a position for several days to take Paris. Two of his Divisions are across the Seine and have moved North. There are no German forces of consequence between us and the capital. Rumors have been prevalent for some days here that the failure to allow the Third Army to press forward and fully realize its capabilities is due to high politics. Some even say the delay is to permit President Roosevelt to arrive and personally to enter the city. Most, however, claim that the Americans are being forced to await the entry of General Montgomery and the British, who, unable to clear a way through the territory assigned to them, are now to swing through the American Sector and thus get ahead. Whatever the reason may be, it does not seem to make much sense to sit around here as if there were serious opposition in front us, thus allowing the Germans to lay mines, disengage troops, and withdraw supplies that otherwise we could mop up with ease.

Nobody had been able to tell us exactly where General Le Clerc's Second Armored French Division is located. Like the Scarlet Pimpernel, it is said to have been seen here, there, and everywhere. This morning, a Frenchman wearing the red képi and American uniform characteristic of a portion of that Division appeared outside our hotel. He was promptly pounced upon, and induced to lead Gravey, Mouthard and myself to an advance element of Le Clerc's, in charge of Colonel Guilebon, an old friend of Mouthard, which we found in a wheat field beyond Nogent le Roy. We gave the Colonel a fill-in on the situation to the North, East, and West of Rambouillet, and, while we were having lunch, his tanks and retainers lurched off, with the intention of going as far as Sceaux.

Lester and Stacy arrived this afternoon from Le Mans. I had been asked to visit the wounded French in the Rambouillet hospital, so we all went together. It was a distressing sight, especially as a majority of them had been injured by American bombing or as a result of strafing on the roads by American planes. We saw the young and attractive wife of one of the doctors who accompanied us. She had been in a cafe a few days before when a plane machine-gunned passing German transport. She had been hit in the legs by bullets and both feet had to be amputated. She merely said, resignedly: "C'est la guerre." The Director of the hospital and his wife opened a bottle of port for us.

About four miles from here is a beautiful property belonging to the Comte de Fels. It was there that Marshal Pétain was brought by the Germans last winter to stay three months. The grounds are magnificent, with the finest hunting alleys one can imagine, radiating from a center like the points of a star. The Château itself is very large and comfortable. The Mayor and the Prefecture asked if we would not like it requisitioned for our use, and thus save it from vandalism. We answered, "Yes."[5]

Bill Hearst[6] appeared this afternoon; also Charlie Vanderblue, Ed Gaskell and John Mowinckel. The ten German tanks up the road were active again today. One of our Resistance men was killed, another captured, and they took fifteen hostages away with them. They fired on a French Major, whom I saw a few minutes afterwards, about three miles from here—he escaped with a hole through his helmet but his head intact.

August 23

Still no word of General Donovan except that he should have reached France on Sunday.

A great frou-frou this morning. A French Reserve Lieutenant and his wife (who had captured two German prisoners yesterday) told me Monsieur Coulougnou, the lessee of the Château du Terrier, was not only a notorious black market operator but a well-known collaborator with the Germans. He looks like a typical Chicago gangster, and is accompanied always by a bodyguard of whom Al Capone, in his halcyon days, would not have been ashamed.

PWD has settled down in his Château, and he entertains constantly all American, British, and Canadian officers and war correspondents. The Countess d'Aymery has corroborated the story told me, and I have passed it on to Colonel de Chevigné, who intends to place him under restraint. It is a pity that our CIC and SCI men are not here, as there are several cases of this sort requiring their attention.

A gush of Allied war correspondents poured into Rambouillet this morning, coming from Twelfth Army Group and from First and Third Armies. They had been told by Colonel Dickson, G-2 of First Army, that General Le Clerc had at last been granted permission to try and enter Paris.

A small patrol from Le Clerc's Second Armored Division came into town today and proceeded north towards Versailles. We gave them the intelligence we had—and it was precise—as to the opposition they might expect. An hour later they returned, having lost one vehicle, two men killed and two wounded. The attractive Lieutenant in charge had been shot in the back, the arm and the leg, and was bespattered with blood. He was, however, in wonderful spirits, and helped drink a bottle of champagne. While we were talking to him, General Le Clerc arrived in a three star jeep. He is tall, spare, handsome, stern-visaged, and a striking figure. All his people were in light vehicles, and went into the Park of Rambouillet. I was pre-

Free French general Jacques LeClerc directs the Liberation of Paris on August 25, 1944. Several days before this picture was taken, LeClerc brusquely interrogated Bruce and Hemingway at Rambouillet on his way into the capital. Hemingway wrote later that when LeClerc had finished questioning the two Americans, he said something to the effect of *"Buzz off you unspeakables."* Courtesy of the National Archives.

sented to the General there, and asked by him to give all the intelligence I could to his G-2, Commander Repiton. This, with the assistance of Hemingway, Mouthard, and Mowinckel, I did.[7]

The correspondents are furious with Le Clerc because he will not tell them his plans. He, in turn, is angry with them and with reason, for they are looking for a story and he is trying to make plans to capture Paris. Apparently, the pressure from the Resistance people in Paris, who are being chopped up by the Germans, was finally too great for the High Command, and they have belatedly decided to capture the capital.

We have three agents outside whom we may send in tonight. Lester has just returned from Chartres where he heard General de Gaulle speak. The General, it is hoped, will come here tonight and join in what may be the triumphal entry tomorrow.

In the afternoon we motored to the Château of the Comte de Fels, and, in so doing, passed miles of tanks, trucks, etc., of the Second Armored Division. These Frenchmen look extremely tough and fit. We also saw Dana Durand, Captain Brown, and others of our SCI group, who are in the special Task Force of Twelfth Army Group. We saw the concierge at the Château and put up a placard on the front door stating it was reserved for General de Gaulle.

An agent has just come in to ask that, if possible, we send a guard into Montfort tonight. The Germans took four men out of there last night, presumably as hostages. Their bodies were found this afternoon, and the inhabitants say the Germans told them they were coming back tonight and take twelve more.

August 24
We got up at six o'clock, and waited around for a couple of hours before joining one of Le Clerc's columns. We passed through Dampierre. At St. Rémy we took cover behind a wall, but found to our discomfiture that the shelling was from our own guns. The day was rainy, and the visibility extremely limited. The column proceeded cautiously through the winding roads of the valley of the Chevreuse. About nine kilometers from Versailles we were halted at a crossroads, so we drove into an adjoining farmyard. There we found Durand, McCayliss and Guillaume. In no time, we were snugly ensconced in a warm kitchen, eating an omelette and drinking a bottle of wine that had been given to us along the road. When we emerged we found Hemingway and the Private Army, including Mouthard, had been engaged in a battle between French tanks and two Boche 88 guns. The latter were demolished, and prisoners taken.

Proceeding along the road, there was a considerable amount of artillery and tank fire, but not much response from the Germans, although we did see one 88 knocked out, and two dead Germans sprawled across its position. It was evident that relying on the intelligence furnished by us and others to them, the French were bypassing those points where any determined opposition could be expected. We came into Villacoubray, and took the high road to Paris. As we were halted at a carrefour about five miles from the capital, a little German car dashed up near where Gravey was standing and, either with grenades or a machine gun burst, badly wounded two French soldiers. This onslaught was daring and rapid—the car was fired on by infantry, tanks, and some of our own men, but escaped.

We then ran into road blocks which were tedious to clear away. A tank had set fire to a big munitions dump. We were forced to halt near it, and the crackle of small arms ammunition, tracer bullets, and the heavy roar of larger stuff exploding was not only annoying but quite dangerous, as missiles were whizzing by in every direction. We finally passed within a few yards of the edge of the dump, and I, for one, found this part of the journey terrifying.

As we went down the hill toward the Seine about five o'clock in the afternoon, the streets were lined with people. All houses were gay with flags, and the population was almost hysterical with joy. Our progress was extremely slow, and there were many long halts as road blocks were cleared, or small pockets of enemy resistance eliminated. During these stops we were mobbed by the bystanders. They gave us fruit and flowers, they kissed us on both cheeks, men, women, and children throwing their arms around us and saying, "Merci, Messieurs" (often adding: "We have waited for you four years.") When they knew we were Americans that seemed to increase their enthusiasm. Although we were passing through a tenement district, the people, on the whole, appeared to be moderately well dressed and fed. The French flag was everywhere—often it had the Cross of Lorraine imprinted on it. There were a good many American and British flags, and a few Russian, in evidence. We yelled ourselves hoarse, shouting "Vive la France" as we passed through the crowds. Everyone thrust drinks at us that they had been hoarding for this occasion. It was impossible to refuse them, but the combination was enough to wreck one's constitution. In the course of the afternoon, we had beer, cider, white and red Bordeaux, white and red Burgundy, champagne, rum, whiskey, cognac, armagnac, and Calvados.

As night fell, we were still a mile short of the Pont de Sèvres, and there was determined resistance in a factory below the bridge at which our tanks were cutting loose. The vehicles were drawn up along the sidewalks. Mouthard found a house in which we distributed ourselves, and we had our rations there. We could cook nothing, since there is no gas, or coal, but the electricity, they told us, is turned on for several hours each day and night.

The people all complain of the high cost of food. For six weeks most of the railroads operating into Paris have been inactive as a result of bombing, sabotage, or for other causes, and the transport of produce to the city from other parts of France has been almost completely suspended.

August 25

There had been some firing during the night and this morning. We did not get under way until 12:30 p.m. when we crossed the bridge. Tanks had preceded us some time before. The Artillery halted two kilometers from the bridge and shelled Mont Valérien thoroughly.

As we drove into a large square near the Bois de Boulogne, we were suddenly halted in front of a café, and it was said snipers were firing with machine guns from some of the upstairs windows of a larger apartment house. In any event, everyone turned loose at the building. I did see flashes several times near the roof as if someone were shooting from there, although I could not actually distinguish a weapon. Ernest, Gravey and I, sheltered in a doorway, Lester and Mac more bravely lay under the jeep. Finally, a tank sent a few shells into the unfortunate house, and we were told to move on. From that point forward, we were surrounded continually by surging masses of cheering people. Kissing and shouting were general and indiscriminate. It was a wonderful sunny day and a wonderful scene. The women were dressed in their best clothes, and all wore somewhere the tricolor—on their blouses, in their hair, and even as earrings.

We stopped once when three German tanks were signalled ahead. We then turned off and, under the guidance of a Spahis lieutenant raced through the side streets until we emerged, just behind the Arc de Triomphe, on Avenue Foch where we parked the cars. The Majestic Hotel, which had been German headquarters, was on fire. At the end of the Champs Elysées a vehicle was burning in the Place de la Concorde, and behind, in the Tuileries Gardens, it looked as if a tank was on fire. Smoke was issuing from the Crillon Hotel, and across the river, from the Chamber of Deputies. Snipers were firing steadily into the area around the Arc de Triomphe, and the French were firing back at them.

We walked across to the Tomb of the Unknown Soldier. It was being guarded by six veterans, standing at attention, and a mutilated ex-soldier, seated in a wheel chair. They had been there all during the fracas at the Majestic. The French Captain in charge asked us if we wanted to ascend to the roof of the Arc. We did so and were greeted by a squad of Pompiers standing at attention. For some reason, their Commander presented me with a pompier's

Bruce and Hemingway repeatedly dodged German snipers disrupting the wild celebrations of the Parisians on Liberation Day, August 25, 1944. Here some other American soldiers and wellwishers, including one under the jeep in the foreground, duck German bullets the next afternoon. Courtesy of the National Archives.

medal. The view was breathtaking. One saw the golden dome of the Invalides, the green roof of the Madeleine, Sacré-Coeur, and other familiar landmarks. Tanks were firing in various streets. Part of the Arc was under fire from snipers. A shell from a German 88 nicked one of its sides.

When we descended, Mouthard led us back toward our car. Seven or eight German soldiers lay dead in a heap on the street. As we made our way forward there was a burst of fire. We found the head of the street, where our car stood, barricaded, while shots were interchanged with a Gestapo headquarters there. As we sheltered beneath a tank, a man dove in alongside of us and asked if we would

like to drink a bottle of champagne at his house. The Spahis lieutenant, Lester, Gravey and I accepted. As we started down Avenue
Foch, firing became general again. Every side street seemed enfiladed.
There was enthusiastic confusion. Almost every civilian had a weapon
and wanted to shoot it. People on roofs were being shot at, and in
many of the top stories of buildings. Some of them were, no doubt,
German snipers dressed in civilian clothes, and some of them the
hated French Milice.[8] We finally made our way to our host's, not
without fear.

Arrived there, we found a most beautiful apartment, with very
fine furniture and Chinese porcelains, his lovely wife, and a magnum of iced champagne. His name was Robert Lalou, 40, Avenue
Foch. He said he had been an aviator in the French Army in 1940.
After another couple of bottles of champagne, our Spahis friend announced he must return to his squadron. We crossed the Avenue
and parted with him. On the corner, we found a retired French
Lieutenant-Colonel entertaining some of our men with champagne,
which was continually renewed by a servant bringing hampers of it
from a nearby apartment. We dallied there for a while and decided
to push on. Hemingway, Red (Hemingway's driver) and myself, finding the Champs Elysées absolutely bare of traffic, passed down it at
racing speed to the Travellers Club. When we entered, we found the
rooms all closed with the exception of the bar. There a number of
the Old Guard had collected, including the President of the Club.
We were the first outsiders to come there since the taking of Paris.
They celebrated by opening champagne. In the midst of this festiv-
ity a sniper began to fire from an adjoining roof. Red shouldered his
musket and made for the roof, but was balked.

We next collected our gang and, not knowing what was ahead except for the usual indiscriminate popping of small arms, dashed to
the Café de la Paix. The Place de l'Opéra was a solid mass of cheering people, and, after kissing several thousand men, women, and
babies, and losing a carbine by theft, we escaped to the Ritz. Except
for the manager, the imperturbable Ausiello,[9] the Ritz was completely deserted, so we arranged to quarter there as well as to take
lodging for the Private Army. This was done. Ausiello asked what he
could immediately do for us, and we answered we would like fifty
martini cocktails. They were not very good, as the bartender had
disappeared, but they were followed by a superb dinner.[10] During
the night, there was almost incessant shooting. The French Forces
of the Interior are well out of hand, and draw on anybody whom
they consider suspicious.

August 26

In the morning, there was no coffee, but we had an omelette and a bottle of Chablis. Then Gravey, Mac and I went to see my old friend Raoul Boyer, the wine merchant, at 5, Rue du Marché St.-Honoré. He was in excellent fettle, and we had some Montrachet with him. He had contrived during the German occupation to keep intact a small store of fine wines. He complained about the high cost of living and how the Germans had stripped France of all kinds of merchandise, food, and drink. His son, Jacques, had left France via Spain two years ago to join the French Air Corps in London, and they have since had no news of him.

Near Boyer's there had been quite a fight in front of the Hotel Oxford and Cambridge, where some Boche vehicles had been destroyed. Near Sulka's, on the corner of Rue Castiglione and Rue de Rivoli, there had been a similar occurrence. Beneath the arcades, charred remains of cars were lying about. On Place de la Concorde, the Ministry of Marine was badly damaged, and the Hotel Crillon had not escaped unscathed. Ken Downs came in later, and said the German officers and soldiers in the Crillon, who formed some service group, had surrendered to him and to Mowinckel. They refused to surrender to the French, to whom, however, Ken was obliged to turn them over. Ken said apparently they had enjoyed a marvelous lunch, washed down with quantities of champagne, and had then, smoking cigars, come downstairs to give themselves up.

At some time during the day I stopped in at Guerlain's, where Monsieur Guerlain very kindly gave me a bottle of Shalimar perfume.

There was a great procession today, starting from the Arc de Triomphe and going to Notre Dame, in which General de Gaulle, walking down the Champs Elysées, figured as the star personage. The crowds were so great that I could see little of it. People were massed in deep and solid array along the whole route. It was said an attempt had been made to assassinate de Gaulle. In the Cathedral a shot was fired, perhaps accidentally, and a near riot resulted during which some civilians were shot and others were crushed to death.

While these events were transpiring, Lester, Gravey and I started from the Ritz up the Rue de la Paix for a quiet walk. It was two and a half hours before we returned, having walked only about eight blocks! As we arrived in front of Cartier's, firing broke out everywhere. The Grand Hotel, the Opera, and most of the buildings along the Rue de la Paix seemed to be the targets of the FFI. Armored cars suddenly appeared, rushing up and down the streets at fifty miles an hour, firing wildly with machine guns at roofs and

Although he did not attend the confused service of thanksgiving at Notre
Dame on August 26, 1944, that was disrupted when snipers opened fire
inside the cathedral, Bruce commented on the proceedings at some length
in his diary. Here General de Gaulle leaves Notre Dame after the service.
Courtesy of the National Archives.

high windows. The glass in the second story of the Café de la Paix
was splintered with bullets. Lester and I retired into a doorway, and
eventually reached the Ritz via the Rue Cambon. There were fusil-
lades all over Paris. The streets are really dangerous, for everyone
with a firearm is trying to use it. The police are impotent, and the
whole situation is disorganized.

At 5:30 p.m., Charlie Neave took us up to see Colonel Roulier,
who has installed the BCRA in the Hotel Majestic. On the ground
floor were several hundred German prisoners, squatting together
miserably. Roulier introduced us to four of our "Pathfinders" who
have done such magnificent work. Two of them were French women

who, like the others, had been parachuted to their destinations. Colonel Henderson of SIS came in, his hands grimy from crawling over the roofs, chasing three snipers with machine guns who had finally evaded him.

We came back to the Ritz and found Joe Haskell and Paul Van der Stricht there. As there were no lights, we all went to bed about ten o'clock. About eleven-thirty there was tremendous excitement. German bombers were dropping their loads on Paris. The Ack-Ack was very feeble, but people were shooting at the airplanes with pistols, rifles, and machine guns. In a few minutes, the sky back of Morgan's Bank was glowing brightly. An alcohol dump was on fire there.

After a noisy hour, the wheezy All Clear sounded. At five o'clock another small flight of bombers came over and the performance was repeated.

August 27

This morning it appeared that last night's damage from bombing was extensive. The Bichat Hospital was hit, and some wounded and sick burned alive. The Panhard factory was struck, and the Halle Aux Vins, with its valuable content of wines, was burned, although to everyone's delight the large stocks of brandy there were saved. There were, of course, casualties in many quarters.

More light was thrown today upon the extraordinary events at Notre Dame yesterday. According to the morning newspapers, about half past four yesterday afternoon, when the Cathedral was packed with an immense crowd, General de Gaulle arrived outside. Before he could enter, machine gun bullets were fired by people hidden behind outside abutments of the edifice. Inside, others fired upon the congregation there. The FFI and the Garde Republicaine fired back. Under the vaults of the Cathedral a real battle began to rage. The worshippers tried to hide beneath the stalls, and behind columns and pillars. Some of them began to sing the Magnificat, others the Ave Maria. Men were pursued down the aisles of the church, and at least three alleged assassins were arrested. General de Gaulle entered and was cheered. The ceremony proceeded.

This morning the city appears quiet. Only seldom is a shot heard. I have been seeing Charlie Neave, Ken Downs, and others, including an MO agent who has successfully distributed his black literature amongst German troops.

Last night there was a little disturbance at the premises of the Chase Bank. The FFI claimed that a German radio set was hidden there. I took a French officer to the premises, and he persuaded them to stop breaking glass and beating up the Concierge. He told them they could obtain authority to make an orderly search. Between two courses at dinner, Lester and I saved General de Chambrun[11] from prison, and the Morgan Bank from being shelled by a Le Clerc tank.

The most unusual requests are made of one here. As I was talking to someone on the street outside the Ritz, a young Frenchman came up to me and introduced quite a nice-looking young man in civilian clothes whom he said was a German soldier who wanted to surrender to the American authorities. The German had formerly enabled the Frenchman to escape when the latter was a prisoner in Germany, and now wanted a favor in return. The story was very complicated; technically, the soldier had once been an American citizen. I finally arranged something about his disposition which was almost as complicated as the story.

Charlie Codman, Bunny Carter, de Besse and several other friends and acquaintances appeared at the Ritz for lunch. It is the last meal that will be served here, as the kitchen has run out of food, so we will have to fall back on our rations again. Almost every restaurant is closed, there is little in the markets, and the food situation is rapidly becoming worse.

British officers have appeared in Paris in swarms.

The streets are very quiet today, although there is still some rooftop fighting, and firing, in certain quarters. There are said to be several thousand Germans and Milice harboring in the subways, which, for lack of power, have been closed for the past twelve days. From there, they can make their way through previously prepared exits into buildings—the Crillon and the Majestic are amongst them—from which they can fire onto the streets if they wish.

Everywhere, as had been the case ever since we entered the city, there are thousands of cyclists. We have been busy today requisitioning office quarters. The Germans requisitioned many office buildings, hotels and private homes. As regards the last category, they took only those dwellings that belonged to Jews, known enemies, or Frenchmen who had quitted the capital. Already, General Pleas Rogers has arrived and set up an officers' mess at the Ambassadeur, another instance of the efficiency of the American Army Service of Supply.

Until recently, the population of Paris does not seem to have been as badly off as one might have expected under German occupation, except for their hatred of it and their constant humiliation by it. The Germans, of course, drained away, by the use of occupation francs, everything that took their fancy, and the labor relève withdrew thousands of young Frenchmen for work in the Reich. Unfortunately, since I have been here the shops have all been closed so it is impossible to compare the quantity and quality of merchandise on sale with that in London.

In the afternoon, swarms of OSS officers came to see us. Russ Forgan, John Haskell, Whitney Shepardson, Jack Harris, Howard Baldwin, Charlie Stearns, John Mowinckel and many others arrived.

Charlie Neave, Colonel Nason,[12] Forgan, Armour and myself dined tonight with Lieutenant Colonel Roulier, head of BCRA in France, at his mess in the Hotel Lapèrouse, near the Etoile. The others present were de Besse and Lieutenant Colonel Henderson of SIS. We had a wonderful dinner of hors d'oeuvres, steak and vegetables, salad and crèpes suzette, with a choice accompaniment of wines taken from German headquarters. Henderson had again been chasing snipers over the rooftops, and said there were still many of them roaming the city.

August 28

After seeing Roulier early this morning on some BCRA business, Lester, Gravey, Mac and myself left the Ritz in our jeep at 9 o'clock for St. Pair, having breakfasted well on K rations. We motored through the now-peaceful Bois de Boulogne, where FFI stalwarts were still ferreting about for hidden Germans and Milice men, past St. Cloud and into Versailles, where the palace appeared to be entirely undamaged. Soon, however, the aspect of things changed, and there was every evidence of intensive bombing and shelling, especially at St. Cyr, which is thoroughly wrecked. One of the surprising things about passing through one of these towns, where for blocks destruction is complete, is to see the inhabitants stand in front of the ruins of what were once their homes, and smile and wave at the passing Allied soldiers. Outside their ruined villages, work in the fields goes on as usual. The peasants, men, women and children, are now engaged in gathering the wheat. They have few horses, and I have not seen a single motorized piece of agricultural equipment in operation since being in France, nor, with the exception of one rusted tractor, have I seen any signs of it in storage. Yet in the great plain of the Beauce, almost every field, by a miracle of diligence, has been kept in cultivation.

We passed through the villages, whose names we knew so well from having supplied intelligence concerning them, such as Trappes, Maison Blanche, Les Essarts and others, to Rambouillet, where we chatted with Mr. Adam, who feels personally aggrieved

In the last month of the war in Europe, Bruce received this certificate from the maquis to honor his support of the Free French. He had written in his diary just after the Liberation of Paris that the Resistance people were in some respects a disorganized nuisance but "it is they who, throughout France, have raised the standard of revolt." Courtesy of the Virginia Historical Society.

that he has not yet been allowed to return to Paris and reopen his night club! We lunched at Nogent le Rotrou, and went on, via Domfront, to Mortain, a region where the fighting had been very bitter. Here for miles there was a devastated countryside, and numbers of scorched tanks, half trucks and armored vehicles.

We arrived at St. Pair about nightfall, dined with Reutershan and slept there, with nothing to disturb us except the distant rumble of heavy bombing or shelling of the Channel Islands.

August 29

Already, the so-called Liberation of Paris seems almost like a dream. I have never imagined a scene that was, all in all, so dramatic, so moving, and so beautiful and picturesque. The day of the German surrender, the weather was incomparable, the sky cloudless, the sun bright and hot. The frenzied joy of the crowds is impossible to describe. Yet during it all, there was an element of danger that added an almost sinister flavor to the feast. A German

88 fired into the crowd on the Champs-Elysées from the Tuileries Gardens at the very moment when the civilians were swarming around the advancing French tanks. It would once have seemed almost incredible that one would witness tanks firing on the Crillon Hotel, and machine guns directed against the Café de la Paix.

It is fitting that it was Le Clerc's Armored French Division that occupied the city and joined the French Resistance Forces, who had for some days been battling there, in cleansing it of the enemy. It is true that the Resistance people, ill-organized and unused to weapons, are a dangerous nuisance in some respects. Yet it is they who, throughout France, have raised the standard of revolt. In conjunction with the advancing Allied Armies, and often in advance or in the wake of them, they have accounted for thousands of Germans, and even freed whole districts and large cities unaided. The tale of their exploits, and of the American-British organization that controlled many of their units will one day be told, and it is filled with heroic tales and extraordinary incidents. Whatever other part OSS may have or may play during this war, its participation in the French Resistance movement represents a proud achievement.

Joe Haskell and Paul Van der Stricht arrived at St. Pair about noon, and they accompanied Lester, Gravey, and myself to the airport beyond Avranches where we boarded a SHAEF plane for England. The weather was bad and we flew about 100 feet above the Channel all the way to England, arriving at Northolt about six o'clock in the evening.

For the past forty-eight hours, there has been comparatively little buzz bomb activity in the United Kingdom. This is probably due to the present swing of a portion of the Allied Armies into the Pas de Calais area, where the majority of the sites are located. During my absence from London, Landsdown House, on Berkeley Square, had been hit by a flying bomb, but no damage had been done to any of our installations and personnel.

12

To the Borders of the Reich

August 30 to December 6, 1944

August 30

Had a talk with Walter Giblin last night. He left this morning for Paris. We are now to make the penetration of Germany our prime objective.

I found the merry-go-round as usual in the office. I saw a stream of people all day—Bastedo, Larry Lowman[1] and Spike Connelly (from Washington), Charlie Winn, Gerry Miller, Harold Coolidge, and many others. Lunched with Joe Haskell at the Connaught. Colonel Billeu of BCRA came to see me in the afternoon to discuss the problem of moving most of his personnel to Paris, and to obtain our help in transporting them.

General Donovan arrived during the afternoon from a trip to Italy with General Spaatz and Ted Curtis. He looked, as usual, extremely well and in fine spirits. He had Lester, John and Joe Haskell, Larry Lowman, Chan Morse, Spike and myself for dinner, and we sat up talking until 1:30 a.m.

August 31

Norman Pearson[2] and Hugh Will talked about Francis Taylor's[3] (Director of the Metropolitan Museum) Commission to track down objets d'art stolen by the Germans. They were interested in the possible use of this Commission as cover for X-2. Lunched alone with General Donovan at Claridge's—interesting talk. Bruce Ottley[4] came to see me about tracing a package of diamonds left, during the German occupation of France, by one of his men in the safe of the American Consulate at Lyons. Many conferences today.

September 1

Went to Norfolk House in the morning to see Tony Biddle about attaching our men to Allied Military Missions to Liberated Countries.

He promised to help with G-3 SHAEF. Then had a physical examination, and found everything satisfactory. Lunched with Tom Cassady at United Hunts Club. Talked to Joe Haskell about sending a plane to bring Allen Dulles out of Switzerland—this will be done, weather permitting.

General Donovan and John Haskell left for the Continent this morning.

September 2

Went with Joe Haskell to see General Betts at Bushey Park. He wanted to know whether the Jedburghs and the Operational Groups would be available for intelligence targets such as the capture of Berchtesgarten.[5] The idea presents interesting possibilities. Then we saw Brigadier Mansell,[6] a British officer, who asked the same question except that he wants them to clean out the Nazi underground after occupation, a task that will involve considerable cellar and street fighting.

I talked this afternoon to the civilian employees who have been here for six months or longer about the work of OSS Field Detachments.

September 3

This is the anniversary of Great Britain having declared war on Germany five years ago. To date, the British Empire has lost in Killed, 242,995; Missing, 80,603; Wounded, 311,500; Prisoners, 290,865. Casualties of merchant seamen in British ships are: Deaths, 29,381; Internees, 4,192. Civilian air raid casualties in the United Kingdom total: Killed (or missing, believed killed), 56,195; Injured and detained in hospital, 75,897. The total of all the forgoing casualties is 1,091,628.

Casualties among the British Empire forces in the four years 3 months of the 1914–18 war totalled 3,490,907—1,089,919 killed and 2,400,988 wounded. Civilian air raid casualties in the British Isles were 1,316 killed and 3,000 injured.

Civilian casualties due to flying bomb attacks in July were announced last night by the Ministry of Home Security as 2,441 killed or missing, believed killed, and 7,107 injured, detained in hospital.

Of the killed, 1,022 were men, 1,187 women, and 232 children; of the injured, 2,746 men, 3,876 women, and 485 children.

There have been no flying bomb attacks in London for several days, and everything is quiet and peaceful.

September 4
Saw Mayo of Supply (Washington) and others.

September 5
As usual, dozens of questions, such as one of officers wanting to marry a Hungarian girl. Coster's two Austrian "Wispies" from Dakar running afoul of MI5, Jimmy Murphy wanting to transfer a girl with language qualifications, two British secretaries wishing to go to Paris, whether female personnel going to France have to purchase uniforms out of their personal funds, Commander Vetlesen exercised over what SHAEF is going to do about Norway, Gerry Miller regarding his personal post-war plans, a Colonel at the War Office trying to locate a paper that should not have been sent to OSS, George Pratt about his Faust agents going into Germany, Alcorn concerned over black market exchange transactions, 8th Air Force inquiring what the hell the General has done with their plane, John Whittaker worried over projected black radio station activities at Paris, Larry Lowman about trying to cut down personnel at Charles Radio Station, and, running through it all, the bothersome mess arising out of the failure to bring Allen Dulles out of Switzerland by plane, a matter in which so many OSS people are now involved, as well as British personalities, that it is almost hopelessly tangled. Lunched with Ed Murrow (CBS) at Bucks, and dined with Leo d'Erlanger at Claridge's.

September 6
More of the Dulles matter. A special plane is standing by which will be sent to fetch him as soon as direct communications are received from him at the reception point. Much skullduggery over a PBY[7] which the General, Vetlesen and Bernt Balchen intend to use on a secret mission in Norway.

September 8
The first of the V-2's arrived today.[8] One landing at Epping, one at Cheswick, and the third exploded in the stratosphere. The hole made by them was about 25 feet in diameter and 15 feet deep. The Warhead is approximately 3,000 pounds. They came from Flushing, were picked up by sound waves, one by Radar.
V-1's are still being shot into London from "pickapack" planes.[9]

September 10
Last night 9:30 p.m. three rockets landed in England. Two of them at Chelmsford Street—one in Estuary. This morning at 9:30

three more—one at Maidstone, two others at North Weald. They were supposed to have come from the Rotterdam area. Mosquito was patrolling, and saw one of those last night. The V-2 went up to stratosphere—took five seconds. Its speed is estimated at 2,200 mph.

[Editor's note: There are no diary entries for September 11–18, 1944]

September 19

Lester and I left Paris this morning with Ken Downs and Bob Lambert.[10] Mac followed us in a jeep, which had "Mississippi" printed in big white letters under the windshield. We lunched at the Hotel Vert Galant at Montmirail on beefsteak and natural champagne. Late in the afternoon we arrived at Verdun, where the 12th Army Group is located. Our SI detachment has a house there, and it was pleasant to see Klots, Kirkpatrick and the others again. We had supper at the officers' mess with Bill Jackson. Afterwards, we talked to Lieutenant Colonel Griswold, a Boston architect, who is now liaison between the OSS Detachment at Seventh Army and the French Divisions in that Army.

The country between Paris and Verdun along the road we followed is comparatively unravaged by war with the exception of such places as the railroad marshalling yards at Vincennes, Chalons-Sur-Marne, and Verdun itself. This last city was heavily bombed by the Germans a few days after the Americans had taken it. The trip today was beautiful across the great open plain of Champagne into the rolling country around Verdun, which is much like the terrain near Gettysburg.

September 20

This morning I called on General Sibert, who expressed himself as continuing to be highly pleased with the work of our SI and SCI detachments.

We then went, near Etain, to Third Army Headquarters. The country outside Verdun which was so fiercely fought over in the last war still shows definite traces of the vast amount of shelling it underwent. Many fields were so churned up that even after the passage of twenty-six years they cannot be brought under the plough. Verdun itself is dour and unattractive.

At Third Army, we saw Colonel Koch,[11] Ed Gaskell, Louis Huot,[12] Bill Turnbull, Rip Powell, and many others. The staff appeared to be very content with the work done for them by our Detachments, and wish them to continue with Third Army indefinitely.

From Etain we went North through Longuyon and Longwy to the city of Luxembourg, where we found Stacy, with his MO group, occupying a large and comfortable house. Colonel Powell, head of Psychological Warfare at Third Army, was staying with him.

The little country of Luxembourg is quite Graustarkian, and very beautiful. It is prosperous, in spite of the Germans having occupied it. Everywhere the flags of the Grand Duchy are flying, and the windows of almost every house and shop display photographs of the Grand Duchess and her consort, the Prince, who was one of the prolific Bourbon-Parme family and a brother of ex-Empress Zita of Austria.[13] The natives speak German, and a Luxembourg dialect as well. Many of them also speak French. The Germans, having incorporated the Duchy into the Reich, treated its inhabitants rather correctly. There was a resistance movement, but small in numbers. In any event, the Luxembourgeois could have done little against the Germans since they had no standing army and no supply of arms. There is fierce fighting going on near the border in the direction of Trier, where the Germans are offering an intense and effective defense against the American Fifth Armored Division.

Tonight we had what I can only describe as a banquet. Most of the things were left behind, either here or in France, by the Germans. We had Portuguese sardines, tuna fish, vegetable soup, roast beef, green salad and German cheese, cake and fruit, with delicious Moselle, Château Pavie (Red Bordeaux) and 1937 Charles Heidseck Champagne.

September 21

Lester, MacMinn and I left this morning, with Stacy and Paul Munster in another jeep, for Brussels. The bridge was out at Longwy, where we made a detour. We then passed through Arlon and Bastogne to Namur (where there had been considerable damage) and via Wavre into Brussels. New Belgian flags were everywhere, but few pictures of the King, who is a prisoner in Germany. The people of Belgium were intensely proud of his first wife and resent his morganatic marriage to a Commoner. They do not seem to hold against him the surrender of the Belgian Army, believing that action to have been inevitable under the then existing circumstances.

There is a great circulation of well-kept private cars in Brussels—most of them assigned to the use of the Secret Army and the Resistance Groups, which, although less active than those in France, are numerous.

Brussels has suffered little war damage. The people appear well clothed and well nourished, although the condition of the children may evidence a lack of proper nutrition. There is an abundance at this season of marvelous fruit, especially of grapes.

As in Paris, a black market flourishes in Brussels. We dined at the Savoy Restaurant. It had a stringed orchestra, and we had soup, mushrooms on toast, roast chicken and fresh vegetables, raspberries and peaches with cream, Chablis, Meursault and Volnay, at a cost of about twelve dollars a head. The luxuriously appointed dining room was crowded with Allied officers, and civilians so well dressed that, in comparison, the people at Claridge's in London would have looked shabby.

We saw Bob Pflieger,[14] Rae Brittenham, Captain Wood and Bates Compton, and spent the night at the Albert Premier, where there was hot water and electricity. The trainways also are operating at full capacity.

September 22

We went to see Bob Pflieger this morning at Resistance Group headquarters, and found him well installed there with Commander Johns, R.N. (of SOE). We then called on Brigadier Williams,[15] Field Marshal Montgomery's very young and reputedly able G-2. He was most cordial and helpful. We met Don Coster and Captain Macy shortly afterwards, and got a considerable amount of business transacted.

I called on Colonel LePage,[16] head of the Belgian Secret Service, whom I had known well in London, but, unfortunately, found him away for the day.

We then left Brussels and stopped at the Hotel du Nouveau Monde at Tirlemont for lunch, where we had wonderful charcuterie, veal, Moselle and beer. Louvain has been badly damaged by American and German bombing. The Germans burned the great library there, supposedly in anger over the famous inscription stating it had been destroyed during the last war by Hun vandalism.

We reached Liege about 2:30 p.m. The old bridges across the Meuse were all down, but our engineers had thrown pontoon bridges across the river. We found John Mowinckel and Major Arnold Baker there, and left Brittenham with them.

The trip up the Meuse to Maastricht in Holland was beautiful. There again, all the bridges were down, and the inhabitants complained of being very short of food. The local beer, however, is superb.

We rejoined Stacy and Paul Munster in Maastricht, where they had been dealing with some agents. We all motored back to Luxembourg, which we reached at nightfall, after passing through (especially for the last 100 kilometers) entrancing country over magnificent roads, unencumbered by any except occasional army traffic. There are said to be small packets of Germans along this route in the forests, but we saw no signs of them.

Ken Mann[17] was at the house tonight, and we enjoyed another of Stacy's "Living Off the Country" banquets.

There are about 150 railroad cars loaded with stuff looted by the Germans in Paris, and abandoned by them here. Stacy, Lester and I took a truckload of necessities from these cars.

September 23
For the first time since we started on our trip, we have had a rainy morning. We went down to see Colonel Tompkins, of the 12th Army Group T force,[18] found him away, and were briefed by Lieutenant Colonel Lyon on the situation. The Germans have patrols about five miles outside Luxembourg City, and everyone seems to feel they would have little difficulty in reoccupying it if they so desired. However, if they did so, they would expose their flanks to our attacks. The Luxembourgeois are thoroughly worried over the possibility of having the Germans bomb them or come back again.

This afternoon we set out in a driving rain and motored to Rheims, where we spent the night at the Lion d'Or Hotel. The Cathedral was only slightly damaged during this war, and the city itself has suffered little. On the way to Rheims, we passed many Maginot line forts and defenses. How anyone could have thought them sufficient to stop powerful and speedy armour is not (in the light of aftersight) now apparent.

The country through which we passed today is rich and highly cultivated with many fine forests. Some of the villages showed evidence of severe punishment in 1940, but the recent German retreat was so rapid that they were left for the most part untouched this summer. Several days ago, near Longwy, we did see one village where each house had been burned by the Germans during their retreat, together with some of the occupants. The neighbors did not know whether this action was capricious, or what was the reason for it.

September 24
Determined to buy some champagne, we tracked down Monsieur Carré of Pommery and Greno, transported him to the factory and

departed with 12 cases of 1937 Brut. We travelled to Paris via Soissons. We had to make several detours where the bridges were down, and arrived in Paris about 2:30 p.m., having motored 950 miles during this trip.

Champagne, which costs in Paris four to five hundred francs a bottle, is 130 francs ($2.60) at the factory. Since the official rate of exchange is 50 francs to the dollar, while the black market rate is about 225 francs to the dollar, it would, in a free exchange market, have been surprisingly cheap.

September 26

Lester, Mac, and I left this morning in a jeep to visit Seventh Army. We went in a driving rain all day through Provins, Nogent, Troyes, Chaumont and Langres to Vesoul. About 8 kilometers from Vesoul we found Colonel Ed Gamble and his detachment billeted in a pleasant small château where we spent the night.

September 27

We spent the day visiting Seventh Army headquarters and the G-2 of each of the three Divisions, the 45th, the 36th, and the 3rd. They were all enthusiastic to the last degree about OSS work there. Gamble is a splendid officer, and a very attractive man.

September 28

We returned today to Paris—a long, gruelling drive of 350 miles, due to detours. It is pleasant to find transport beginning to be re-established on the roads. Many camions, most of them wood-burning, laden with victuals, especially wheat flour, were making their way toward Paris. There were also the usual thousands of bicycles. Every automobile, cart, or carriage was thronged with people making their way back to the capital and bringing with them an assortment of household belongings ranging from canary birds to kitchen utensils. Children along the route have as yet abated little in their enthusiasm, and wave vigorously at every passing soldier. We lunched today, as we had two days ago, at Bar-sur-Aube.

[Editor's note: There are no entries in the diary from September 29 to October 27]

October 28

Left by plane today for London, and landed at Bovington, near Chesham, where I found Angier Duke,[19] with a beautiful French poodle, in charge of the field. Arrived at the office about 5:00 p.m., where I had numbers of conversations, and afterwards had a good dinner with a magnum of champagne at Claridge's, where I am staying.

October 29

Lester, Whitney, Charlie Neave, Dr. McLeod, Bill Jackson, and others met this morning and we attempted to solve the knotty problem of where to train deep penetration agents. Most of them from now on will be recruited on the Continent. However, parachute facilities are not available in France, and security conditions in France and Belgium are unsatisfactory to the last degree. The problem is to be further examined. Lester, Whitney, and myself prepared a slate of names of candidates to be submitted to General D. as replacements for Forgan, Bruce, Giblin, and Armour, when they are respectively relieved, and also for the vacancy as head of SI, ETO. Jackson is proceeding in an orderly way to organize his staff, and we all expect good things of it.

Last night and tonight there were quite a lot of V-1s and V-2s— seven of the latter fell in England. The forward speed of the V-2 is estimated to be about 2,200 m.p.h., and, as the propulsion continues even after it is headed downward, its landing speed is believed to be about 900 to 1,000 m.p.h., which may account for the terrific noise it makes upon impact.

London looks very shabby. The effect of flying bombs is manifest everywhere now, especially because of the enormous number of shattered windows.

October 30

The personnel strength of OSS, ETO stood a few weeks ago at a high of 3,410. It has now been reduced by two hundred, and we are hopeful of carrying through some drastic reductions. It is the old difficulty of whose ox is gored. Everyone recognizes the necessity of making cuts, but wants the operation performed on his neighbor's branch and not on his own. Of this personnel, 350 are in the Paris office and 450 in the Field Detachments.

Lunched today at Bucks with Lester, Raymond Guest, and a British Wing Commander who had been a pilot for elephant hunting expeditions in East Africa before the war. Raymond was in his usual excellent form, enlivened, but not stimulated noticeably beyond his usual temperament, by a bottle of champagne. I gave him my Springer Spaniel, Stars, on condition he transport the dog to America and make him the founding father of a new line there.

Dined with Whitney Shepardson at Claridge's, where we settled the future to our taste.

October 31

Much office work this morning, after much noise from V-1s during the night. I lunched with Ronnie Tree at the Turf Club, and dined with Alan Scaife and a gay company at Claridge's. Saw Adele Cavendish, Bridget Poulett,[20] Dottie Beatty, and other reminders of yesteryear.

November 1

I was due to return to France today, but all flights were cancelled because of bad weather. I then met Mr. Sawyer,[21] the newly appointed American Ambassador to Belgium. I found him and his wife very genial and agreeable. He offered to take me on his private plane to Brussels this afternoon. We set out for Bovington airport, but after several hours there were postponed until the morrow. George Waller was also in the Ambassador's party, as well as Lieutenant Colonel George Bird, who had charge of the trip for ATC. I had last seen Mr. Waller in Athens twenty-five years ago, when I was in the Army Courier Service, carrying despatches for the Peace Conference. At that time he and the Consul, Alec Weddell[22]—later Ambassador to Spain—had been very kind to me. Waller was a poetaster and quite a conversationalist. He occupied, through his friend, a brother of the King of Greece, a fine palace, and in true Alabama fashion offered lavish hospitality. Since then, he had been in Japan, and later in Central America, whence he had been posted to Luxembourg where he spent almost twelve years which were to his liking. Ejected by the Germans, he is now returning with eagerness to the country he loves best.

November 2

This time we were successful in flight. We left Bovington about 1:00 p.m., and two and a half hours later were in Brussels, considerably delayed by losing our way when our radio failed. We flew over the clouds much of the time, but we came down low as we crossed the Belgian border, and were thus afforded a fine view of that intensely cultivated and highly industrialized country. We also flew over Germany by mistake when the clouds again interposed themselves, and a few German ack-ack shells soon sent our pilot scuttling back on the right path.

I went to Ray Brittenham's office-flat, where I spent the night. Bob Pflieger took me to a club where we indulged in cocktails and talk. The Belgian Government is weak, and may soon fall. Here, as in France, the Communists have the best organized party, but are not yet prepared to make a bid for power. Several V-1s fell in Brussels tonight.

November 3

After meeting a lot of our people, I set forth with Major Van der Graacht in his jeep for Luxembourg. He is an architect and a great friend of Billy Delano.[23] I found him a delightful companion, and the hours passed quickly, although it was bitter cold. At Luxembourg City, we found Kirkpatrick, Mowinckel, et al, in their SI villa. At 12th Army Group I settled many questions with John Haskell. General Sibert had, unfortunately, just left, and I propose to join him and Allen Dulles in Pontarlier tomorrow, the General having very kindly left word that I can use his plane.

November 4

A heavy fog this morning, making flying impossible. Therefore, I gladly accepted Trafford Klots' invitation to motor to Paris with himself and Lieutenant Russell. He had a German Staff officer's Packard, and, except for a stop at Verdun, we had an uninterrupted trip. All through Luxembourg and the Vosges we saw fine, sleek, black and white cattle, and evidences of agricultural prosperity. Traff had recently been in Germany. He thinks they will fight bitterly, especially the young people who are thoroughly indoctrinated in the Nazi philosophy. He cited the case of an eight-year-old boy who had a few days ago approached three American soldiers, cooking their rations in a field, and hurled a hand grenade at them, killing them all.

Van der Graacht, after contact with his Dutch friends, had given me a similar picture. The Germans have flooded all they could of Holland, looted it with complete thoroughness, destroyed the public utilities, tortured and massacred thousands of individuals, and now have left about five million Dutch to face famine. If conditions there are as represented, the situation is indeed desperate. Montgomery is accused by the Dutch of always delaying too long, of reducing cities to ashes long after the German garrisons have left them, and of proceeding so cautiously that he has become the victim of his own overwhelming preponderancy in armor.

[Editor's note: There are no diary entries for November 5–12]

November 13

After our two-day meeting of the Field Detachments, Allen Dulles, Royal Tyler, and myself left Paris early this morning with Mac, in the Cadillac, for Switzerland. McCarthy came along in the other car that brought Dulles and Tyler into France.

We stopped for a short time to admire the beautiful cathedral at Sens. Royal, amongst his many other accomplishments, such as archaeologist, banker, diplomat, etc., is an amateur and authority on historical monuments, art, and kindred subjects. Travelling with him is like taking a witty, urbane, human Baedeker as a courier.

We lunched a few miles beyond Avallon at a country inn called the "Relais" something; I am ashamed to have forgotten its name, for I shall never forget how good was the fare. The five of us had excellent charcuterie, an omelet, a beefsteak with Brussels sprouts and French fried potatoes, salad, and a great slab of Gruyère cheese and fresh fruits. Two bottles of Chablis and the same number of 1937 Red Musigny, followed by the best of coffee and Armagnac, were not the most neglected feature of the meal.

We motored through the picturesque Burgundy country, passing south of Dijon, and arrrived at Bellegarde after dark. There had been a heavy fall of snow and the mountain roads were difficult to negotiate. We finally reached the Château Gaillon at Annemasse, where we found Captains Crockett and Bourgoin. I spent the night there, while Allen and Royal proceeded to Geneva.

November 14

It was wonderful to get into civilian clothes this morning. My visa arrived, and Allen drove me up to Geneva, where I saw Max Shoop and Larimer Mellon.[24] Allen and I took the train from there to Bern. He has a charming apartment at 23 Herrengasse, where I dined and spent the night. After dinner, his principal officers, who are stationed in various parts of Switzerland, came in and we sat up late discussing our mutual concerns. The streets are covered with snow, but the weather is bracing and agreeable.

November 15

The Foreign Minister, Mr. Pillet, whose resignation will shortly take effect, lunched at Allen's with Leland Harrison[25] and myself as the other guests. He is an admirable and entertaining conversationalist. He was quite frank in expressing his views on many subjects. He regards unemployment as the greatest potential menace to Swiss political stability, thinking it would incite Communist elements to

In November 1944 Bruce visited OSS's man in Switzerland, Allen Dulles, who later became director of the CIA. Courtesy of the National Archives.

action. To avoid it, he thinks the Allies should give facilities for the importation of a certain amount of coal, iron, and cotton. His justification of Swiss neutrality was interesting and obviously sincere. He regards a stable Switzerland as a very important factor in the reconstruction of Europe. He feels that any drastic change of government in France would be calamitous, especially if it resulted from a Communist coup d'état.

This afternoon Allen took me to see General Guisan,[26] the Commander-in-Chief (and incidentally the only General) of the Swiss Army. He is a fine-looking, vigorous man of seventy, very genial, and gives the impression of possessing great force of character. He, also, talked very frankly about Swiss problems. He is very anxious to have a military mission with the American Armies, as a matter of prestige and also to study new developments in warfare, but not, he asserted with indignation, to pass on any news of what they might see to the Germans. He discussed the Rhine water level question, in which Allen is so interested, at considerable length.[27]

Tonight I had a most pleasant dinner with Leland, since A. was entertaining an acquaintance whom it was desirable for him to see without me.[28] Leland has an attractive house which Nancy[29] and he have furnished with their own things.

November 16

I arose at quarter of seven and left with Robert Shea[30] and a chauffeur at 7:40 to motor to a train at Neuchatel. My short stay in Bern had been of great interest and value to me, and increased, if that is possible, the admiration and affection I feel for Allen. He is one of the chosen ones of the earth, in my opinion, and I hope his highly unusual talents will continue to be used by the Government.

We motored through a countryside covered in snow. About 15 miles from Bern, what I had dreaded as inevitable came to pass. As we were coming down a long, winding, hillside road, the Packard skidded, got completely out of control, and careened into a ravine, where it toppled over on one side with a crash. We were lucky in coming to rest where we did, as the ravine was narrow enough in that place to hold us, wedged between two trees—twenty yards further on would have been a disastrous ending for us.

We crawled unhurt out of our smashed machine, and Shea exercised his German to such good effect on the telephone that a taxi (unexpected in a country where there is practically no gasoline available for any use) came to fetch us. The King of Speed Demons was at the wheel. He took the icy curves at sixty miles an hour, and finally removed his chains so he could go faster. Speaking no German, I was helpless, but Shea reassured me by saying the driver had twice won the Swiss Grand Prix in winter automobile racing. We missed our train by half a minute, and took advantage of the interval to walk around Neuchatel. Everything in Switzerland is carefully rationed. It is a triumph of good management that, as an importing country, they have managed during the war to maintain their high standard of living. We saw enormous cheeses, of the Gruyère type, but were unable to buy them for want of coupons. Only clothing seemed very expensive. There was a profusion of bicycles, watches, and small precision instruments at reasonable prices.

From Neuchatel we took a clean, comfortable, and modern train to Les Verrieres. There we had a rigorous Swiss customs examination, and a less exacting French one across the border. Major Simon met us with a jeep and motored us to Pontarlier, where he gave us lunch. Afterwards, Shea and I were taken by his driver to Besançon, the French First Army Headquarters, where we recaptured Mac and the Cadillac, which had driven General Davet around from Anne-masse. Mac was vastly impressed by the excellence of the French Messes to which the General had introduced him.

We motored from Besancon to Contrexeville, passing through various Spas, where we arrived after dark. Stoneborough occupied a spacious and comfortable villa there in which we spent the night.

November 17

I went to Vittel, where I called on Colonel Harrison, the G-2 of Sixth Army Group. He was generous in praise of his small OSS Detachment. After seeing Colonel Erskine, the CI officer, and Lieutenant Colonel Torielli, the OI officer, we went on beyond Epinal to visit Colonel Gamble's Detachment at Seventh Army. There everything was, as usual, in apple pie order. I saw the G-2 Colonel Quinn[31] (from Crisfield, Maryland), who, as before, sang the praises of OSS very loudly. Ed Gamble had a banquet tonight for his officers, and we made speeches. Commander Quirk had appeared from Aachen with two bottles of Moselle—one a 1937, the other a pleasant 1942—and our landlady (whose husband had been killed by American bombing) contributed two cobwebbed bottles of Red Burgundy. Together with the local supplies, this made the speeches satisfactory to all concerned.

Tonight the sky was bright with the flames from St. Dié and other burning villages. The Germans have adopted a scorched earth policy. All males between the ages of 15 and 60 have been evacuated from this territory. Women, children, and old men have been left. The cattle have been driven off, and supplies of food taken away or destroyed. The country is heavily mined. Our Lieutenant Duff, two nights ago, was passing a couple of agents through the lines. While crossing a field in the dark he stepped on a mine. His foot was blown off. His leg has been amputated.

The Germans are using booby traps freely. An American soldier yesterday went into a house just abandoned by the enemy. Hearing a cat miaowing from the locked closet of a bedroom, he opened the door. The cat sprang out. There was a cord around her neck. The charge exploded. The soldier was killed.

November 18

I went this morning to Nancy, where Third Army Headquarters are located. I found Jacques Beau and the others in a Chinese pagoda. I called on Colonel Koch—the G-2—who pronounced himself well satisfied with the OSS work at his Army.

I also saw Bunny Carter and George Murnane, Jr. We had a fine trip to Paris—a relief after previous snow and rain. It had cleared. The sun shone brightly during the afternoon. We went along fast on the St. Dizier route to the Port de Vincennes, and arrived at Paris before nightfall.

[Editor's note: There are no entries in the diary for November 19–20]

November 21

Ken Downs, Franz Weiskeim (an Austrian now a Lieutenant in the British Army), and I set off this morning with Mac in the Cadillac. It was a beautiful day, and we motored past the Chocolat Menier factory at Grand Champs Sur Marne at St. Menehault, where we lunched at the Hotel du Vert Galant. The last time I had been there we had enjoyed some excellent local champagne. Now the cellars were bare, and we had to be content with beer. We went through a country thoroughly flooded by the recent almost incessant rains, pasty gloomy Verdun, arriving in Luxemburg City about dark. Bill Jackson was there for dinner. It was amusing seeing the names drivers have painted on their trucks and jeeps. One great lorry was marked "Urgent Virgin," while Mowinckel's jeep is called "Pet de Nonne," which, besides being the name of a delicate cake, means something better left untranslated.[32] When he first entered Paris with it, he aroused the enthusiastic interest of the female population, although certain carping critics considered this baptism sacrilegious.

Tonight there were one, or more, German planes overhead. We heard no bombs—perhaps they were dropping agents—but there was quite a display of anti-aircraft fire.

November 22

This morning the Cadillac was hors de combat. We had a puncture yesterday, and the brakes had gone completely out of commission. Accordingly, Franz and I borrowed the famous Pet de Nonne and her driver. We went through a driving rain to Stacy's establishment, somewhere between Verviers and Malmédy. As usual at Stacy's, we were regaled with a magnificent banquet. Bob Pflieger was there with Captain Nicodème, of the Belgian Sûreté. Ken finally arrived in the big car, and I saw my old friends in the Lloyd detachment.

Yesterday 105 buzz bombs had passed over this house; many of them bound for Liège. This evening there were many more. One heard the angry roar, and then the explosion, that often rattled the windows of the house.

November 23

This morning, Ken and I went out in a jeep with Walter Kerr driving, a charming and talented Herald-Tribune newspaper correspondent who had made a name for himself in Russia and who now is a Corporal in MO. We headed for the First Division, always called by its members "The Division." Crossing the border into Germany, we saw many evidences of fierce fighting. However, except for a good number of wrecked houses and the Dragon's teeth of the advance part of the Siegfried Line, there were fewer signs of destruction than I had anticipated. It was raining in torrents, as it continued to do all day, and that may have explained the absence of many cattle in the fields. Despite this, we saw some cattle—all sleek and well-fed—as well as an abundance of poultry.

We stopped at Spa at Seventh Corps Headquarters, where we received permission to visit the First Division and Aachen.

We arrived at the First Division, whose name is, appropriately, "Danger," during their lunch time. After a chat with General Huebner,[33] we had an excellent Thanksgiving turkey lunch, and stayed for an hour afterwards talking to General Taylor, the Deputy Commander. Ken has countless friends in his old Division, and we visited around the CP. There I also saw Don Whitehead of the AP, who was so kind and helpful to me in Sicily—also Miss Carson of INS, whom I had last seen in Rambouillet.

On the road to Brand, we were passed by General Terry Allen, to whom Ken had been aide when he commanded the First Division, and whom I had known in Sicily. He invited us to stop in at his 104th Division CP (Timber Wolf).[34] We had a very pleasant conversation, and he presented us each with a bottle of White Horse Whiskey. General Collins came to see him, and we exited. Around the First Division there was heavy artillery fire from our batteries. Its men have been in the line since July. They are worn and have had heavy casualties. Even the Headquarters has never been out of artillery range from the enemy. The 104th is a new Division, first tested in Holland. Under the inspiring leadership of the dynamic General Allen, it should prove to be a crack outfit.

We found Aachen—Aix-la-Chapelle—an almost entirely ruined city. I have seen bad destruction, such as at St. Lo, but never before a large city—for it possessed about 130,000 inhabitants—in such a state of wreckage. The buildings were not rubble, but they were gaunt skeletons. The completeness of the devastation was appalling. About ten thousand of the inhabitants are supposed to have returned, but, unless they live in the cellars, I cannot conceive how they are sheltered. We arrived at dark, in the incessant rain, at Stacy's, where we found Dana Durand.

The V-1s have made a cacophonous symphony all evening, exploding loudly but we do not know where.

The leaves are now almost all off the hardwood trees, but such as remain are a lovely yellow or russet color, and remind me of autumn in the woods at home. However, this continual drench of rain, which has for weeks been only rarely interrupted, is depressing, and makes even the countryside seem dreary and gloomy.

November 24

We set off in the rain this morning to Maastricht, where we found Lieutenant Colonel Sutherland established on a very favorable basis with the Ninth Army. Maastricht was crawling with American troops. The recent deluge had swept away one of the two temporary bridges, and there was a resulting bottleneck of traffic.

After lunching with Arthur at the mess, we went on to Eindhoven. Ides Van der Graacht has done fine work there. The town itself was stripped of merchandise by the Germans, and the food situation for civilians is bad. Conditions in the north of Holland are desperate. The Germans are deporting large numbers of able-bodied males and looting indiscriminately. The shortage of food there is said to be appalling.

Eindhoven is an industrial town where almost everything depends on the Phillips Company, the officers of which have been useful to us both in America and here. At dinner, the Dutch officers present discussed the failure of the British to join up with the paratroopers at Arnheim.[35] Had this been done, they feel Holland would have been quickly cleared of Germans. They were severe in their criticism of British tactics and strategy.

November 25

We left Eindhoven this morning in the rain. The whole countryside is flooded. Almost endless rows of British tanks were on the road, perhaps being taken away from the sodden ground. In this procession, it took us three hours to traverse the 80 miles to Brussels. From there, we went to Mons, Valenciennes, Cambrai, Roye, and so to Paris, which we reached about 7:30 p.m.

[Editor's note: There are no diary entries for November 26 to December 1]

December 2

Left this morning with Ken Downs, Trafford Klots and Mac in the Cadillac. It rained all day. We lunched at Nogent-le-Rotrou and arrived at Rochefort in Brittany after dark. Rochefort is south of Vannes, and German patrols from the remaining enemy pockets there have recently been within two kilometers of this town of 2,000 inhabitants.[36] We stopped at one of the twenty-two bar-restaurants that adorn the town. Trafford's father had refurnished and decorated it, and presented it to Traff—now named by us "The Duke of Brittany"—on his twenty-first birthday. It is, without exception, the most attractive little inn I have ever seen. We were introduced to the favorite Breton beverage—Eau de Vie de Cidre. It is very potent, like applejack, and nicknamed by Americans "Jersey Lightning." We then proceeded up the street to another bar, also redecorated by the senior Klots, where we were again struck by Lightning. Everywhere Trafford went the women kissed him and the men crowded around to shake his hand. We were soon attended by a retinue of FFI who fight Germans during the day and come to the villages on Saturday night to take a restorative. The Bretons are much addicted to hard liquor. Drunkenness and the results of it are quite apparent over weekends.

We arrived at the Château, the former stables of the great Château which Richelieu had destroyed when he was curbing the powers of the arrogant nobles. It is a lovely building, largely constructed in the 13th Century. Part of a company of American troops are billeted in it. They have with them, messing, sleeping with them, and wearing GI clothes, two recent German deserters, one reputed to be an architect from Stuttgart, speaking excellent French, and the other a bestial-looking, typical SS youngster. Our soldiers are very naive about this sort of thing, and we propose to have this unusual situation examined.

We had dinner in the kitchen—eggs, meat, salad, cheese, a magnum of champagne, coffee, and Lightning. The old servants were wonderful. They all sat around, chatting with us, telling us how local boys taken as hostages had been shot by the Germans, about the exploits of the FFI, and kindred topics. I went to bed about twelve, but Traff and Ken sallied into the town where they discovered a local dance taking place and stayed up until all hours.

December 3

We all arose at 6:30 a.m. and went to 7 o'clock Mass in a glorious little church. We then fell into the spirit of the country and had a coupe de vin at a pub Mr. Klots had given to one of the former house chambermaids. Then we inspected Rochefort and found it altogether admirable. It is apparently remarkable for its flowers in summer, and is a favorite resort for artists. We called on a local shoemaker who had sheltered two of our agents. Within the Château grounds are two villas, a studio, an old tower with a dungeon beneath, and a subterranean passage leading into the town. The views are beautiful—slate rock, mountains reminding one of Scotland, and a constricted, well-watered valley between the hills. The interior of the Château is without furniture, but is lovely.

We left about eleven and motored to Josselin, the home of Alain de Rohan, who is a prominent FFI. It was built, I believe, in about the 12th Century and is a magnificently impressive feudal keep, perched on a promontory above the river. It was restored inside by Alain's grandfather. The Rohans have owned it now for seven hundred odd years and are great swells. The Duchess, his mother,[37] is a charming woman, as is his wife, who speaks excellent English. We lunched well in a dining room adorned by a life-sized stone horse upbearing a life-sized stone Rohan. "King I cannot be, Prince I would not be, Rohan I am" is the not over-modest remark attributed to a remote ancestor, while the family motto is "I do as I please."

Having left the abode of this uninhibited family, we started on our 300-mile jaunt to Paris, passing through Rennes, Le Mans, Chartres, Rambouillet and Versailles. We reached Rue Weber long after dark and ate some cold things, accompanied by Lightning and the genial presence of Ernest Hemingway as a guest.

4 December
Flew to London.

5 December
Remained in London at Claridge's.

6 December
Flew back to France.

Later in December, Traff Klots and I ran into the Battle of the Bulge. I was ordered home, and reached Washington on Christmas Day, after narrowly escaping being killed in a snowstorm over Maine.[38]

Epilogue

As the final entry reveals, David Bruce stopped his journal well before the war ended and hinted only cryptically about being swept up in Hitler's desperate last offensive through the Ardennes. After coming back to the United States in late 1944, Bruce rejoined the OSS Washington headquarters he had left almost two years before. He served there in the last spring of the war as chairman of the agency's planning group and returned once more to Europe in the summer of 1945 before leaving OSS. By then the guns had fallen silent for the first time in almost six years, and in London the "sinister, droning noise" of the buzz bombs had finally ceased. When he took off his Army Air Corps uniform for the last time, in November, Bruce had completed forty-nine months of service with COI and OSS.

Although he labeled his journal "personal," Bruce did not intend it to be a secret diary in which his deepest worries and frustrations found written expression. The diaries he kept, at least after his transfer to London in 1943, were meant to provide a record that he was willing to share with others in his inner office. For that reason, and for obvious security reasons, he necessarily diluted and foreshortened some episodes. We are the poorer for the omissions. Despite his pleasure in keeping a diary, an appetite he indulged throughout his career, Bruce was a private man who did not easily unburden himself in unguarded prose. He excelled as a diarist, however, in compiling an account still capable, after half a century has passed, of bringing to life the climax of World War II in western Europe. Through his eyes it is possible once more to experience the invasion of Normandy, the tumultuous liberation of Paris, the unnerving rocket attacks on London, and the race across northern France to the borders of the Reich.

The continuing fascination of these subjects, especially the secret affairs of OSS, produces a constant stream of new books, and most

Early in 1945, shortly after Bruce had returned to duty in Washington—and noticeably grayer around the temples than when he first went overseas—he received a medal from a grateful General Donovan for his work in directing OSS's London office for almost two years. Courtesy of the Virginia Historical Society.

of them give Bruce credit for his contribution. Despite the need to improvise in the chaos of wartime, and despite the frequent hostility of both the American military and the British cousins, David Bruce hammered together an effective organization during his tenure as head of OSS in the European theater of operations. He was not just an urbane, confident patrician who could reassure the service chiefs and intelligence mandarins of London, though that contribution in itself brought much benefit to an agency often dependent on British good will. More important, as his colleagues repeatedly suggested in their memoirs, he was an effective leader, a man who could persuade others to do what he wanted them to do, a man who valued men and women for their intelligence and capacity to achieve, not for their background or credentials. Although Bruce stood near the top of the list of socially prominent Americans in OSS, it would have been a mistake for members of the organization to think that Donovan made him head of OSS/London as mere ornamentation.

If Bruce received general acclaim for his leadership, the agency he served did not so easily win favor for itself. OSS endured its share of criticism, in part, because of the ample supply of dilettantes who found their way into its ranks. In the early months, critics devised endless derogatory permutations for the service's acronym, "Oh So Social" and "Oh So Silly" being examples of the kinder variety. When, early in the game, a new employee was troubled by the number of inept dabblers attracted to OSS, mostly looking for an exciting but comfortable berth for the war's duration, he sought Bruce's counsel. The advice Bruce gave provides some insight into his attitude: "Colonel Donovan is so great a leader that he attracts to himself not only the finest men, but often a sorry lot who ride on his coat-tails." If, however, the reliable officers do "our job so supremely well . . . they—the undesirables—will drop away or be ignored."[1]

The successes that ultimately came to OSS are all the more remarkable in light of the agency's shaky beginnings. As a new organization, OSS faced formidable obstacles. Failures, like enemies, were legion. In the early years, the agency overrated the extent of Nazi fifth-column activity. Indeed, COI/OSS owed its existence, in part, to an inflated opinion of the role that such subversion played in past German victories—subversion that might, by analogy, be harnessed in aid of future American efforts. Once established, the agency lurched from one confrontation to another with enemies in the State Department, the FBI, and the military intelligence services who, in Bruce's words, "forgot their internecine animosities and joined in an attempt to strangle this unwanted newcomer at birth."[2] In the field much of its early work was a shambles. Despite its best efforts in parts of Asia, it never amounted to much in the war against Japan. Further, not being central to the Ultra secret—the British unscrambling of the German Enigma codes guarding information of the highest order—OSS could not claim for itself the most dramatic intelligence coup of the war in Europe.

Despite its maladroit beginning and some amateurish blunders along the way, the agency achieved much of value. If its contribution to winning the war will probably always provoke lively debate, some accomplishments are beyond dispute. It gave vital support to the Resistance forces in France just before D day, an investment that repaid the Allies handsomely as saboteurs thwarted the approach to the Normandy beachhead of such formidable units as the Panzer Lehr division. The success of the Jedburgh and Sussex operations, designed to insert joint OSS-British teams of agents behind German lines at the time of the invasion, justified the tedious months of planning by Bruce's staff in England. During the rapid liberation of France, OSS proved especially effective in collecting tactical intelligence in the field. The measure of this success can be gauged by the warm reception Bruce recorded in his diary when he visited American divisions with OSS field detachments. Such praise from military skeptics earlier in the war would have been hard to come by. Finally, OSS collected vital information on conditions in Germany and moved well ahead of the British services in placing agents in the Reich near the end of the war. If OSS never became a centralized agency collecting strategic intelligence, at least it mastered the intelligence game at the tactical level.

Even the British had to concede that OSS performed well after Normandy. Their condescension gave way—in some cases to admiration, in others to apprehension—as they saw what unlimited American dollars and a little practical experience could produce. Despite their ongoing spats over turf, the various British secret agencies and OSS forged valuable links for future Anglo-American cooperation. These ties proved crucial in the shadow warfare that loomed as Western attention began to shift eastward even before the ashes of Berlin had cooled. Parsimonious in the honors they bestowed on their OSS allies at the end of the war—only ten were given in all—the British made sure to make a Commander of the British Empire of the man who effectively created OSS/London and guided it through its toughest challenges.

The Office of Strategic Services did not long survive the war, however. Its enemies in Washington, always vigilant for a chance to discomfit its enthusiastic, abrasive founder, finally succeeded in gutting Donovan's creation in the year of Allied victory. The efforts of its supporters unavailing, OSS expired in October 1945 on President Truman's orders. Its component branches were disbanded or transferred to other federal agencies.

Responding to this blow, Donovan and his friends renewed their campaign for a permanent, peacetime intelligence establishment, and Bruce joined their lobbying in print and in private argument. Writing that "an efficient strategical intelligence service is the country's first line of defense," he helped reverse the climate of opinion engendered by what he called the "witchburners" in the press opposed to any form of successor to OSS. In an article published in

1946, he outlined the feeble attempts to gather intelligence between the wars that left America ill-prepared for the great conflict it had just survived: "While [Secretary of State Cordell] Hull breathed tranquilly over his Eden, primitive forces throughout the world had become unloosed, and were threatening the very foundations of our national existence."[3] Only with OSS, argued Bruce, did the nation acquire an effective tool for collecting and applying intelligence, foolishly discarding it as soon as victory was won.

The following year Truman reversed himself—in the face of a changed geopolitical map and his own growing unease about Soviet expansion—and set in motion the process that created the Central Intelligence Agency. Building on the experience of its wartime predecessor, the new agency recruited an initial cadre of talent from the officers who had learned their espionage tradecraft in OSS. Although the CIA was a different entity, facing different problems in a different world, and although he criticized it bitterly at times, Bruce took great satisfaction in the foundation that he and his OSS colleagues had laid.[4]

As they did for millions of Americans, the war years marked a turning point for David Bruce in his personal life as much as in his career. He and Ailsa Mellon Bruce had drifted apart long before Pearl Harbor. Their friends were not surprised, then, when a wartime divorce ratified their separation. If the war brought a formal end to his first marriage, it also made possible a second and happier one. Evangeline Bell, the daughter of an Anglo-American diplomatic family who had attended school in Europe and learned the easy command of half a dozen languages, worked for OSS first in Washington and then in London. With their marriage in 1945, she became the ideal companion for Bruce as he embarked on a career in government service abroad that fulfilled the promise of his youth.

Bruce's first appointment after the war—as assistant secretary of commerce under his friend W. Averell Harriman—quickly led him back into foreign affairs, first as head of the Marshall Plan in France and then as ambassador there. After tours as undersecretary of state and American representative to talks on European cooperation came ambassadorial appointments to Bonn and the Court of St. James's. These achievements confirmed Bruce's membership in the most select group of American diplomats. Though a Democrat, he was a man above party and served Democratic and Republican administrations equally.

As often happens when a diplomat of exceptional talent retires, the respite is short-lived. The year after returning home from the London embassy, Bruce agreed to come out of retirement and lead the American delegation to the Paris peace talks on Vietnam. A second retirement ended with appointment in 1973 as the first American emissary to the People's Republic of China. Yet a third time he answered a president's call to leave his well-earned repose: his final ambassadorship took him, appropriately, to Brussels, as envoy to the North Atlantic Treaty Organization, successor to the alliance he served so ably in OSS.

When David Bruce died on December 5, 1977, two months before his eightieth birthday, tributes came from all over the world in testimony to his personal charm, his character, and his service to his country. Of that service, most friends understandably recalled his career at the center of postwar diplomacy. Although Bruce himself took satisfaction in his work during those years, he never discounted the effect of his earlier decision—as he expressed it to a reunion of OSS veterans almost thirty years later—"to follow the Pied Piper" into COI/OSS.[5] That experience fixed for good in his mind the intention first articulated after World War I, and temporarily sidetracked between the wars, to enter foreign service.

As the last secretary of state he served said of Bruce, "his bearing made clear that he served a cause that transcended the life span of an individual; he exuded the conviction that his country represented values that needed tending and that were worth defending."[6]

Abbreviations

A-2	U.S. Army Air Force Intelligence
ATC	Air Force Transport Command
BCRA	Bureau Central de Renseignements et d'Action
BCRAL	Bureau Central de Recherches et d'Action à Londres
BSC	British Security Coordination
CBS	Central Base Section
CE	Counterespionage
CI	Counterintelligence
CIA	Central Intelligence Agency
CIC	Combat Information Center
CO	Commanding Officer
COI	Coordinator of Information
CP	Command Post
DE	Destroyer Escort
DNI	Director of Naval Intelligence
ETO	European Theater of Operations
ETOUSA	European Theater of Operations, United States Army
FANY	First Aid Nursing Yeomanry (British)
FFI	Forces Française de l'Interieur
FUSAG	First United States Army Group
G-2	American army designation for intelligence section
G-3	American army designation for personnel section
JIC	Joint Intelligence Committee (British)
LCT	Landing craft, tank
LCV	Landing craft, vehicle
MI5	British Security Service
MI6	British Secret Intelligence Service (same as SIS, Broadway)
MO	Morale Operations branch (OSS)
MOI	Ministry of Information
MTB	Motor Torpedo Boat
NATO	North African Theater of Operations
OG	Operational Group (OSS's commando units)
OI	Oral Intelligence branch (OSS)

ONI	Office of Naval Intelligence
OSS	Office of Strategic Services
OWI	Office of War Information
PAC	Pilotless Aircraft (same as V-1)
PT	Patrol Torpedo boat
PW	Psychological Warfare
PWD	Psychological Warfare Division
PWE	Political Warfare Executive
R&A	Research and Analysis branch (COI/OSS)
RAF	Royal Air Force
RN	Royal Navy
SCI	Special Counter Intelligence (a joint operation of MI5 and X-2)
SEAC	Southeast Asia Command
SF	Special Forces
SFHQ	Special Forces Headquarters (established in January 1944 with the merger of SOE and OSS SO)
SHAEF	Supreme Headquarters Allied Expeditionary Force
SI	Secret Intelligence branch (COI/OSS)
SIS	Secret Intelligence Service (British, also called MI6, Broadway)
SO	Special Operations branch (OSS)
SOE	Special Operations Executive (British, also called Baker Street)
SS	Schutzstaffel
UK	United Kingdom
USAAF	United States Army Air Force
USSTAF	United States Strategic Air Force
USMC	United States Marine Corps
USNR	United States Naval Reserve
V-1	Hitler's first "vengeance weapon" (*Vergeltungswaffen*), the pilotless, jet-powered, flying bomb
V-2	The second German "vengeance weapon," a true rocket unlike the V-1
WAC	Women's Army Corps
X-2	Counterintelligence branch (OSS)

Notes

INTRODUCTION

1. Newspaper clipping dated July 1921 in scrapbook in Louise E. F. Bruce Papers, Virginia Historical Society.

2. David K. E. Bruce to Louise E. F. Bruce, July 29, 1940, Louise E. F. Bruce Papers, Virginia Historical Society.

3. Address by David K. E. Bruce to the American Red Cross National Convention, April 1941, transcript, David K. E. Bruce Papers, Virginia Historical Society.

4. Quoted in Bradley F. Smith, *The Shadow Warriors: O.S.S. and the Origins of the C.I.A.*, 95.

5. Malcolm Muggeridge, "Book Review of a Very Limited Edition," *Esquire*, May 1966, 94.

6. Quoted in R. Harris Smith, *OSS: The Secret History of America's First Central Intelligence Agency*, 1 from Drew Pearson's "Washington Merry Go-Round" column for December 3, 1941.

CHAPTER 1

1. A Virginian, Nancy Yuille had married Viscount Adare, later sixth Earl Dunraven and Mount-Earl, whose family's estate was at Adare, near Foynes; Helen Kirkpatrick, reporter for the *Chicago Daily News*, whom Bruce had seen in England during the Battle of Britain; David Gray (1870–1968), writer and U.S. minister to Ireland (1940–47); Col. Kingman Douglass, Sr., USAAF (1896–1971) later served as assistant director of the CIA.

2. MI6's Charles Howard "Dick" Ellis (b. 1895), an aide to William Stephenson ("Intrepid"), British liaison with Donovan in Washington. Ellis later admitted passing confidential material to the Germans before the war.

3. Air Commodore Lionel G. S. "Lousy" Payne, deputy to the head of MI6; Fisher Howe (b. 1914) helped organize the COI London office and later served in the State Department.

4. Newspaperman Percy Winner (1899–1974), posted at Rome in the 1920s when Bruce was vice-consul there, worked for COI in London and as assistant to the American ambassador.

5. Brig. Gen., later Sir, Stewart Graham Menzies (1890–1968), head of MI6. See Anthony Cave Brown, *"C": The Secret Life of Sir Stewart Graham Menzies, Spymaster to*

Winston Churchill. The British Secret Intelligence Service was known by several names: SIS, MI6, or Broadway, for the address near the St. James's Park underground station.

6. Sibyl Halsey Colefax (d. 1950), wife of Sir Arthur Colefax and one of London's smartest hostesses during the 1930s; Oliver Lyttleton (1893–1972), a member of the War Cabinet as minister of state in Cairo (1941), later in Ministry of Production, created Viscount Chandos in 1954; Oliver Frederick George Stanley (1896–1950), secretary of state for war (1940) and then for the colonies (1942); Lord Louis Mountbatten (1900–1979), later supreme Allied commander in Southeast Asia, Earl Mountbatten of Burma, and his wife, Edwina Ashley (1901–1960).

7. Spanish marqués Robert de Casa Maury (d. 1968), an RAF wing commander, and his wife, Winifred Dudley Ward, née Birkin. Of her long affair with the Prince of Wales, Mountbatten said, she was "a good influence on him. None of the others were. Wallis's influence was fatal" (Joseph Bryan III and Charles J. V. Murphy, *Windsor Story* [New York: William Morrow, 1979], 72).

8. Tory politician, later Baron, Richard Austen Butler (b. 1902), minister of education (1941–45). "RAB" and Sydney Elizabeth Courtauld (d. 1954) had married in 1926; Capt. Victor Alexander Cazalet (1896–1942), a Conservative M.P., died in a plane crash with General Sikorski, the head of the Polish government in exile.

9. London merchant banker Sir Charles Jocelyn Hambro (1897–1963), head of Special Operations Executive, also known as Baker Street, for the location of its offices near the address made famous by Sir Arthur Conan Doyle; earlier in 1942 SOE had sent Anthony Keswick to Washington to assess the strength of COI vis-à-vis its bureaucratic enemies; an official in the Ministry of Economic Warfare, the Hon. Sir David Bowes-Lyon (1902–1961) was brother-in-law of George VI and uncle of the future Elizabeth II; journalist Peter Ritchie Calder, later Baron Ritchie-Calder (b. 1906).

10. FDR appointed Republican governor of New Hampshire John Gilbert Winant (1889–1947) to succeed Kennedy as ambassador to Britain. Winant served from early 1941 until 1946; FDR's special envoy to Britain in 1941, railroad heir William Averell Harriman (1891–1986), like his friend Bruce, became one of America's most prominent postwar diplomats; Col. Euan Rabagliatti of MI6; Donovan had sent William Whitney to head COI's London mission in autumn 1941.

11. Daughter of a famous hostess and intimate of Edward VII, Audrey James (d. 1968) had a brief affair with the Prince of Wales. Her husbands included Marshall Field III, of Chicago, and Peter Pleydell-Bouverie. Evelyn Waugh described her as a "strained, nervous, cross-patch of a woman" (Bryan and Murphy, *Windsor Story,* 74–75).

12. Virginia Cowles (b. 1912), American journalist and special assistant to Ambassador Winant, later married Aidan Crawley, M.P., and settled in England. She had viewed aerial dogfights with Bruce at Dover in August 1940.

13. Like his friend Bruce, Thomas "Tommy" Hitchcock, Jr. (d. 1944), a renowned polo player who later shared a flat with Bruce in London, married into the Mellon family. Later chief of tactical research for the U.S. Ninth Air Force, he died when the plane he was testing crashed.

14. Laura, née Charteris, wife of Viscount Long, later married Michael Canfield and the duke of Marlborough.

15. In 1920 Barbara Lutyens had married Capt. David Euan Wallace, M.P. (d. 1941), friend and brother-in-law of the head of MI6. She later married American writer and OWI official Herbert Agar, whom Bruce mentions June 13, 1944.

16. Esmond Cecil Harmsworth, second Viscount Rothermere (1898–1978), had succeeded his father, the first viscount and founder of the Harmsworth publishing empire, in 1940; Ann, née Charteris, wife of the third Baron O'Neill, sister of Lady Long, and future wife of Rothermere and of Ian Fleming; gentleman Virginia farmer, son of a Liberal M.P., and a cousin of Churchill, Raymond Richard Guest (b. 1907) directed OSS operations in France and Scandinavia; Harold Fowler (1887–1957) served with the British and American air forces in World War I and with the Royal Canadian Air Force and the USAAF in World War II; Bernard Shirley "Bunny" Carter (1893–1961), American banker in Paris before the war and in New York and Paris afterwards.

17. Lt. Gen. Carl "Tooey" Spaatz (1891–1974), chief of air force Combat Command (1942), later commander in chief, U.S. Strategic Air Force in Europe.

18. Vice Adm. John Henry Godfrey (1888–1971), director of British naval intelligence (1939–42); a handsome portrait of Bruce by Robert Lutyens belongs to the Virginia Historical Society in Richmond; Wallace Banta Phillips (1886–1952), formerly with naval intelligence in Washington, OSS director of special information services (1941–43), president of the American Chamber of Commerce in London, and resident of Claridge's.

19. Anthony Joseph Drexel Biddle, Jr. (1897–1961), American envoy to the London governments-in-exile of Poland, Belgium, the Netherlands, Norway, Greece, Yugoslavia, Czechoslovakia, and Luxembourg; Adm. Alan Goodrich Kirk (1888–1963), formerly director of naval intelligence, later chief of staff of American naval forces in Europe and ambassador to Belgium and the Soviet Union; Adm. Harold Raynsford Stark (1880–1972), chief of naval operations, commander of U.S. naval forces in Europe; Maj., later Sir, Desmond Morton (1891–1971), advisor to Churchill on German rearmament during the 1930s and his personal assistant when Churchill became prime minister; in 1915 Elizabeth Vere Cavendish had married Robert "Bobbety" Viscount Cranborne, later fifth marquess of Salisbury.

20. Gen., later Baron, Hastings Lionel Ismay (1887–1965), chief staff officer to the prime minister. Ismay said of this time, "I spent the whole war in the middle of the web" (*Dictionary of National Biography*, 1961–1970, 570).

21. Col. Garland Williams, formerly with the New York Narcotics Commission, helped negotiate in June 1942 a protocol for collaboration between COI and British SOE; John Hanbery-Williams (1892–1965), deputy chairman of Courtaulds Limited, with the Ministry of Economic Warfare in 1942, later deputy head of SOE and knighted.

22. Bruce added to the typescript by hand the word "secret."

23. Roundell Cecil Palmer, earl of Selborne (1887–1971). A friend of Churchill, he replaced Hugh Dalton as Minister of Economic Warfare in 1942, and thus supervised SOE; Fred Astaire's sister and first dancing partner, Adèle, wife of Lord Charles Cavendish and later Kingman Douglass, whom Bruce mentions May 20, 1942.

24. Probably Antony Head (1906–1983), then on General Ismay's staff, formerly with the Life Guards in France, later made a viscount. His wife was the portrait painter Lady Dorothea Ashley-Cooper.

25. Robert Arthur James Cecil, Viscount Cranborne (1893–1972), secretary of state for dominion affairs, later fifth marquess of Salisbury and leader of the House of Lords. His son Robert (b. 1916) succeeded him in the title.

26. William Edward Stevenson (b. 1900), delegate of the American Red Cross in London, not to be confused with William Stephenson ("Intrepid"), head of British secret operations in the Western hemisphere; Gerald Wilkinson, MI6's man in

Manila and Douglas MacArthur's British liaison officer; in 1923 Helen Gascoigne Drury, sister-in-law of press baron Max Aitken, Lord Beaverbrook, had married the Hon. Evelyn Charles Joseph Fitz-Gerald.

27. The crown prince of Norway (b. 1903) succeeded his father, Haakon VII, in 1957 as Olav V.

28. Nancy Perkins Tree (b. 1899), a Virginian, niece of Lady Astor and wife of Conservative M.P. Ronald Tree, later married Claude Lancaster. In 1933 the Trees bought Ditchley Park, ancestral English home of the Virginia Lees. Arthur Jeremy Tree (b. 1935) was their younger son.

29. Col. Claude Granville "Juby" Lancaster (b. 1899) later married Nancy Tree after her divorce; Hamish Hamilton (b. 1900), founded his publishing firm in 1931 and was seconded from the army to the Ministry of Information. His second wife was Countess Yvonne Pallavicino.

30. Albert Boergner, of the Free French, provided information to the OSS Secret Intelligence branch in London.

31. Whitney Hart Shepardson (1890–1966), international businessman, special assistant to U.S. ambassador in London in 1942, first OSS Secret Intelligence chief in London.

32. Stella, dowager marchioness of Reading (d. 1971), later baroness of Swanborough, founder of Women's Voluntary Services for Civil Defence. Her work impressed Bruce when he was in London in 1940, and she wrote a glowing letter of thanks to his American superior about his Red Cross work.

33. Elizabeth Valetta Bettine Montagu-Stuart-Wortley (d. 1978) had married the eighth earl of Abingdon in 1928; another Anglo-American couple, Rudolphe de Trafford and Katharine Balke, of Cincinnati, had married in 1939; Air Vice Marshal Charles Edward Hastings Medhurst (b. 1896), assistant chief of air staff, intelligence (1941) and policy (1942).

34. Brig. Richard Gambier-Parry, head of MI6's communications division; Lt. Col. James W. Munn, commandant of SOE's training facility at Beaulieu, Hampshire, and later head of training for MI6, also advised OSS on training of its personnel; Brig. Gen., later Maj. Gen. Sir, Colin McVean Gubbins (1896–1976), joined SOE in 1940 and became executive head in 1943; Ian Lancaster Fleming (1908–1964), personal assistant to the director of British naval intelligence throughout the war, by the end of which he had attained the same rank as his fictional character, Commander Bond; Nancy Langhorne, Viscountess Astor (1879–1964), a Virginian who married the second Viscount Astor and was the first woman to sit in the House of Commons.

35. Cyril John Radcliffe, later Viscount Radcliffe (1899–1977), director general of the Ministry of Information; Robert Hamilton Lockhart (1887–1970), deputy undersecretary of state at the Foreign Office, head of the Political Warfare Executive, knighted 1943; Dorothy Power Hall, a Virginian, had married the second Earl Beatty in 1937; Loelia Mary Sysonby had married the second duke of Westminster in 1930.

36. Maj. Felix Henry Cowgill, chief of counterespionage for MI6, located at St. Albans, north of London.

37. U.S. diplomat H. Freeman Matthews (b. 1899), of Baltimore and Princeton, became counselor at the London embassy in 1941, minister in 1942.

38. Henry David Reginald Margesson (1890–1965), Conservative M.P., secretary of state for war (1940–42), was created a viscount in 1942; Maj. R. B. Brooker, an SOE training instructor, also advised OSS on training courses for its personnel; Margaret Sheila Chisholm, an Australian, formerly Lady Loughborough and, in 1942, wife of

Sir John Milbanke; Margaret Armstrong Drexel (d. 1952), an American, widow of the fourteenth earl of Winchilsea and Nottingham.

39. Loyd V. Steere (b. 1898) continued in the State Department after the war in posts relating to European agriculture.

40. Field Marshal, later Baron, Sir Philip Walhouse Chetwode (1869–1950), chairman of the executive committee of the joint Red Cross and St. John war effort; probably Maj. Gen. Sir John Kennedy (b. 1878), retired from the British army in 1936.

41. Bruce added the last sentence to the typescript by hand.

42. Bruce added to the typescript by hand the word "secret."

43. Possibly Wing Commander Woolf Barnato (1895–1948), heir to a South African diamond fortune and prominent figure in British motor racing.

44. Bruce added to the typescript by hand the phrase "deputy to 'C' in SIS" (the head of SIS, or MI6, was traditionally known as "C"). Years later Bruce described Col. Claude Dancey (1876–1947) as "a crusty old curmudgeon who could not stand any interference or rivalry from the Americans" and "did everything he could . . . to sabotage our relationship and our plans to set up American teams for France" (David Schoenbrun, *Soldiers of the Night: The Story of the French Resistance*, 295).

45. Bruce added to the typescript by hand the identification in parentheses describing William Samuel Stephenson (b. 1896), Canadian industrialist, code name "Intrepid," director of British Security Co-ordination in the Western Hemisphere (1940–46), knighted in 1945.

46. Millard Preston Goodfellow (1892–1973), newspaper publisher, deputy director of OSS; Irving Peter Pflaum (b. 1906), a foreign correspondent who worked for COI and OSS in London, Portugal, and Spain.

47. On this day FDR signed the executive order creating OSS out of COI.

48. Maj. Gen. James Eugene Chaney (1885–1967), commanding U.S. army forces in British Isles; Brig. Gen. Charles L. Bolte (b. 1895), chief of staff under Maj. Gen. Chaney in command of U.S. forces in Britain.

49. On this day Donovan made a presentation about COI, now OSS, to the British War Cabinet.

50. Comdr. Kenneth H. S. Cohen, RN (b. 1900), of MI6, later worked with OSS on the Sussex program.

51. Victor Cavendish-Bentinck, later duke of Portland (b. 1897), Foreign Office chairman of the British Joint Intelligence Committee.

52. Harold Adrian Russell "Kim" Philby (1912–1988), who later defected to the Soviet masters he had served while in the British secret service; possibly Capt., later Admiral of the Fleet Sir, George Elvey Creasy (b. 1895), director of antisubmarine warfare for British naval intelligence; Air Chief Marshal Sir Philip Bennet Joubert de la Ferté (1887–1965), an assistant air chief of staff, later commander in chief, RAF coastal command.

53. New York and Paris banker and USAAF Col. Julian Allen (1900–1967).

54. The words in parentheses were added in Bruce's hand to the typescript and refer to the disastrous Allied raid of August 18, 1942, on the French Channel port of Dieppe. Bruce's handwritten corrections may have been added some years after the diary was typed. It is possible he and Donovan knew the target when they watched the rehearsals.

55. Richard Heppner (1909–1958), an attorney from Donovan's law firm, later an OSS officer in China and deputy assistant secretary of defense under Eisenhower.

56. Entries for June 24 and 25 added to original typescript by Bruce by hand.

CHAPTER 2

1. In early 1942 German submarines devastated shipping along the American Atlantic coast. About the time Bruce was in Miami, the losses began to be reduced when a system of convoys was instituted.

2. Probably Lt. Col., later Col., Samuel Francis Clabaugh (b. 1890), assistant U.S. military attaché, London (1941), with U.S. armed forces in Middle East (1942–43).

3. A port on the Brazilian coast closest to West Africa, not the province of the same name in southern Africa.

4. It is likely that some of the Pan American people Bruce met worked for OSS. He was in charge of the network of agents that OSS had established throughout Africa and had been a member of the Pan American board of directors in the 1930s.

5. Secretary of the Civil Aeronautics Board and well versed in Washington intrigue, Col. Thomas Early was an early recruit in COI and became the agency's executive officer; the American vice-consul at Accra, Walter Stratton Anderson, Jr. (b. 1912), had held similar posts elsewhere in Africa since 1939.

6. Years later another passenger sent Bruce an excerpt from notes he had taken during the stop at El Geneina: "Went hunting for gazelles with Purcell (Columbia grad student, history). Stuck in mud, walked back with David K. E. Bruce—flies—flies—flies" (Ross A. McFarland to David K. E. Bruce, Apr. 17, 1973, David K. E. Bruce Papers).

7. After wartime service with OSS, Lt. (jg), later Comdr., Turner Hudson McBaine, USNR (b. 1911) practiced law in San Francisco; the Mena House hotel, near the Sphinx and Pyramids outside Cairo.

8. Lt. Gen. Lewis Hyde Brereton (1890–1967) organized the Ninth U.S. Army Air Force in Egypt and later served in Europe; possibly Maj. Gen. Aymer Maxwell (b. 1891), with the British army in the Middle East until 1944; Cornelius Vanderbilt "Sonny" Whitney (b. 1899), who had been on the board of directors of Pan American with Bruce, was with the USAAF in Egypt; Christopher Grey Tennant, second Baron Glenconner (1899–1983), former naval officer, head of SOE in Cairo; Capt. Cuthbert Francis Bond Bowlby, RN (b. 1895), MI6 assistant chief staff officer, later head of MI6 operations in Algiers; Comdr. William Bremner, MI6 deputy to Capt. Bowlby; Lt. Col. John Teague, with MI6 in Cairo, later in Iraq.

9. Lt. Col. John Eugene, Count de Salis (1891–1949), soldier and diplomatic official; Ahmad Hasanayn (d. 1946), chief of the Egyptian Royal Cabinet.

10. Bruce added the last sentence by hand to the ribbon copy. Apparently at a different time he added to the carbon copy, "Saw flashes from artillery fire in the desert." Rommel began his last offensive in North Africa about a week later. Its failure led to the successful British drive against the Afrika Korps later in the autumn.

11. Michael Robert Wright (1901–1976), British diplomat, later knighted and appointed ambassador to Norway and Iraq; British diplomat, later Conservative M.P., Henry Lennox d'Aubigné Hopkinson (b. 1902), acting counsellor of embassy, office of minister of state in the Middle East.

12. Lt. Col. Paul West had recently arrived in Cairo as chief of OSS operations there.

13. Theodore A. Morde, assistant to Lt. Col. West. According to one account, Morde very shortly began, on his own initiative but possibly with OSS knowledge, a scheme to persuade the German ambassador to Turkey, former Chancellor Franz von Papen, to engineer a coup against Hitler. The terms Morde offered—German hegemony in central Europe—could have led to considerable diplomatic em-

barrassment if his report to FDR about his overtures were leaked (Anthony Cave Brown, *The Last Hero: Wild Bill Donovan*, chap. 23).

14. Bruce added the last three sentences by hand to the typescript.

15. Capt., later Lt. Col., Harry Raymond Turkel (b. 1906), chief of army intelligence for Africa and with the Middle East Wing, Air Transport Command.

16. Bruce added the last three sentences by hand to the typescript.

17. Possibly Lt. Col. Earl Christian Lory (b. 1906), who took his Ph.D. at Johns Hopkins and before the war directed a medical research institute in Pittsburgh. After the war he became dean of Montana State University; Warwick Potter, New York investment broker and OSS officer.

18. William Phillips (b. 1878) U.S. diplomat and Bruce's predecessor as head of OSS in London (July-December 1942); possibly Col. L. Franck, who earlier in the war handled liaison for SOE with the Combined Chiefs of Staff in Washington; David Williamson, special assistant to William Phillips, Bruce's predecessor as head of OSS/Europe.

19. Possibly auto manufacturer Errett Cord (1894–1974), president of Cord Corp.

20. Sir Edwin Savory Herbert (1899–1973), director of postal and telegraph censorship for the Ministry of Information, later a life peer, Baron Tangley of Blackheath.

21. Probably Col. Gustav Guenther (d. 1944), formerly head of OSS operations in Cairo. See diary entries for June 15 and 17, 1944; possibly Ellery Huntington, a wealthy Wall Street lawyer and political crony of Donovan.

22. The Dunraven Arms inn lies in the shadow of the ancestral estate of the earls of Dunraven, to which title Nancy Adare's husband was heir.

23. Bruce's wife owned a country home at Syosset, Long Island.

CHAPTER 3

1. Donald Coster, an advertising executive before the war and OSS officer in Casablanca and London, later worked in the CIA and in foreign aid programs; Col. William Alfred Eddy, USMC (1896–1962), college professor in the U.S. and Middle East before the war, president of Hobart and William Smith College.

2. Lt. Col. W. Arthur Roseborough, lawyer, head of the Western Europe division of OSS Secret Intelligence branch in Washington, then in Algiers; a wealthy attorney, Theodore Ryan was later active in Connecticut politics after his OSS service; Charles Sherlock Vanderblue (b. 1903), West Point class of 1929, after wartime work in OSS served in the State Department.

3. David King, businessman, former French foreign legionnaire, and one of the original U.S. intelligence agents in Casablanca, later served with OSS in London; New York attorney Paul R. M. van der Stricht (b. 1908) was one of OSS's first special operations officers to serve an apprenticeship with his British cousins in SOE.

4. Eisenhower had been appointed Allied commander in chief in North Africa in November 1942.

5. After the war Katharine "Tatty" Spaatz married Walter Bell, a British official with MI6, whom Bruce mentions July 28, 1944.

6. Marie Rose Antoinette Catherine de Robert d'Aqueria d'Erlanger. Her son was Sir Gerard John Regis Leo d'Erlanger (1906–1962), British investment banker and airline entrepreneur.

7. George Smith Patton, Jr. (1885–1945), was then commander of the Seventh Army in Sicily.

8. The son of wealthy Italian immigrants in St. Louis and the husband of a friend of Donovan's wife, OSS Lt. Col. Guido Pantaleoni disappeared behind enemy lines in Sicily a few days later.

9. A former newspaper correspondent in Rome, John Whittaker served in OSS's Psychological Warfare branch; Max Corvo recruited fellow Sicilian-Americans to work as OSS agents in Sicily and Italy.

10. A World War I pilot and vice-president of Eastman Kodak, Brig. Gen. Edward P. Curtis, Sr. (1897–1987) served with Spaatz in North Africa and Europe; Lt. Gen. Walter Bedell Smith (1895–1961), secretary to the Joint Chiefs and U.S. secretary to the Combined Chiefs of Staff before becoming Eisenhower's chief of staff in 1942. President Truman appointed him director of CIA in 1950; Brig. Gen. George C. McDonald (1898–1969), director of intelligence, Twelfth Air Force, had been assigned to the military mission of COI in 1941 and was later director of intelligence, USSTAF.

11. An urbane Bostonian and World War I aviator, Col. Charles Russell Codman (d. 1956) had known Patton before the war.

12. A flamboyant American journalist, Hubert Renfro Knickerbocker (1898–1949) had reported on wars throughout the 1930s and had distinguished himself during the Ethiopian conflict by engaging in a drunken fist-fight in Addis Ababa with a fellow correspondent, Evelyn Waugh, who got his revenge by basing a character in his novel, *Scoop*, on his opponent. See Martin Stannard, *Evelyn Waugh: The Early Years, 1903–1939* (New York: W. W. Norton, 1986), 406, 474.

13. Newspaperman Don Whitehead (1908–1981) covered the Mediterranean and European theaters (1942–45).

14. Maj. Gen. Terry Allen (1888–1969) later served in Europe with the 104th Division.

15. At a critical point in the invasion of Sicily, when the First Division seemed in danger of being pushed back into the sea by the Germans, Allen issued the order, "we attack tonight," that earned for him a reputation for audacity and the nickname "Terrible Terry."

16. Brig. Gen. Theodore Roosevelt, Jr. (1887–1944), son of President Theodore Roosevelt and a friend of Donovan.

17. Frances Day was a popular actress, American by birth but British by choice.

CHAPTER 4

1. After participating in the Normandy invasion, Rear Adm. Arthur Dewey Struble (b. 1894) served in the Pacific theater.

2. The USS *Davis* later repulsed a German E-boat attack on June 12 and was heavily damaged, probably by a mine, when escorting a supply convoy to the Normandy beachhead on June 21. The ship survived and returned to Atlantic convoy duty.

3. The three passages in this day's entry marked in parentheses do not appear in the version of the diary belonging to the Virginia Historical Society, otherwise complete, but do appear in the typescript of the small portion of Bruce's diary (May 31 to June 9, 1944) in the Donovan Papers at the U.S. Army Military History Institute.

4. Deputy commander of U.S. naval forces at Normandy, Vice Adm. Morton Lyndholm Deyo (1887–1973) held similar posts during the Iwo Jima and Okinawa campaigns.

5. FDR appointed Republican publisher Frank Knox (1874–1944) to his cabinet as secretary of the navy in 1940 to enlist bipartisan support for his pro-British

foreign policy; Adm. Husband Edward Kimmel (1882–1968) had commanded the U.S. Pacific and combined fleets in 1941.

6. Lt. Gen. Walter Campbell Short (1880–1949), commander of the army's Hawaiian Department.

7. Retired Rear Adm., later Sir, Richard Hugh Loraine Bevan (1885–1976) rejoined the Royal Navy in 1939 and was flag officer in charge of Northern Ireland (1942–45); Lt. Gen. Sir Alan Gordon Cunningham (b. 1887).

8. British commander in chief in the Middle East Gen., later Field Marshal, Sir Claude John Eyre Auchinleck (1884–1981).

9. Before his death in a plane crash, Maj. Gen. Orde Charles Wingate (1903–1944) achieved wide fame as a practitioner of irregular warfare behind Japanese lines in Burma. One of his later disciples, who had served under him in Palestine, was Moshe Dayan. Wingate was related to Lawrence of Arabia.

10. Wilfred Scawen Blunt (1840–1922), poet, traveller, and vigorous critic of British imperialism.

11. Churchill, Roosevelt, and Stalin met at the Tehran Conference at the end of November 1943.

12. James Albert Edward Hamilton (1869–1953), third duke of Abercorn and first governor of Northern Ireland (1922–45).

13. Maj. Gen., later Lt. Gen., Staford Leroy Irwin (1893–1955); Brig. Gen. Aln Dudley Warnock (b. 1894).

14. Sir Basil Stanlake Brooke, later Viscount Brookeborough (1888–1973), described in the *Dictionary of National Biography* as "a lazy man of limited ability and considerable charm," became prime minister of Northern Ireland in 1943. His more well known uncle, not cousin, Field Marshal Sir Alan Francis Brooke (1883–1963), later Viscount Alanbrooke, was chief of the Imperial General Staff.

15. The fourth marquess of Dufferin and Ava (1909–1945) had been undersecretary of state for colonies (1937–40) and was killed in action in Burma. Maureen Constance Guinness had married the marquess in 1930.

16. The three passages in this day's entry marked in parentheses do not appear in the version of the diary belonging to the Virginia Historical Society, otherwise complete, but do appear in the typescript of the small portion of Bruce's diary (May 31 to June 9, 1944) in the Donovan Papers at the U.S. Army Military History Institute.

17. Maj. Gen., later Gen., Joseph Lawton Collins (b. 1896), commander of U.S. Seventh Corps, later chief of staff.

18. For a different view of Gen. Mark Wayne Clark (1896–1984), see Martin Blumenson, *Mark Clark* (New York: Congdon and Weed, 1984); Lt. Gen. Ira C. Eaker (1896–1987), commanding general of U.S. Eighth Air Force in Britain and of Mediterranean Air Forces.

19. In February 1944 the Allies bombed the abbey of Monte Cassino, which they erroneously thought was being used by the Germans as a part of their defensive lines blocking the Allied advance on Rome. The Germans had, in fact, observed the abbey's neutrality and did not occupy the buildings until after it was reduced to rubble by the bombing.

20. Brig. Gen. Lucian King Truscott, Jr. (1895–1965), led the assault troops in the invasion of southern France.

21. Rear Adm. John Lesslie Hall, Jr. (1891–1978), commanded American amphibious landings in Sicily, Normandy, and later Okinawa; Rear Adm. Don P. Moon (1894–1944) had earlier commanded a destroyer squadron in the Atlantic and participated in the invasion of North Africa.

22. Maj. Gen. Eugene M. Landrum (b. 1882); Maj. Gen. Raymond Oscar Barton (1889–1963); Brig. Gen. Henry A. Barber, Jr. (1896–1956).

23. James Phinney Baxter (1893–1975), president of Williams College, director of COI's R&A branch (1941–42), and deputy director of OSS (1942–43).

24. Eisenhower's broadcast was prerecorded on May 28.

25. USS *Corry* hit a mine and, under fire from shore batteries, was abandoned.

26. The preceding sentence marked in parentheses does not appear in the version of the diary belonging to the Virginia Historical Society, otherwise complete, but does appear in the small portion of Bruce's diary (May 31 to June 9, 1944) in the Donovan Papers at the U.S. Army Military History Institute.

27. The Germans had threatened to unleash new weapons, chiefly rockets, against the Allies.

28. Lt. Comdr. Edward A. Michel, Jr.

29. Much later Bruce recalled, in a highly embellished letter, this foray to the beach. At Donovan's insistence, according to this version, the two officers made their way to the front line and beyond so that the general could interrogate French civilians in the zone between the contending armies. The two Americans soon found themselves crouching behind a hedgerow with machine-gun fire not far off. Faced with the possibility of capture, Donovan kindly offered Bruce one of his suicide pills when he discovered that his associate had not brought his along. Rummaging through his kit, Donovan found that he too had no pills, apparently having left them at his London hotel: "Solicitous for the health of Claridge's personnel, he told me to wireless as soon as we returned to the ship that any medical supplies left in his room should be gathered carefully together and deposited with the hall porter." Bruce wrote that he omitted this incident from the diary, which would be available to others at his London headquarters (David K. E. Bruce to Whitney Shepardson, Aug. 16, 1958, retained copy, David K. E. Bruce Papers).

30. Like the incident about the suicide pills, Bruce omitted details about this encounter. He later wrote that Donovan and Royce "heartily disliked each other" and that Bradley "ordinarily amiable, must have known there were strict orders against D. being anywhere near Normandy." When Donovan offered to have Bruce attached to the First Army, Bradley replied, "Bill, I would be very glad to have Bruce at my headquarters later on, but suppose you now go back to wherever you came from" (David K. E. Bruce to Whitney Shepardson, Aug. 16, 1958, retained copy, David K. E. Bruce Papers).

31. Robert Heyler Thayer (1901–1984), lawyer, U.S. Navy commander (1941–45), later with foreign service.

32. Hitler made good on his threat to employ the so-called vengeance weapons with the first V-1 attack six days later.

33. In 1943 the Germans had used a new radio-controlled glider bomb to good effect against the U.S. invasion fleet at Salerno and against the Italian fleet on its way to surrender to the British.

34. The USS *Meredith* was struck by a mine while on patrol off Normandy and sunk on June 9 following an air attack. While escorting freighters to Guadalcanal on October 15, 1942, the earlier *Meredith* was sunk by planes from the Japanese carrier *Zuikaku*, a veteran of Pearl Harbor later sunk at Leyte Gulf.

35. Ira Wolfert (b. 1908) followed the American armies through France, Belgium, and Germany.

CHAPTER 5

1. The head of intelligence at Bradley's First Army, Col. Benjamin A. "Monk" Dickson, opposed Donovan's people at every turn throughout the campaign for France.

2. Donovan's instincts were good; among OSS's greatest contributions to the war effort were those made by the field units providing tactical intelligence to American combat divisions in the campaign for France.

3. The First United States Army Group, FUSAG, was composed of the real U.S. Third Army and the fictitious U.S. Fourteenth and British Fourth Armies, part of the massive plan to deceive the Germans about the Normandy invasion.

4. The code name for the head of the British Secret Intelligence Service (1939–52), Sir Stewart Menzies.

5. For more on the MI6 decision, see Cave Brown, "C", 625.

6. Lester Armour (1895–1970), Chicago banker, deputy chief of OSS/London; former Berlin official for United Press, Frederick Oechsner headed black propaganda for OSS; Rae H. Smith (b. 1896), manager of the London office of the J. W. Thompson advertising agency before the war and chief of OSS Morale Operations in the European theater; by the end of the war, Chicago investment executive James Russell Forgan (1900–1974) had succeeded Bruce as commanding officer of OSS in the European theater.

7. The American minister, David Gray, clashed repeatedly with OSS agent Ervin R. "Spike" Marlin (b. 1909); later a federal judge, Chicago attorney Hubert Will, worked for the head of OSS Counterintelligence in London.

8. Bureau Central de Renseignements et d'Action, the principal Gaullist agency coordinating secret operations and intelligence.

9. Gen. Pierre Marie Koenig (1898–1970) headed de Gaulle's French forces in both Britain and the underground.

10. A filmmaker before the war, Gilbert Renault-Roulier, code name "Colonel Rémy," became de Gaulle's top secret agent.

11. Diplomat Aaron Switzer Brown (1913–1969) served in Dublin from 1943 to 1945.

12. Lt. Edward J. Lawler, USNR (b. 1908), formerly with the IRS, assistant to the chief of Counterintelligence in London, and OSS's replacement in Ireland for Marlin.

13. Journalist and author Herbert Sebastian Agar (1897–1980), special assistant to the American ambassador in London and director of the British section of the Office of War Information. He later married Barbara Lutyens Wallace, whom Bruce mentions May 23, 1942.

14. "Paul Hagen," an alias for Dr. Karl Frank, a German emigre psychologist whose nomination as a member of an OSS-sponsored anti-Nazi front organization caused some concern in OSS because of Frank's left-wing political past (Smith, *OSS*, 208).

15. The V-1 flying bomb had long been expected by Allied intelligence, which had been receiving information for some time on Hitler's often-promised secret weapons.

16. Colonel de Basse taught special tradecraft to candidates training for the Sussex operation, which inserted agents into France around the time of the invasion; probably Capt. Roger Guattary, who interviewed Sussex candidates for the French forces and was later attached to an OSS field detachment.

17. David Sarnoff (1891–1971), a pioneer of the radio and later the television industry, chairman of RCA Corporation.

18. Brig. Gen. Edwin Luther Sibert (b. 1897), head of intelligence in the European theater and later assistant director of the CIA; Patton's chief of staff, Maj. Gen. Hugh J. Gaffey (1895–1946).

19. Brig. Gen. Thomas J. Betts, deputy to Eisenhower's chief of intelligence, Maj. Gen. Kenneth Strong. Eisenhower had moved the headquarters of SHAEF out of central London to Bushy Park, near Kingston, to get away from the distractions of the center of town.

20. A partner in Russell Forgan's firm, investment banker Walter M. Giblin (1901–1964) was chief of the OSS service branch in the European theater.

21. Walter Kerr returned to journalism as a foreign correspondent after the war. See diary for November 23, 1944; European correspondent John Elliott (b. 1896) served with OSS Morale Operations branch.

22. Bruce refers to the second, more deadly German "vengeance" weapon, the V-2 rocket, which OSS knew was being prepared for attack on London.

23. A special service was being held in the Guards Chapel, on Birdcage Walk between Buckingham Palace and Parliament Square, when the V-1 hit, killing or wounding nearly two hundred.

24. Virginia publisher Capt., later Lt. Col., Stacy Lloyd (b. 1908) of OSS Secret Intelligence branch, shared a flat in Belgravia with his neighbor and Bruce's brother-in-law, Paul Mellon, while they both served in Bruce's organization.

25. In 1944 future associate justice of the Supreme Court Arthur Joseph Goldberg (1908–1990) was a labor union attorney serving as a major in the OSS; chief trial counsel for the National Labor Relations Board, George O. Pratt (b. 1903) took over in November 1942 as chief of the Labor branch set up by Arthur Goldberg for OSS/London.

26. Chicago banker Thomas G. Cassady (d. 1972), former naval attaché at Vichy in charge of the Medusa operation, who transferred to OSS in 1942. Consisting of several hundred agents in France controlled by OSS/Madrid and the Free French, Medusa was perhaps the largest secret American intelligence network in Europe.

27. American-born Alfred Chester Beatty (b. 1875) made a fortune in mining enterprises, collected Oriental manuscripts, became a British subject, and was later knighted. He seconded mining engineers to the British secret services while they were still on his payroll.

28. Major Edward P. Gaskell, commanding officer of the OSS Secret Intelligence field detachment with the Third Army; Pittsburgh industrialist Alan Magee Scaife (1900–1958), temporary head of OSS Secret Intelligence branch in London and a cousin of Bruce's wife; Lt. Col. Andre Bilbane was in the operations section of an OSS Special Intelligence field detachment with Third Army; before appointment as Eisenhower's deputy chief of staff, Maj. Gen. Royal Bertram Lord (1899–1963) had served in key support and supply posts.

29. Communications Zone: the Allied term for the area of liberated territory behind the active zone of combat.

30. Joseph Farrell Haskell (b. 1908), a career army officer who had worked in the planning for the Normandy invasion. As head of Special Operations, he was one of the keys to the success of OSS/London (see Smith, OSS, 174).

31. The Jedburghs—teams made up of a radio operator, a French officer, and either an American or British officer—parachuted into occupied France to help ensure that Resistance activities meshed with the Allied invasion.

32. Col. A. D. Reutershan handled the duties of the head of OSS Services branch in Paris; Col. Theodore D. Palmer (b. 1896), former assistant deputy director of Secret Intelligence branch in Washington and later OSS chief of personnel in the European theater.

33. Playwright George Brewer, Jr., conducted a successful OSS Special Operations network in Stockholm.

34. Comdr. George L. Graveson, USNR (b. 1904) helped establish the OSS Communications branch in London in September 1942 and later became head of the unit.

35. University professor and president of the Foreign Policy Association, Dr. William Percy Maddox (1901–1972) was Bruce's Secret Intelligence chief.

36. Film director Comdr. John Ford (1895–1973) lent his talents to both COI and OSS, and in 1944 was chief of OSS's field photographic unit.

37. District attorney, later judge, Murray Irwin Gurfein (b. 1907), with OSS Psychological Warfare Division.

38. Col. Waller Booth, Jr., formerly with OSS Secret Intelligence in Spain and commanding officer of the Proust program; the Proust program sent units of French military personnel recruited by OSS and SIS to France to produce intelligence helpful for the Allied invasion at Normandy.

39. Maj. Gen. Harold Roe Bull (1893–1976), assistant chief of staff, G-3, SHAEF, later worked for the CIA.

40. Col. Guy Westmacott, MI6 was attached to Eisenhower's headquarters.

41. Station Charles began operation in November 1943 and kept in contact with OSS agents in France (see *War Report of the OSS [Office of Strategic Services]*, vol. 2, 163–65).

42. Many women members of the British First Aid Nursing Yeomanry (FANY) were assigned to the various secret services, including OSS and SOE.

CHAPTER 6

1. Col. Franklin O. Canfield (b. 1910), a Standard Oil lawyer after the war, was in charge of recruiting OSS men for the Jedburgh teams; Lt. Albert E. Jolis (b. 1912), a diamond merchant with contacts among non-Communist trade unionists in Europe, worked for the OSS Labor branch in London and later headed "Milwaukee Forward," an operation aimed at penetrating Germany; financier William Turnbull worked in the forging and counterfeiting operation of OSS/London.

2. An OSS wireless station, set up for work associated with the D-day invasion—specifically the Sussex teams in France.

3. Col. William Harding Jackson (1901–1971), deputy head of intelligence on Gen. Bradley's staff, later deputy director of the CIA; possibly Lt. Col. John H. Colby, who was involved with OSS field detachments. A less likely possibility, William Egan Colby (b. 1920), later director of the CIA, was at this point a major not a lieutenant colonel; Chicago journalist Kenneth Downs commanded a field detachment for OSS Secret Intelligence branch.

4. Maj. Gen. William Benjamin Kean (b. 1897), chief of staff, First U.S. Army; Col., later Maj. Gen., Samuel L. Myers (b. 1905) had served in the North African and Sicilian campaigns.

5. Ogden Livingston Mills (1884–1937), secretary of the treasury following Bruce's father-in-law, Andrew Mellon.

6. Alfred G. Toombs, a civilian employee of OSS with Morale Operations attached to Twelfth Army Group.

7. Possibly Col. Malcolm Henderson, who had been with MI6 in North Africa earlier in the war.

8. Col., later Brig. Gen. Truman C. Thorsen (b. 1895).

9. Lt. Mercader, the Calvados Resistance chief working with OSS field detachments.

10. Gen. Karl Wilhelm Von Schlieben and Adm. Hennecke.

11. Bruce unaccountably fails to mention the role of OSS officer Pat Dolan, whom he mentions July 24, in securing the surrender of the Germans at the arsenal.

12. The Todt Organization, under the direction of German minister for armaments and munitions Dr. Fritz Todt, was charged with the task of building coastal defenses in France against the day when the Allies would invade. After Todt died in a plane crash in 1942, Albert Speer succeeded him.

13. Maj. Arnold-Baker, a British liaison officer with an OSS Secret Intelligence unit attached to FUSAG.

14. Stanhope B. Mason, chief of staff of General Huebner's First Division.

CHAPTER 7

1. In 1943 Lt., later Capt., John G. Hayes, Jr. (b. 1912), had helped establish an administrative office for Secret Intelligence branch in London; Lt. (jg) Henry H. Proctor, USNR (b. 1908) was in charge of the air dispatch section of field intelligence in the Sussex operation.

2. Attorney Spencer Phenix (b. 1890) later served on the staff of the U.S. military government in Germany.

3. P. E. J. Manuel, head of Bureau de recherches et d'Action à Londres, which cooperated with the special section of British SOE that supplied Gaullist resistance forces in France.

4. Louie F. Timmerman, a civilian employee of OSS in the Secret Intelligence branch.

5. Hazel Cropsey worked in the administrative section of the Secret Intelligence branch at OSS's London headquarters; Maj. Harold Jefferson Coolidge (1904–1985), Harvard zoologist with OSS/Washington office; writer James Vincent Sheean (1899–1975) had been informally associated with OSS activities in North Africa.

6. Sir Samuel Findlater Stewart (b. 1879), temporary director general of the Ministry of Information.

7. South Carolinian Gertrude Legendre had charge of Bruce's Message Center, through which passed all OSS radio traffic. Touring the front lines in late September, she and her OSS colleagues were captured by the Germans. She reached Switzerland near the end of the war.

8. At the outbreak of the war, Thomas Archibald Stone (b. 1900), a cousin of Legendre, rejoined the Canadian foreign service, from which he had resigned, apparently as a cover for intelligence work, according to Bruce's comment. He later became Canadian ambassador to the Netherlands.

9. Economist Chandler Morse headed OSS's London R&A branch; Brig. Gen., later Maj. Gen., Robert A. McClure (1897–1957), chief of Psychological Warfare Division, SHAEF.

10. Lt. Col. William P. Davis, chief of Special Operations, Algiers, worked with the British to merge SO and SOE in Algiers in 1944 into the Special Project Operations Center (SPOC); Maj. Peter J. Ortiz was also a veteran of the French foreign legion.

11. Bruce's longtime friend, Conservative M.P. Ronald Tree (1897–1975), with whom he had roomed during his Red Cross work in 1940. During the war Tree served as parliamentary private secretary to three ministers of information. He made his country home, Ditchley Park, available as a secret getaway for Churchill.

12. Brendan Rendall Bracken (1901–1958), later Viscount Bracken, editor, M.P., and one of Churchill's closest associates. As head of MOI, he was one of the chief supervisors of PWE; Maj. John "Jack" Strange Spencer Churchill (1880–1947), the prime minister's younger brother.

13. See Winston S. Churchill, *The Second World War* (Boston: Houghton Mifflin, 1948–53), vol. 6, 44. The Allies, in fact, were already bombing German cities indiscriminately. The great fire storm of July 1943 at Hamburg, for example, was only the beginning of what awaited German urban centers.

14. Capt. Ernest L. Byfield (b. 1914) served on the training staff for the Sussex operation.

15. In May 1944 Britain's SOE and OSS's Special Operations branch merged to form a new unit called Special Forces Headquarters, directly under SHAEF (see *War Report*, vol. 2, 144–45).

16. Joseph Walshe had visited OSS headquarters in London in spring 1944 and recommended to Bruce's associates that OSS send an officer to Dublin to work with the Irish on security matters. OSS was reluctant to do so. See T. Ryle Dwyer, *Irish Neutrality and the USA, 1939–47* (Totowa, N.J.: Rowman and Littlefield, 1977), 198.

17. Col. Dan Bryan had been appointed head of Irish military intelligence in 1941; Paddy Carroll, chief superintendent of the Irish Garda Crime Branch.

18. Detroit banker Gerald E. Miller (b. 1903), appointed chief of OSS Special Operations branch in London in late 1944; Russell Grace D'Oench (1901–1959), grandson of the founder of W. R. Grace & Co., assisted Bruce's Secret Intelligence chief, Dr. William Maddox.

19. Brig., later Maj., Gen. Sir Kenneth William Dobson Strong, Eisenhower's British intelligence chief, not to be confused with the American army's chief of intelligence in Washington and bête noire of OSS, Maj. Gen. George V. "George the Fifth" Strong.

20. *New York Times* military correspondent Hanson Weightman Baldwin (b. 1903); a fellow member with Bruce of the Virginia House of Delegates, a leader of the internationalist campaign to aid Britain before Pearl Harbor, and a key officer in OSS's Sussex program before transferring to SHAEF, Francis Pickens Miller (1895–1978) was later a candidate for Virginia governor and U.S. Senator.

21. Lt. Col. Robert Hayden Alcorn (b. 1909) joined COI in 1941 and was administrative-executive officer to Bruce in London; Howard Cady was later assigned to the Paris OSS secretariat.

22. On July 6, 1944, more than 150 people died after a fire swept the main Ringling Brothers and Barnum & Bailey circus tent at Hartford, Connecticut.

23. Pennsylvania attorney and USAAF Lt. Col. James Moorhead Bovard (1901–1982) later served as trustee of Carnegie-Mellon University and of the foundation named for Scaife's wife, Sarah Mellon Scaife.

24. Lt. Gerald J. Hodgkinson (b. 1917), an accountant assigned by OSS to Special Funds branch.

25. David Field Beatty (1905–1972) succeeded his father, the commander of the British battle cruiser fleet at Jutland, in the title as Earl Beatty in 1936; Dorothy Rita Furey Bragg, an American and the widow of an RAF sargeant, married Lord Beatty in 1946.

26. Capt., later Maj., Charles Katek (b. 1910), chief of Czechoslovak section of Secret Intelligence branch in London.

27. American Brig. Gen. Pleas Blair Rogers (1895–1974), organizer and commander of Central Base Section in England.

28. Brig. Gen. A. Franklin Kibler, later head of personnnel for Twelfth Army.

29. Comdr. William Ladd, Office of Naval Intelligence liaison officer with Counterintelligence.

30. Later a deputy to the director of CIA, John Adams Bross (b. 1911), along with Canfield and van der Stricht, were the first American Special Operations officers accepted as apprentices by SOE.

31. SOE's Brig. Eric Edward Mockler-Ferryman (b. 1896) had been intelligence chief to Eisenhower in North Africa.

32. Dr. Taylor Cole, a Duke University political science professor and chief of Secret Intelligence branch in Stockholm.

33. A successful Illinois printer, Lt. Col. Willis C. Reddick ran Bruce's London counterfeiting and forging shop.

34. Col. Clifford J. Heflin (b. 1915) commanded the air force unit, code name "Carpetbagger," that delivered supplies to agents on the Continent. Although not officially an OSS officer, he was occupied exclusively with assisting Special Operations branch.

35. Capt. Owen D. Johnson served in OSS in France and Germany.

36. Lt. Col. Henry P. de Vries (b. 1911), a lawyer, was chief of the division of strategic intelligence in the London Secret Intelligence branch.

37. The Labor division, within Secret Intelligence branch, attempted "to enlist the support of labor in all countries, chiefly for purposes of intelligence, but also for sabotage and subversion" (see *War Report*, vol. 1, 183–85).

38. Margaret Thompson Schulze married Anthony Biddle in 1901. She worked in the Red Cross in London while her husband was emissary to the governments in exile.

39. In March 1941 the teenaged Prince Peter was placed on the throne as Peter II of Yugoslavia (1923–1970) after a coup toppled the pro-Axis government. As a consequence, the Germans invaded the country in April and sent the young king into exile in London.

40. Princess Alexandra of Greece married King Peter in March 1944.

41. Princess Aspasia (1896–1972), widow of King Alexander I of Greece. On January 14, 1945, another diarist wrote, "And there are some tiresome telegrams about Yugoslav affairs. What a bore these kings are! (In the case of King Peter, the nigger in the wood-pile is Princess Aspasia, his mother-in-law)" (Harold Macmillan, *War Diaries: Politics and War in the Mediterranean, January 1943–May 1945* [New York: St. Martin's Press, 1984], 648).

42. Edward R. Murrow (1908–1965) organized CBS radio's network of foreign correspondents before the war and became known to all Americans for his reports on the Battle of Britain in 1940; Oscar Nathaniel Solbert (1885–1958) left the army for business before the war but then rejoined and served as head of the Office of War Information and of special services at SHAEF.

43. Constantine A. Fotic (1891–1959), last Yugoslav ambassador to the United States before the coalition government of 1944, which contained Titoist as well as royalist elements. Fotic opposed Tito from exile after the war.

44. The OSS had a hand in the appointment of Ivan Subasic (1892–1955), former governor of Croatia, as premier of the 1944 Yugoslav government-in-exile. He later served as foreign minister in the postwar coalition government but soon broke with Tito.

45. Dr. Milan Gavrilovic, Yugoslav minister to Moscow, 1940–41.

46. By the date Bruce wrote "Bastille Day." Donovan had arranged a special, dramatic delivery of over 300 planeloads of supplies for the French Resistance to mark the occasion.

47. The British wanted to control all OSS activity in the Southeast Asia Command, the acronym for which American wags said stood for "Save England's Asiatic Colonies."

British Capt. G. A. Garnon Williams was placed in charge of all special operations in SEAC (see Smith, *Shadow Warriors*, pp. 260–61).

48. The code name for the headquarters of the U.S. Eighth Air Force, at Bushy Park, Teddington, a London suburb. On the radio equipment, see *War Report*, vol. 2, 287–90 and Cave Brown *"C"*, 548–49.

49. Maj. Gen. Frederick L. Anderson, Jr. (1905–1969), deputy commander for operations, USSTA; Maj. Sally Bagby, aide to Gen. Spaatz.

50. Philip Horton (b. 1911) taught English at Harvard before the war and as a civilian employee of OSS helped build a reports division for the London headquarters. He later worked for the CIA.

51. OSS gave the code name "George Wood" to the German source providing high-grade secret information to its Swiss station.

52. Capt. Leo Loxtercamp, OSS/London security branch.

53. Hawaiian pineapple executive and OSS deputy director Atherton C. Richards (b. 1894) was among the inner circle of Donovan's top administrators.

54. Helen Hitchcock Clark, sister of Bruce's cousin-in-law Tommy Hitchcock, the polo celebrity and Bruce's roommate in London who died testing the new P-51 fighter, had two sons in the air force, Avy and Tommy. Despite Bruce's hopeful comments, Tommy Hitchcock Clark was killed when his plane went down. His Uncle Tommy Hitchcock was awarded a posthumous Distinguished Flying Cross.

55. On OSS's limited and disheartening operations in Czechoslovakia, see *War Report*, vol. 2, 133–34.

56. Possibly Rear Adm. John Wilkes (1895–1957).

57. Justin McCortney O'Brien (1906–1968), a Harvard French professor who worked in OSS's Sussex program.

58. Biologist Maj. Graham Erdwurm (b. 1917), OSS Counterintelligence administrative officer in London.

59. Quentin Roosevelt (d. 1948), a grandson of President Theodore Roosevelt, returned to China after wartime work for OSS there.

60. Bernard Yarrow (1900–1973), OSS liaison with the governments-in-exile in London, later senior vice-president of Radio Free Europe; Maj. George H. Andrews (b. 1916), regular army, adjutant of OSS/European theater; Maj., later Lt. Col., Charles B. Stearns, acting executive of OSS London Services branch.

61. Trafford P. Klots (1913–1976), an artist who divided his time between Baltimore and his Breton chateau, was assigned to a field detachment of Secret Intelligence branch; Far Shore: the French coast across the Channel from England.

62. Probably American businessman Kenneth L. Lindsey (d. 1969), a member of the American Red Cross Committee in Great Britain when Bruce was the delegate in charge (1940–41); probably Daniel B. Grant (d. 1948), like Lindsay, on the committee of American businessmen who ran their country's Red Cross operations in England during the Blitz. In 1943 he was assigned to SHAEF.

63. Ossewa Brandwag was a pro-Axis organization in South Africa, against which Premier Jan Smuts later took firm action because of OSS reports (see *War Report*, vol. 2, 43).

64. Dick Goldsmith White (b. 1906) later became head of MI5 and still later head of MI6 and thus "C," knighted 1955.

65. After his OSS work, Charles P. Kindleberger (b. 1910) became one of America's most distinguished economists; Maj. Walt Whitman Rostow (b. 1916), later a leading American economist and economic historian.

228 NOTES TO PAGES 113–25

66. Bradshaw Beverley Byrd (b. 1920) was wounded shortly after D-day. His father, Sen. Harry Flood Byrd, Sr., former governor of Virginia, dominated Democratic politics and Virginia public affairs for four decades.

67. A former officer in the tsar's army and hotelier to the fast set in New York, Lt. Col. Serge Obolensky (b. 1890) had helped OSS liberate Sardinia and was with the maquis at the time of the Normandy invasion.

CHAPTER 8

1. Brig. Gen., later Maj. Gen., Earl Seeley Hoag (b. 1895) had served on the War Department general staff (1940–43).

2. Sgt. Victor E. Kirouac, an instructor for training OSS field detachments.

3. Harvard historian and OSS Counterintelligence officer Dana Durand, Jr., later worked for the CIA.

4. Probably Akeley P. Quirk, a Standard Oil lawyer with OSS Counterintelligence.

5. American businessman Col. Charles F. Neave (1894–1961) had charge of the forward echelon in France of OSS/London's Secret Intelligence branch. He should not be confused with Airey Neave, of MI9, whom Bruce mentions August 20; Maj. John Bertram Oakes (b. 1913), with OSS Counterintelligence in London, later an editor of the *New York Times*.

6. Bruce's brother-in-law Paul Mellon (b. 1907), philanthropist and president of the National Gallery of Art.

7. A newspaper reporter in civilian life, head of OSS's Morale Operations branch Patrick Dolan had personally convinced the German garrison of the Cherbourg fortress to surrender and later rescued Dr. Leo Baeck from Theresienstadt concentration camp (see Brown, *Last Hero*, 551–53, 651–56).

8. Robert J. Casey (1890–1962) had been with the *Chicago Daily News* since 1920 and had reported on the war in Europe, North Africa, and the Pacific since 1940; Lawrence E. Lesueur (b. 1909), a foreign correspondent for CBS since 1939, covered the London Blitz and the fighting in Russia.

CHAPTER 9

1. Harvard historian Crane Brinton (1898–1968), an authority on the French Revolution, worked in R&A; Henry Nathan Sporborg (b. 1905), a director at Hambro's Bank and the sole deputy chief of SOE under Gubbins; Maj. John Hackett, representative of SOE at PWE and director of an SOE school training psychological warfare agents.

2. W. Lane Rehm, chief paymaster of OSS and head of Special Funds branch.

3. Louise Hepburn, head of registry for OSS/London Secret Intelligence branch, later married William Maddox, chief of the branch.

4. New York attorney William Casey (1913–1987), then Secret Intelligence branch chief in London, was appointed director of the CIA by President Reagan. He was the last head of CIA who could draw on personal experience in OSS.

5. British vice-consul in New York early in the war, Walter Bell (b. 1909) was with MI6. After the war he married Katherine Spaatz, daughter of Gen. Carl "Tooey" Spaatz.

6. On July 20 a bomb demolished the conference room at Hitler's East Prussia headquarters during a meeting. With this attack, the coup long plotted by German military officers began. When news reached Berlin that Hitler survived the blast, however, the attempt to overthrow the Nazi regime collapsed.

7. OSS gave the code name "Breakers" to the plot against Hitler, about which OSS/ Switzerland had acquired substantial information before the attempt of July 20, 1944.

8. Probably Lt. Gen. John Clifford Hodges Lee (1887–1958), commander of Services of Supply and Communications Zone in the European theater; British Maj. Gen. Robert Edward Laycock (b. 1907), chief of Combined Operation.

9. James Murphy, a Washington attorney, old friend of Donovan and OSS Counterintelligence chief. North Africa was not part of Bruce's jurisdiction.

10. Investment banker Maj. Alexander Brown Griswold (b. 1907), son of Baltimore lawyer and banker Benjamin Howell Griswold, Jr., had attended the same prep school as Bruce.

11. Central Base Section.

12. Allied intelligence about German rocket research led to the bombing of the main facility at Peenemünde. These raids retarded but, in the end, did not stop the work of Werner Von Braun and his associates to develop a rocket capable of hitting London.

13. Carlton Joseph Huntley Hayes (1882–1964), Columbia history professor and ambasssador to Spain (1942–45).

14. New York architect William Adams Delano (1874–1960) had helped Bruce re-model Staunton Hill; Idesbald van der Gracht (b. 1902) established his own architec-tural firm after earlier work for Delano & Aldrich. Head architect for the War Department before active duty, he served in the State Department after the war.

15. Henry Alexander Murray (b. 1893), director of Harvard Psychological Clinic and OSS major.

16. Possibly Lt. Col. Arthur E. Sutherland, Jr., head of a Secret Intelligence branch field detachment with the Ninth Army.

17. Chicago attorney Raymond Lee Brittenham (b. 1916), head of the Belgian desk at OSS/London, ended the war as a major and became senior vice-president at ITT.

18. Maj., later Lt. Col., Joseph Dasher (b. 1903) headed the Polish desk of Secret Intelligence branch in London. The day after this entry Polish resistance forces rose in Warsaw against the German occupiers, expecting aid from the Red Army, which had reached the capital's suburbs. Stalin, no friend of the Polish patriots, allowed the Germans to do his dirty work for him. The revolt was crushed while the Red Army watched from the outskirts of the city.

19. Ricardo Mazzerini oversaw Secret Intelligence branch's Italian section in London. In 1942 he engaged in a complicated and risky abuse of Vatican diplomatic privilege, whereby Vatican representatives in Tokyo passed information on bombing targets to OSS via Irish diplomats in Rome and Dublin.

20. Bruce was vice-consul in Rome from 1926 to 1927.

21. Capt. Frank Alexander Slocum (b. 1897) served in this position throughout the war, after which he maintained his ties with Norway through the Foreign Office.

22. George Taylor, an Australian, served as chief of staff to the head of SOE.

23. Ensign George D. Forney, USNR, security officer for OSS in the European theater.

24. P. G. H. Hedley-Dent, later secretary of the Bank of London and South America.

25. Col. Bartholomew "Barty" Pleydell-Bouverie (1902–1965), head of Bill Ste-phenson's BSC office in Washington and chief liaison with Donovan.

26. Comdr. George Unger Vetlesen, a Norwegian-American millionaire and friend of the Norwegian king, headed the Norwegian division of OSS Special Operations in London.

27. Brig. Gen. Cornelius Wendell Wickersham (b. 1884), Eisenhower's deputy on German affairs.

28. Vice Adm. William Alexander Glassford (1886–1958), FDR's personal representative to French West Africa (1943), deputy commander of U.S. naval forces in Europe (1944).

29. North African theater of operations.

30. Maj. Louis P. Dups had become the chief of operations section in London Secret Intelligence branch in July.

31. Maj. Gen. Clayton Lawrence Bissell (1896–1972), assistant chief of staff, U.S. Army intelligence.

32. Hallett Johnson (1888–1968) was the State Department's assistant chief, Division of Defense Materials. His daughter, Priscilla Livingston Johnson, was a draftsman in the map division of R&A London. Here Bruce confused Johnson's and Norris's work at the London office.

33. Mary Theresa Norris had arrived in London in March 1944 as a secretary for James J. Gorman, a civilian employee in OSS Security branch. She apparently was successful in defying her parents and stayed with OSS/London until transferring to OSS/Paris in September.

34. Lawyer and diplomat Allen Welles Dulles (1893–1969), later director of the CIA, performed some of the most successful OSS work of the war at his Swiss base.

35. Possibly Margaret Van Buren Mason, wife of Samuel Sloan Colt, president of Bankers Trust; businessman Amory Houghton (b. 1899), deputy chief of the U.S. Mission for Economic Affairs in 1944 and later ambassador to France.

36. Psychologist Robert Brodie Macleod (1907–1972) had become chief of the Continental division of Secret Intelligence branch in Europe in July.

37. Patrick Huskinson (b. 1897), president of the air armament board, Ministry of Aircraft Production; Charles Vivian Winn (b. 1918) later reached the rank of Air Vice Marshal in the postwar RAF.

38. Pilot of Adm. Richard E. Byrd's flight over the South Pole, Norwegian air force officer Bernt Balchen (1899–1973) joined the U.S. Air Force after the fall of Norway and served with the Eighth U.S. Air Force and OSS/Scandinavia.

39. Greek-American importer Ulius Amoss (1894–1961) had been relieved of his duties as OSS executive officer in Cairo in 1943. " 'He knew nothing,' declared one OSS executive, 'and messed up everything he touched' " (Smith, OSS, 124, 124n). He later operated a private spy network.

40. Lt. Col., later Col., Sylvester C. Missal, chief surgeon for OSS and supervisor of OSS medical services in Washington.

41. Lt. (jg) Fossel was with the Norwegian desk of the London Secret Intelligence branch.

42. Capt. Stephen Vinciguerra was on the training staff of the Sussex and Proust projects.

43. Foreign service officer Herschel V. Johnson (1894–1966) served as U.S. minister to Sweden during the war.

CHAPTER 10

1. A pilot in World War I, between the wars Col. Merian C. Cooper (1894–1973) became a successful film director, producing, among others, "King Kong." He served

OSS as a special assistant to Donovan; Col. John Speaks (d. 1965) served with the RAF in World War I, the Kosciusko Squadron in the Russo-Polish War, and as an assistant to Cooper in his film enterprises.

2. Capt. Benjamin Welles (b. 1916), son of Undersecretary of State Sumner Welles, with Special Operations branch in the Middle East, Counterintelligence in London, and head of an SCI field detachment in France.

3. Henry Adams's *Mont-Saint-Michel and Chartres* (Boston and New York: Houghton Mifflin, 1904).

4. Henry Morganthau, Jr. (1891–1967), Roosevelt's secretary of the treasury (1934–45), was an early advocate of American entry into the war to aid the western Allies but is unfortunately perhaps best remembered for his draconian and absurd plan to "pastoralize" Germany after the war. Bruce had reason to be less than kind in his comments about him: Morganthau was a principal in the politically motivated income tax case against Bruce's father-in-law, Andrew Mellon, at the beginning of the New Deal.

5. Capt. Alan C. Conway (b. 1913), commanding officer of OSS signal detachment, later communications operations officer in London; Maj. Gen. Robert W. Crawford (b. 1891).

6. A medical diagnostic test to detect syphilis.

7. Robert Blum (1911–1965), a Yale instructor before the war, worked in OSS Counterintelligence and for U.S. economic missions in Europe and Southeast Asia after the war; Lt. Col. Robert I. Powell (1900–1963), a wealthy architect and commanding officer of a Special Operations detachment with Third Army; Col. André Dewarin, code name "Passy," had been de Gaulle's chief of intelligence, as Bruce said.

8. Probably a reference to the comments of a certain Standardenführer SS Bickler at a conference of seventy Sicherheitsdienst (SD) officers on July 1, 1943 (see Cave Brown, "C", 500, 808n).

9. Count Paul Munster, friend of the duke of Windsor and kinsman of the earl of Dudley, was attached to a Morale Operations field unit.

10. Marcus E. Armistead, a supply officer with the Field Photography branch in London.

11. Col. Charles C. Blakeney, with Psychological Warfare branch.

12. Brest held out until mid-September 1944, the garrisons at Lorient and St. Nazaire until the end of the war.

13. With a Secret Intelligence field detachment in 1944, John Wallendahl Mowinckel (b. 1920) served after the war as a foreign correspondent and then State Department official; Michel Brault, code name Jérome, national head of the Maquis.

14. The agent who survived was André Rigot. His five colleagues were André Noel, age 23, Aristide Crocq, age 26, Marcel Biscaino, age 23, Roger Fosset, age 25, and Evelyne Clopet, age 22.

15. Bruce crossed out this last sentence in the typescript.

16. Gen. Philippe Leclerc (1902–1947), head of the French Second Armored Division, later received the formal German surrender at Paris.

17. Capt., later Maj., Jacques H. Beau (b. 1905) was involved in the Sussex operation and field detachments of the Secret Intelligence branch.

18. Col., later Brig. Gen., Hobart Raymond "Hap" Gay (b. 1894), chief of staff, Third Army.

19. On August 15 Operation "Anvil" landed an American–Free French invasion force east of Marseilles, where it met little opposition.

20. Wendell Gibbs was a civilian employee of OSS with the Morale Operations branch.

21. Field Marshal Erwin Rommel had been wounded on July 17. After the July 20 attempt to kill Hitler, Rommel was one of the many high German officers implicated. Given a choice, he committed suicide on October 14.

22. Maj. Gen. Elwood Richard "Pete" Quesada (b. 1904), innovative chief of Ninth Tactical Air Command.

23. Foreign correspondent Joseph Driscoll (1902–1954) had reported on the war in the Pacific and in Europe.

24. Investment banker George Murnane, Jr. (b. 1917) ended the war as a major and became a partner with Lazard Frères & Co. in 1945; coauthor in civilian life, with Drew Pearson, of the syndicated column "Washington Merry-Go-Round," Lt. Col. Robert Sharon Allen (b. 1900) was in 1944 the intelligence operations executive for Third Army headquarters.

25. Michel Pasteau, an engineer who used the code name "Mouthard," was an important member of the BCRA and did not look kindly on the amateurish methods of typical Resistance fighters. Bruce persuaded Pasteau to stay with his group until they reached Paris (David K. E. Bruce to Carlos Baker, Dec. 13, 1965, retained copy, David K. E. Bruce Papers).

CHAPTER 11

1. During the early years of the war Ernest Hemingway (1899–1961) set up a counterespionage network in Cuba. He went to London in 1944 on assignment for *Collier's* and recovered from a London motor accident in time for the march on Paris.

2. Pvt. Archie Pelkey of Canton, N.Y.

3. Himself an escaped POW, Airey Neave (1916–1979) served with MI9, the British agency that abetted such action by captured Allied servicemen. An M.P. after the war, Neave became minister for Northern Ireland in Margaret Thatcher's first cabinet and was killed by IRA terrorists at the House of Commons in 1979.

4. Bruce kept the document, written on the letterhead of the arrondissement de Rambouillet and inscribed with the names and titles of the local dignitaries, throughout the mad dash to Paris. It is now among the Bruce Papers at the Virginia Historical Society.

5. On meeting the Comtesse de Fels in London years later, Bruce recorded in his diary; "I hadn't seen Marte de Fels for some years. She said she and her husband are still grateful to me for saving Château Voisin during the war" (diary entry for December 16, 1966, David K. E. Bruce Papers).

6. Probably William Randolph Hearst, Jr. (b. 1908), heir to the Hearst publishing empire, a friend of Bruce and a war correspondent (1943–45).

7. Hemingway recalled the encounter in typically more flamboyant terms, saying he would never forget Leclerc's greeting: "*Buzz off, you unspeakables*, the gallant general said, in effect, in something above a whisper, and Colonel B[ruce], the resistance king, and your armored-operations correspondent withdrew" (Carlos Baker, *Ernest Hemingway: A Life Story* [New York, Charles Scribner's Sons, 1969], 413).

8. A branch of the Vichy security forces especially detested by the Resistance because it recruited thugs who, being French and knowledgeable about local personalities, were more of a threat than the German occupation troops.

9. Claude Auzello and his wife, Blanche, had run the Ritz since the 1920s.

10. One of the diners wrote, "Among my souvenirs is the paper bearing the signatures of Colonel David K. E. Bruce, Brigadier Edwin L. Sibert, Ernest Hemingway,

Commander Lester Armour, U.S.N.R., G. W. Graveson, Captain Paul F. Sapiebra, Captain John G. Westover, and J. F. Haskell. Above the signatures is the caption: 'We think we took Paris.' The date was August 25, 1944" (S. L. A. Marshall, "How Papa Liberated Paris," *American Heritage* 13 [April 1962]: 5).

11. Probably Gen. Jacques de Chambrun, a supporter of the pro-German Pierre Laval during the confusing French political scene from 1939 to 1940, before the phony war ended and the Third Republic collapsed.

12. Howard Baldwin (b. 1894), a journalist with Morale Operations who later became acting chief of that branch in October 1944; Lt. Col. Leonard H. Nason, French liaison officer with OSS Secret Intelligence branch.

CHAPTER 12

1. Probably Lt. Philip Bastedo, USNR, an OSS liaison officer with SHAEF; Col. Lawrence W. Lowman (b. 1900), vice-president of CBS in civilian life and chief of OSS Communications division.

2. A Yale English professor, Norman Holmes Pearson (1909–1975) headed OSS's Counterintelligence unit in London.

3. Francis Henry Taylor (1903–1957), director of the Metropolitan Museum, member of the Commission for Protection and Salvage of Artistic and Historic Monuments in War Areas, headquartered at the National Gallery. OSS established an X-2 "Art Looting Investigating Unit" that worked with the commission and under the direction of OSS/London (*Secret War Report,* 92–93).

4. Probably Bruce Ottley, a London merchant banker employed by MI6.

5. That OSS units were considered useful for the task of capturing Hitler's Bavarian resort, with or without its resident, indicates the enhanced stature of OSS in the eyes of the military when they had had a chance to see the practical intelligence work OSS could perform after the breakout from the Normandy beachhead.

6. British Brig. Raymund John Mansell (b. 1903), attached to SHAEF.

7. The PBY, an American airplane used extensively for reconnaissance work.

8. Like the more primitive V-1 buzz bombs, the V-2 long-range rocket was known to the Allied intelligence services as no idle Nazi propaganda threat. Bombing raids on the rocket production and launching sites delayed but could not prevent their appearance as an instrument of war.

9. The V-1 could be launched from planes as well as from the ground. The Germans resorted increasingly to the former method as the Allies occupied more of the Continental launching sites.

10. Owner of a New York textile import firm, Robert Lambert had recruited agents in French North Africa for the Sussex program, which sent OSS agents into occupied France.

11. Col. Oscar W. Koch (d. 1970), chief of intelligence for Patton's Third Army.

12. Acting chief of SO in Cairo, Maj. Louis Huot organized an OSS mission to Tito. Huot acted effectively but abrasively, without the approval of Brig., later Sir, Fitzroy Maclean, Churchill's personal liaison with the Yugoslav partisan leader (see Cave Brown, *Last Hero,* 444–51).

13. Charlotte, grand duchess of Luxembourg, had married Felix, prince de Bourbon de Parme in 1919. His sister, Zita, was the wife of the last Hapsburg emperor, Charles I, who reigned from 1916 to 1918.

14. After the war businessman Robert Pflieger (d. 1955) was president of the American Chamber of Commerce in Brussels.

15. Possibly Comdr. Philip Johns, who had been Lisbon head of station for MI6; Brig. Gen., later Sir, Edgar Trevor Williams (b. 1912), later editor of the *Dictionary of National Biography.*

16. Baron Fernand LePage, head of intelligence for the Belgian government in exile and more recently in liberated Belgium.

17. Ohio Steel executive Kenneth Mann had earlier worked with Secret Intelligence branch in Algiers.

18. OSS developed T-Force, or Target-Force, groups to expedite the exploitation of enemy documents as soon as they were captured.

19. Angier Biddle Duke (b. 1915) ended the war as a major in the Air Transport Command. He was later chief of protocol for the White House and State Department and was U.S. ambassador to Spain and Denmark at the time Bruce was ambassador to Great Britain.

20. Bridgett Poulett (b. 1912), daughter of the seventh Earl Poulett.

21. Former lt. gov. of Ohio Charles Sawyer (1887–1979), ambassador to Belgium and minister to Luxembourg, later secretary of commerce. He had married his second wife, Elizabeth L. de Veyrac, in 1942.

22. Alabaman George Platt Waller, Jr. (1889–1962), joined the foreign service in 1913 and was in charge of the American legation in Luxembourg in the 1930s; Alexander Wilbourne Weddell (1876–1948) capped his diplomatic career with the embassies in Buenos Aires and Madrid. He left his estate and a generous endowment to the Virginia Historical Society, of which he was president and Bruce a vice-president.

23. For some unexplained reason Bruce deleted this sentence from the typescript, perhaps because the information was given when he first mentioned van der Gracht on July 31.

24. Paris representative of the Dulles law firm before the war, Max Shoop (d. 1956) was Allen Dulles's advisor on French affairs. He went to Switzerland when the Germans occupied France and aided the French Resistance from there; William Larimer Mellon, a relative of Bruce by marriage and OSS Secret Intelligence branch official in Spain and Switzerland, later ran a clinic for the poor in Haiti.

25. Swiss federal president and foreign minister Pilet Golaz; Leland Harrison (1883–1951) began his diplomatic career before World War I and had been minister to Switzerland since 1937.

26. In 1939 the Swiss Parliament elected Henri Guisan (d. 1960), a farmer and militia colonel from a French-speaking canton, general of the Swiss forces. He served throughout the world war that began two days after his election.

27. Because German destruction of dams on the upper Rhine could flood the Allied crossing of the river downstream, OSS established listing posts to monitor the water level for indication that dams upstream had been breached (*Secret War Report,* 331–32).

28. Dulles had had secret talks with German contacts for some time. Perhaps Bruce's reference was to one such meeting.

29. Anne C. Coleman had married Leland Harrison in 1925. Known to her friends as "Nancy," she was the godmother to Bruce's second wife, Evangeline Bell Bruce.

30. Attorney Robert Shea, Dulles's OSS man at Basel, later served the CIA in Rumania and Switzerland.

31. Lt. Col. William Quinn, later director of the War Department's Strategic Services Unit, which took over part of OSS when that agency was dissolved, and afterwards deputy director of CIA.

32. Mowinckel recalled arriving at the headquarters of British MI6 in Paris, a convent: "I had named my jeep the 'Pet de Nonne,' which is the name of French cream

puffs. Literally translated, however, it means 'Nun's Fart.' All the nine nuns broke into laughter as they saw the name painted on my windshield" (Cave Brown, *Last Hero*, 574).

33. Maj. Gen., later Lt. Gen., Clarence R. Huebner (1888–1972), later commanding general of the U.S. Army in Europe.

34. The division earned the nickname Timber Wolves because of their expertise at night fighting.

35. In Montgomery's operation "Market Garden," September 17–26, 1944, the Allies failed to link up with the paratroops dropped at Arnhem and thereby lost the attempt to capture bridges across the lower Rhine.

36. Isolated German garrisons held out at nearby Lorient and St. Nazaire until the end of the war.

37. Alain Louis Auguste Marie de Rohan-Chabot, thirteenth duke de Rohan (b. 1913); Marguerite de Rohan, wife of the twelfth duke.

38. The last two sentences were added, in Bruce's hand, sometime after the final entry to the diary was typed.

EPILOGUE

1. Stanley P. Lovell, *Of Spies & Stratagems* (Englewood Cliffs, N.J.: Prentice-Hall, 1963), 18–19.

2. David K. E. Bruce, "The National Intelligence Authority," *Virginia Quarterly Review* 20 (Summer 1946): 363.

3. Bruce, "The National Intelligence Authority," 358.

4. For one of the best accounts of the origins of OSS and its linkages with the CIA, see John Ranelagh, *The Agency: The Rise and Decline of the CIA*.

5. From a speech at the annual dinner of Veterans of OSS, May 26, 1971, David K. E. Bruce Papers.

6. Henry Kissinger, *White House Years* (Boston: Little, Brown, 1979), 521.

Note on Sources

The following note describes the most important sources for researching David Bruce's role in OSS and for annotating his wartime diaries. It is not presented as a bibliography on secret intelligence or the Office of Strategic Services.

The most important manuscript sources were the papers of David K. E. Bruce at the Virginia Historical Society in Richmond, Virginia. The same institution owns a manuscript collection cataloged under the name of his mother, Louise Este Fisher Bruce, containing information on Bruce's work for the Red Cross during the Blitz. Equal in importance to Bruce's private papers were the official records of the Office of Strategic Services, Record Group 226, at the National Archives in Washington, D.C. There were also some materials, including OSS documents, in the papers of William J. Donovan at the U.S. Army Military History Institute at Carlisle Barracks, Pennsylvania.

For identifying the people Bruce mentioned in his diaries, the most helpful sources were the manuscript collections mentioned above. The standard biographical directories were helpful too: the British and American volumes of *Who's Who* and *Who Was Who*, the *Dictionary of National Biography*, and the *Dictionary of American Biography*.

Books on Allied intelligence operations in World War II are without number. The few mentioned here appear because they were especially helpful in describing OSS operations pertinent to Bruce's work or in identifying his OSS colleagues. Intelligence operations are summarized in *War Report of the OSS (Office of Strategic Services)*, introduction by Kermit Roosevelt, 2 vols. (New York: Walker and Co., 1976) and *Secret War Report of the OSS*, edited by Anthony Cave Brown (New York: Berkeley Publishing Corporation, 1976). Although written before official records were widely available, R. Harris Smith's *OSS: The Secret History of America's First Central Intelligence Agency* (Berkeley and Los Angeles: University of California Press, 1972) identifies many of the key players. A fuller account is Bradley F. Smith's *The Shadow Warriors: O.S.S. and the Origins of the C.I.A.* (New York: Basic Books, 1983). Parts of the OSS experience are considered by William R. Corson's *Armies of Ignorance: The Rise of the American Intelligence Empire* (New York: Dial, 1977); Joseph E. Persico's *Piercing the Reich: The Penetration of Nazi Germany by American Secret Agents during World War II* (New York: Viking, 1979); David Schoenbrun's *Soldier's of the Night: The Story of the French Resistance* (New York: Dutton, 1980); and Robin W. Winks's *Cloak and Gown: Scholars in the Secret War, 1939–1961* (New York: William Morrow, 1987). Perhaps the best overall summary and assessment of OSS appears in the early pages of John Ranelagh's *The Agency: The Rise and Decline of the CIA* (New York: Simon and Schuster, 1986).

Several biographies of Donovan have appeared: Corey Ford, *Donovan of O.S.S.* (Boston: Little, Brown, 1970); Richard Dunlop, *Donovan, America's Master Spy* (New York: Rand McNally, 1982); and Anthony Cave Brown's *Last Hero: Wild Bill Donovan* (New York: Times Books, 1982). Cave Brown also wrote an account of one of Donovan's leading British counterparts in *"C": The Secret Life of Sir Stewart Graham Menzies, Spymaster to Winston Churchill* (New York: Macmillan, 1987). For the British side, see F. H. Hinsley et al. *British Intelligence in the Second World War: Its Influence on Strategy and Operations*, 3 vols. (New York: Cambridge University Press, 1979–1984) and two books under the psuedonym Nigel West, *MI6: British Secret Intelligence Service Operations, 1909–1945* (New York: Random House, 1983) and *The Circus: MI5 Operations, 1945–1972* (New York: Stein and Day, 1983).

Index

North, Bud, 122–23, 142
North, John R., 77
North Africa, 15, 42, 45, 126, 148; lack of organization of OSS operations in, 127; Rommel's victories in, 13
North Africa Theater of Operations (NATO), 131
North Atlantic Treaty Organization (NATO), 3, 208
Northern Ireland, 159
Northolt, England, 23, 137, 181
North Weald, England, 185
Norway, 129, 151, 184; invasion of, 6; OSS secret mission to, 184

Oakes, John Bertram, 118
Obolensky, Serge, *113*, 114
O'Brien, Justin McCortney, 110
Oechsner, Frederick, 71, 73, 76, 99, 102, 111, 126, 136
Office of Naval Intelligence (ONI), 106
Office of Strategic Services, 2, 108, 131, 179; activities against Germany, 112; agents in Normandy, 103; agents in Sicily, 44–45; Art Looting Investigation Unit, 182; assessment of, 205–7; attempts to streamline operations, 112; Berlin mission, 127; Censorship and Documents Branch, 107; cooperation with British intelligence, 3, 71, 206; Counter-intelligence branch (X-2), 13, 71, 79, 86, 89, 106–7, 111–12, 122, 129–30, 133, 135, 182; created by executive order, 15; disagreement with MI6 over agents in Czechoslovakia, 104; Document Section, 129; efficiency of field detachments, 112; employment of German POWs as agents, 110; establishment of lab in Calcutta with MI6, 134; European branch, 35, 204; Executive Committee meetings, 78, 99, 105, 110; expiration of, 206; Field Detachments, *119*, 133, 183, 190, 193; Field Photography, 124; formed from COI, 13; and French resistance, 74, 77–78, 79–80, 82, 99,

181; hostility to MI6, 204; in Africa, 14; in Tangiers, 42; interbranch animosity, 80; Labor Branch, 108, 143; lack of organization in North Africa, 126; London office, 1, 106, 109, 207; Madrid branch, 76; manpower of, 110; Medical Unit, 135; meeting of branch heads, 70–71, 83, 130; meeting of branch representatives, 106; Morale Operations Branch (MO), 13, 73–74, 76–77, 88, 99, 102, 105, 119, 124, 126, 136, 142, 152, 177, 186, 198; Operational Groups, 114; operations in Algiers, 36–37; operations in Denmark, 126; operations in Mediterranean theater, 129; operations in Normandy, 87; operations in North Africa, 35–41; operations in Paris, 190; operations in Southeast Asia, 108; operations in Stockholm, 109; Oral Intelligence Branch (OI), 196; personnel, 190; places agents in Germany, 206; planning group, 203; plans for establishing a permanent intelligence agency, 132; plans for occupation of Germany, 136, 182; plans to establish a recruitment and training headquarters in Europe, 105; plans to set up joint lab in Calcutta with MI6, 129–30; possible impairment of independence of, 103; preparations for D day, 47–57; propaganda leaflets, 41; proposal to merge three intelligence branches, 134; Psychological Warfare (PW), 88–89, 143, 186; relations with David Gray, 72, 74, 79, 99; relations with French Secret Intelligence Service, 111; Research and Analysis Branch (R&A), 13, 98–99, 124; Research and Development Branch, 107; Secret Intelligence Branch (SI), 13–14, 71, 73–74, 77, 79–80, 99, 101, 103–5, 107, 109–13, 117–18, 125–31, 133–34, 140–41, 143, 154, 159, 185, 190, 192; Security Office, 109, 132–33; Special Operations Branch (SO), 13, 71, 76, 78, 80, 99, 100, 105, 127, 130–31, 135;

OSS AGAINST THE REICH

was composed in 10/12 New Baskerville
on a Xyvision System with Linotron 202 output
by BookMasters, Inc.;
printed by sheet-fed offset
on 50-pound Glatfelter B-16 acid free stock,
Smyth sewn and bound over .088″ binders' boards in Holliston
Kingston Natural cloth, with 80-pound Rainbow Antique endleaves,
wrapped with dust jackets printed in three colors on 80-pound
enamel stock and film laminated
by BookCrafters, Inc.;
designed by Will Underwood;
and published by

THE KENT STATE UNIVERSITY PRESS
Kent, Ohio 44242